HBJ SPELLING

SIGNATURE EDITION

SILVER

Thorsten Carlson

Richard Madden

HBJ SPELLING

SIGNATURE EDITION

 HARCOURT BRACE JOVANOVICH, PUBLISHERS

Orlando   San Diego   Chicago   Dallas

Acknowledgments

For permission to reprint copyrighted material, grateful acknowledgment is made to the following sources:

Harcourt Brace Jovanovich, Inc.: Letter forms from *HBJ Handwriting.* Copyright © 1987 by Harcourt Brace Jovanovich, Inc. Definitions and the pronunciation key in the "Spelling Dictionary" are from the *HBJ School Dictionary.* Copyright © 1985, 1977 by Harcourt Brace Jovanovich, Inc.

Merriam-Webster, Inc.: From the entry "senate" in *Webster's Ninth New Collegiate Dictionary.* © 1986 by Merriam-Webster Inc., publisher of the Merriam-Webster® Dictionaries.

Random House, Inc.: From the entry "senate" in *The Random House College Dictionary,* Revised Edition. Copyright © 1984, 1980, 1979, 1975 by Random House, Inc.

COVER DESIGN Graphic Concern, Inc.

ART CREDITS

Key: T, Top; B, Bottom; L, Left; C, Center; R, Right.

Page 4, ALL, Bob Shein; 5, Tony Giamas; 8(B), Tom Powers; 12, ALL, 13, Michael O'Reilly; 14, Blaise Zito Assoc.; 16, ALL, 17, Michael O'Reilly; 20, ALL, Bill Colrus; 25, 27, 28, Blaise Zito Assoc.; 30, Bob Shein; 36, Tim Lundgren; 38(TL), 38(TR), Tom Powers; 38(BL), Bob Shein; 40, Blaise Zito Assoc.; 42(T), Bill Colrus; 42(B), Blaise Zito Assoc.; 43, Bill Colrus; 45, Blaise Zito Assoc.; 46, Tom Powers; 48, Art Cummings; 49, 53, 54, 56, Blaise Zito Assoc.; 57, Bill Colrus; 50(B), Tom Powers; 61, John Dyers; 64(T), Bob Shein; 67, 68, ALL, Bill Colrus; 69, Blaise Zito Assoc.; 70, Art Cummings; 74, Tim Lundgren; 77, 78, 79, 80, Blaise Zito Assoc.; 82, ALL, Tim Lundgren; 86(T), Bill Colrus; 86(B), Bob Shein; 87, Kyuzo Tsugami; 89, Blaise Zito Assoc.; 90, ALL, Kyuzo Tsugami; 92, Tim Lundgren; 94(T), Tom Powers; 94(B), Bob Shein; 95(T), Tom Powers; 97, Tony Giamas; 98, John Dyers; 102, 105, 106, Blaise Zito Assoc.; 108, ALL, Bill Colrus; 109, Tim Lundgren; 110, Art Cummings; 112(T), Tom Powers; 112(B), Bob Shein; 115, Blaise Zito Assoc.; 116, ALL, Bob Shein; 120, 121, Michael O'Reilly; 122, Tom Powers; 123, Blaise Zito Assoc.; 124, ALL, John Dyers; 128, 129, 130, 131, 132, 134, Blaise Zito Assoc.; 135, 138, Bob Shein; 139, Bill Colrus; 140, Arthur Friedman; 141, Blaise Zito Assoc.; 142, Bill Colrus; 146, Blaise Zito Assoc.; 150, Kyuzo Tsugami; 151, 154, ALL, 155, 156, 157, 158, 163, 164, 166, 167, 168, 170, 184, 185, ALL, 188, 189, 195, 203, Blaise Zito Assoc.

PHOTO CREDITS

Key: T, Top; B, Bottom; L, Left; C, Center; R, Right.

Cover Photography, Ken Lax; Page 6, Jeff Rotman; 8, Bernard Wolf/DPI; 9, HBJ Photo; 21, Jim Smith/Blaise Zito Assoc.; 22, Sandra Still/Shostal Assoc.; 24, 26, Jim Smith/Blaise Zito Assoc.; 30, Focus on Sports; 30(B), HBJ Photo; 31, C, Bear/ Shostal Assoc.; 34(TL), HBJ Photo; 34(TR), Ruth Dixon; 34(BL), 34(C), Joseph Barnell/Shostal Assoc.; 34(BR), Wil Blanche/ DPI; 34(B), HBJ Photo; 35, Russ Kinne/Photo Researchers; 39, HBJ Photo; 48, Focus on Sports; 49, Eric Carle/Shostal Assoc.; 50, Granger Collection; 51, 52, Jim Smith/Blaise Zito Assoc.; 56(T), Phillip Boyer/Photo Researchers; 60(T), S.L. Craig/Bruce Coleman; 62, Tony Linck/Shostal Assoc.; 64(B), Joe Munroe/Photo Researchers; 65, Mimi Forsyth/ Monkmeyer Press; 66, Robert Caputo/Fund for Animals; 72(L), Saala/EPA; 72(TR), Museum of Modern Art, NY/Andre Meyer Bequest; 72(B), Jim Smith/Blaise Zito Assoc.; 73, Gianni Tortoli/Photo Researchers; 83, Wil Blanche/DPI; 84, Focus on Sports; 95(B), London Daily Mail/Photo Researchers; 98, HBJ Photo/David Phillips; 103, Bettmann Archives; 104, Jim Smith/Blaise Zito Assoc.; 113, Yvonne Hemsey/Gamma-Liaison; 114, Farrell Grehen/Photo Researchers; 117, Editorial Photocolor Archives; 120, Robert Koropp/The Image Bank; 125, Wide World; 126, Editorial Photo Archives; 130(T), Jim Smith/Blaise Zito Assoc.; 134(T), HBJ Photo; 138, Doris S. Baum/DPI; 142(T), Robert E. Foley; 142(B), Robert Lee/Photo Researchers; 143, Wally McNamee/Woodfin Camp and Assoc.; 145, Roger Werth/Woodfin Camp and Assoc.; 146(T), Columbia Artists Management; 150(T), Bill Gillette/Stock Boston; 150(B), Freda Leinwand/Monkmeyer Press; 151, R.D. Ullmann/Taurus; 167, HBJ Photo/David Phillips; 171, Leonard Lee Rue, III/Shostal Assoc.; 174, Bob Daemmrich; 176, Robert Villani/Blaise Zito Assoc.; 177, Jim Smith/Blaise Zito Assoc.; 179, Granger Collection; 182(L), James H, Karales/Peter Arnold; 182(R), Three Lions; 187, T. Lipton/Shostal Assoc.; 189, Jim Smith/Blaise Zito Assoc.; 196(T), HBJ Photo; 196(B), Robert Villani/Blaise Zito Assoc.; 197, Jim Smith/Blaise Zito Assoc.; 199, E.R. Degginger/Bruce Coleman; 201, Lee Boltin.

PRODUCTION AND LAYOUT Blaise Zito Associates

Printed in the United States of America
ISBN 0-15-327076-4

Contents

Study Steps to Learn a Word

 SAY the word. Recall when you have heard the word used. Think about what it means.

 LOOK at the word. Find any prefixes, suffixes, or other word parts you know. Think about other words that are related in meaning and spelling. Try to picture the word in your mind.

 SPELL the word to yourself. Think about the way each sound is spelled. Notice any unusual spelling.

 WRITE the word while looking at it. Check the way you have formed your letters. If you have not written the word clearly or correctly, write it again.

 CHECK your learning. Cover the word and write it. If you did not spell the word correctly, practice these steps until the word becomes your own.

Skills Check

Name_____**Date**_____

A. Write the letter of the misspelled word.

1. ____ **a.** album   **b.** diseaze   **c.** language
2. ____ **a.** initial   **b.** appoint   **c.** allready
3. ____ **a.** lawndry   **b.** journey   **c.** ignore
4. ____ **a.** colum   **b.** comedy   **c.** rescue
5. ____ **a.** experience   **b.** material   **c.** autamatic

B. Write the correct spelling for each pronunciation.

6. /shōl′ dər/ _____
7. /hīt/ _____
8. /ri·sēv′/ _____
9. /kwiz/ _____
10. /plej/ _____
11. /yoo′ zhoo·əl/ _____
12. /fôr′ in/ _____
13. /mis′ ter·ē/ _____

C. The words in each column end with the sounds at the top of the column. Write the correct spelling of the whole word.

/ər/	/ən/
14. partn _____	17. chos _____
15. rum _____	18. pige _____
16. burgl _____	19. org _____

/əl/

20. approv _____
21. quarr _____
22. triang _____

D. Write the plural of each word.

23. tomato _____
24. radio _____
25. batch _____
26. hero _____
27. mouse _____
28. ox _____
29. auto _____
30. lens _____

number right

A. ____ (5)

number right

B. ____ (8)

number right

C. ____ (9)

number right

D. ____ (8)

2

E. Add the inflectional ending in ( ) to each word. Write the word.

31. occur + (ed) _____

32. appear + (ing) _____

33. picnic + (ed) _____

34. reply + (ed) _____

35. study + (ing) _____

36. lie + (ing) _____

F. Match the words in the two lists to write three compound words.

earth   body   **37.** _____

some   ever   **38.** _____

where   quake   **39.** _____

G. Add one of these prefixes to each word. Write the new word.

re-   in-   im-   pre-

40. polite _____   **41.** mind _____

42. caution _____   **43.** visible _____

H. Add a suffix to each word. Write the new word.

-ly   -ion   -ity   -ment

44. easy _____   **45.** locate _____

46. appoint _____   **47.** active _____

I. Complete each sentence with a word that means the same as the word or words in ( ).

48. The cast bowed to the (people watching) _____.

49. We had a long telephone (talk) _____.

50. I brought a (easily carried) _____ TV.

number right

E. ____ (6)

number right

F. ____ (3)

number right

G. ____ (4)

number right

H. ____ (4)

number right

I. ____ (3)

total
right ____ (50)

1 Short Vowel Sounds

UNIT WORDS

1. lather
2. atlas
3. jest
4. method
5. instead
6. whim
7. mock
8. pondered
9. tongue
10. grudge
11. campus
12. novel
13. tremble
14. hinder
15. notch
16. symbol
17. jealous
18. southern
19. sponge
20. plaid

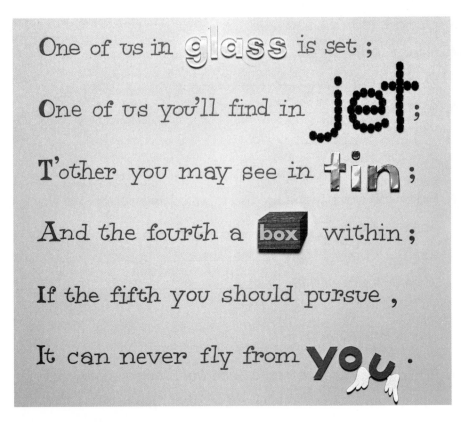

One of us in glass is set ;

One of us you'll find in jet ;

T'other you may see in tin ;

And the fourth a box within ;

If the fifth you should pursue ,

It can never fly from you .

The Unit Words

These lines are from a poem called "The Five," written by Jonathan Swift, the author of *Gulliver's Travels.* Even though Swift never identifies "the five," it is not hard to figure out that they are the five vowel letters.

The five vowel letters are used to spell the many vowel sounds we use in English. Sometimes the letters *y* and *w* are also used to spell vowel sounds, as in *symbol* and *grow.*

The short vowel sounds are usually spelled with one vowel letter each. However, two letters are sometimes combined to spell a short vowel sound, as in *plaid.* The chart below lists the ways the short vowel sounds are spelled in the Unit words.

SOUND	SPELLINGS	EXAMPLES
/a/	a, ai	lather, plaid
/e/	e, ea	jest, jealous
/i/	i, y	whim, symbol
/o/	o	mock
/u/	u, o	grudge, sponge
	ou	southern

Spelling Practice

A. Complete the following exercises using the Unit words.

1. Write the four words that have the sound /a/ you hear in *glass*.

_____ _____

_____ _____

2. Write the five words that have the sound /e/ you hear in *jet*.

_____ _____ _____

_____ _____

3. Write the four words that have the sound /i/ you hear in *tin*.

_____ _____

_____ _____

4. Write the four words that have the sound /o/ you hear in *box*.

_____ _____

_____ _____

5. Write the five words that have the sound /u/ you hear in *up*.

_____ _____ _____

_____ _____

6. Circle each word you wrote for **1–5** in which the short vowel sound is spelled with two vowel letters.

B. Here's a spelling game to try. Start by writing a Unit word. Then, by subtracting one letter at a time, write new words until you finally write a word of only one letter. You may rearrange the letters at each step, but you may not add new ones. Look at the example.

campus → camps → maps → map → am → a

7. In five steps, change *atlas* into the word *a*.

_____ → _____ → _____

→ _____ → _____

C. Write the Unit word that is related to each group of words below.

8. block, help, prevent   _____

9. forgot, thought, considered _____

10. sign, token, badge   _____

11. magazine, narrative, story _____

12. foam, laundry, soap   _____

Using the Dictionary to Spell and Write • Guide Words

<table>
<tr><td>

UNIT WORDS

lather
atlas
jest
method
instead
whim
mock
pondered
tongue
grudge
campus
novel
tremble
hinder
notch
symbol
jealous
southern
sponge
plaid

</td></tr>
</table>

The dictionary is a valuable reference tool. You use it most often to find the spelling, pronunciation, or meaning of an unfamiliar word.

Entry words in a dictionary are listed in alphabetical order. Listing words in this way makes it easy to locate a word quickly. Since hundreds of words begin with the same letter, you must look for the first different letter of a word to find it in the dictionary.

A. In alphabetical order, write the Unit words that come between these words.

1. desert

_____

heat wave

_____

_____

irritable

2. meteor

_____

_____

_____

observatory

3. skein

_____

_____

_____

trace

The two words in boldface type or color at the top of a dictionary page are called **guide words.** They tell you the first and last entry words on that page. All the other entry words on the page are listed alphabetically between the guide words.

B. If each group of words below appeared on a single dictionary page, what two Unit words could be the guide words? To answer the question, find the Unit word that comes just before or after each group in alphabetical order. You must alphabetize before you begin.

4. jeep, jostle, knack, lament

_____   _____

5. warden, triple, unicorn, vacuum

_____   _____

6. pledge, pneumonia, plywood, plastic

_____   _____

sponge/spunj/*n.*

Writing on Your Own

Your club wants to raise money for a trip to Washington, D.C. The club members are going to wash cars all day Saturday. Write a paragraph to tell members how to wash a car. Use these and perhaps some other Unit words in your directions: *lather, sponge, method, instead, hinder.*

WRITER'S GUIDE For a sample how-to paragraph, turn to page 262.

Spelling on Your Own

UNIT WORDS

Write the Unit words on a separate sheet of paper. Then, for at least five of the words, write a common expression or phrase that includes the word. Here is an example: grudge—hold a grudge.

MASTERY WORDS

scrap
threat
chest
timid
flock
thunder

Write the Mastery word that has the same vowel sound as each word below. The vowel sound may be spelled differently.

1. give _____

2. add_____

3. hot _____

4. one _____

5. met (two words) _____ _____

Write the Mastery word that fits each meaning below.

6. shy _____

7. a small piece _____

8. a group _____

9. a loud, rumbling noise _____

Guide words are the two words in boldface or color at the top of a dictionary page. Guide words tell you the first and last words on a page.

10. Write the three Mastery words that begin with *t* in alphabetical order.

_____ → _____ → _____

11. Write the two words that would be the guide words if the six Mastery words were the only words listed on one dictionary page.

_____ _____

12. Write the two Mastery words that would be on a page with these guide words: *thread, thus.*

_____ _____

BONUS WORDS

sulky
sympathize
watchful
stealthy
statue
prism
hectic
leopard

Write the Bonus word that fits each definition.

1. a figurine

2. a geometric figure

3. alert

4. a large cat

5. sly

6. cranky

7. share feelings

8. rushed, confused

Alliteration means "the use of words that begin with the same sound." Tongue twisters often use alliteration. Write a tongue twister using the four Bonus words that begin with the same sound.

7

2 Long Vowel Sounds

UNIT WORDS

1. erode
2. easel
3. ninety
4. slight
5. inflate
6. senior
7. concrete
8. complaint
9. oppose
10. exile
11. greedy
12. mellow
13. sustain
14. magnify
15. guarantee
16. heroic
17. betray
18. coaxed
19. tyrant
20. pertain

The Unit Words

The English language contains about forty sounds. These sounds are listed in the pronunciation key at the front of the **Spelling Dictionary.** Since our alphabet has only twenty-six letters, one letter does not always represent just one sound. As our language has developed, some letters or combinations of letters have come to spell more than one sound.

The long vowel sounds, /ā/, /ē/, /ī/, and /ō/, are frequently spelled with a vowel-consonant-e pattern, as /ā/ in the word *inflate*. The chart below lists the other spellings for the long vowel sounds in the Unit words.

SOUND	SPELLINGS	EXAMPLES
/ā/	ai	complaint
	ay	betray
/ē/	e	senior
	ea	easel
	ee, y	greedy
/ī/	igh	slight
	y	tyrant
/ō/	o	heroic
	oa	coaxed
	ow	mellow

REMEMBER THIS

Sometimes English words that were borrowed from French have the sound /g/ spelled with *gu*. *Guarantee* and *guard* are examples. This sentence may help you remember the *u* in *guarantee*.

A g<u>u</u>arantee g<u>u</u>ards **U** against loss.

Spelling Practice

A. Complete these exercises using the Unit words.

1. Write the six words that have a long vowel sound spelled with a vowel-consonant-e pattern.

_____ _____ _____

_____ _____ _____

2. Write the four other words that have /ā/.

_____ _____

_____ _____

3. Write the five words in which /ē/ is not spelled with a vowel-consonant-e pattern.

_____ _____ _____

_____ _____

4. Write the two words in which /ī/ is spelled with *y*.

_____ _____

5. Write the word that rhymes with *bite*. _____

B. Write the Unit words in which these letters spell /ō/.

6. o _____   **7.** oa _____   **8.** ow _____

C. Complete each sentence using a Unit word.

9. Did Benedict Arnold _____ his country?

10. In parts of the world, there is not enough water to _____ life.

11. Wind and water were able to _____ the towering sandstone hills in Monument Valley, Utah.

12. Take notes only on the information that will _____ to your report.

D. Write the Unit word that fits each group of words below.

13. gravel, sand, bricks _____

14. paint, brush, palette _____

15. freshman, sophomore, junior _____

16. zero, thirty, sixty _____

17. brave, courageous, fearless _____

18. contract, expand, deflate _____

19. giving, selfish, generous _____

Proofreading • A Business Letter

UNIT WORDS

erode
easel
ninety
slight
inflate
senior
concrete
complaint
oppose
exile
greedy
mellow
sustain
magnify
guarantee
heroic
betray
coaxed
tyrant
pertain

Steve wrote this letter to complain about an error. He failed, however, to correct his own errors. His letter has six mistakes in spelling and four mistakes in the punctuation and capitalization of a business letter. Read the letter carefully.

1. Find Steve's spelling mistakes. Then circle the misspelled words.

2. Mark Steve's capitalization and punctuation mistakes, and insert any missing punctuation.

---

157 Maple Drive
Buffalo, New York 14219
September 11, 19--

Perplexing Puzzles, Inc.
7 Oakdale Avenue
New York, New York 10012

dear Perplexing Puzzles;

I am writing this letter of complant to advise you of the slite error you made in packaging your jigsaw puzzle showing the tyrent Napoleon before he began his exil on the island of Elba. You guarante that each package contains the five hundred pieces needed to complete the puzzle. After several hours of working on the puzzle, however, I finally joined the last piece—number four hundred and ninty-nine. Please rush me by return mail the upper left-hand corner of puzzle number 503N.

Yours Truly

Steven Sonders

Steven Sonders

---

3. Write the six misspelled words correctly.

_____   _____   _____

_____   _____   _____

 WRITER'S GUIDE See the editing and proofreading marks on page 258.

Writing on Your Own

Everyone has a day now and then when things just seem to go wrong. Write a funny poem about that sort of day for your classmates. Use one of the Unit words in each line of the poem. When you are finished, you may want to read your poem aloud to your classmates.

 WRITER'S GUIDE For a sample poem, turn to page 272.

Spelling on Your Own

UNIT WORDS

Write each Unit word. Next to each word, write the number of syllables you hear as you pronounce it. You will find two one-syllable words, fifteen two-syllable words, and three three-syllable words.

MASTERY WORDS

Write the Mastery words that have each vowel sound below.

1. /ē/ (two words) _____ _____

2. /ī/ (two words) _____ _____

3. /ō/ (two words) _____ _____

4. /ā/ (one word) _____

Write the sound that is spelled by *y* in each word below.

5. daily _____   **6.** style _____

A **consonant cluster** is two or three letters written together, such as *scr* in *scrap*. You hear a consonant sound for each letter in a consonant cluster.

7. Write the four words that have consonant clusters.

_____   _____

_____   _____

8. How many sounds do you hear in *growth*? _____

Finish the paragraph below using the Mastery words.

Across the United States, from one __9__ to the other, there has been a rapid __10__ in the number of people who enjoy roller skating. Almost __11__, you can see people skating to work or to play wearing nearly every __12__ of clothing imaginable. So __13__ up your wheels and join the fun!

9. _____   10. _____   11. _____

12. _____   13. _____

daily
coast
grease
style
growth
desire

BONUS WORDS

1. Copy and complete the chart below. List each Bonus word according to the vowel sounds it contains.

ā	ē	ī	ō

2. The prefix *re-* sometimes means "again," as in *revival. Revive* means "live again." Write five other words that have the prefix *re-* meaning "again." Check your words in a dictionary. Then use each word in a sentence.

rodent
kerosene
revival
furlough
reclaim
abbreviate
impeach
poultry

3 Words with *ie*, *ei*, or *eigh*

UNIT WORDS

1. thief
2. series
3. conceited
4. deceive
5. weight
6. eighteen
7. fierce
8. pierce
9. friendly
10. forfeit
11. weird
12. siege
13. receipt
14. mischief
15. priest
16. neighborhood
17. yield
18. shield
19. leisure
20. fiery

The Unit Words

Write *i* before *e*
Except after *c*
Or when sounded as /ā/
As in *neighbor* or *weigh*.

The spelling rule above is probably familiar to you. The rule is useful in helping you spell words such as *thief, conceited,* and *weight.* But other words just don't seem to fit into this spelling pattern. Words such as *leisure, forfeit,* and *weird* are exceptions to the rule and must be memorized.

In the Unit words, four different sounds are spelled by *ie.*

/ē/ as in *thief*
/e/ as in *friendly*
/ī/ as in *fiery*
/i/ as in *fierce*

REMEMBER THIS

Fiery may be pronounced two ways: /fīr′ē/ or /fī′ər•ē/. In the second pronunciation, you hear the sounds /ər/ as a separate syllable. This pronunciation can help you remember to spell *fiery* with the letters *er.*

Spelling Practice

A. Complete the following exercises using the Unit words. Use each word only once.

1. Write the three words in which /ā/ is spelled with *eigh*.

_____   _____   _____

2. Write the three words in which *c* is followed by *ei*.

_____   _____   _____

3. Three Unit words do not follow the "*i* before *e* except after *c*" rule. Write the words.

_____   _____   _____

4. Write the word that has /ī/. _____

5. Write the word that has /e/. _____

B. Complete the paragraphs below using Unit words in which the sound /ē/ or /i/ is spelled with *ie*.

　　In ancient times and during the Middle Ages as well, a place of worship was a safe place or shelter for those in trouble. A __**6**__ would __**7**__ runaway slaves from their masters and protect refugees from warring nations. Not even a __**8**__ warrior would dare try to __**9**__ the closed doors of a temple or commit an act of __**10**__ under the roof of a sanctuary. No army would lay __**11**__ to a church or temple even to force the surrender of an opposing king or general. It was also thought to be a sacrilege to __**12**__ even a known __**13**__ to the hands of the law.

　　The right of sanctuary, however, no longer exists. Through a __**14**__ of reforms in the modern penal code, this custom has been discontinued.

6. _____   **7.** _____   **8.** _____

9. _____   **10.** _____   **11.** _____

12. _____   **13.** _____   **14.** _____

C. Each sentence contains two words in parentheses. Write the correct word to use in each sentence.

15. Maria was so glad the police caught the (thief/theater).

_____

16. He had been responsible for a (serious/series) of robberies in her neighborhood.

_____

17. He wouldn't be making any more (mischief/mistake) in her town now.

_____

Spelling and Language • Synonyms

When words mean the same or nearly the same thing, we call them **synonyms.** *Jest* and *joke* are synonyms.

UNIT WORDS

thief
series
conceited
deceive
weight
eighteen
fierce
pierce
friendly
forfeit
weird
siege
receipt
mischief
priest
neighborhood
yield
shield
leisure
fiery

A. Write the Unit word that is the synonym for each word.

1. ferocious _____
2. blazing _____
3. neighborly _____
4. eerie _____
5. vain _____
6. robber _____
7. mislead _____
8. relaxation _____
9. protect _____
10. surrender _____

B. The word in ( ) in each sentence below is a synonym for a Unit word. Write the Unit word that could be substituted for each word.

11. My little brother is always getting into (trouble) _____.

12. Sandy and I live in the same (locality) _____.

13. The howling wind made a (strange) _____ noise.

14. The General's plan was to set up a long-term (blockade)

_____ of the enemy town.

Sometimes you can sharpen your writing by substituting one word for a group of words in a sentence. Look at the sentences below.

The horses <u>ran quickly</u> across the field.
The horses <u>raced</u> across the field.

C. Write the Unit word that could be substituted for the underlined words in each sentence below.

15. Tanya asked the storekeeper for a <u>written note of the purchase</u>.

16. A <u>consecutive number</u> of accidents happened before the town installed a stop sign on the corner.

17. Earl has lost <u>many pounds</u> since he began to train for the marathon.

15. _____   16. _____   17. _____

Writing on Your Own

Imagine that you have just spent your first day in a new school. Write a letter to a friend about it. Describe what happened and tell how you felt about it. Compare the new school to another school you have attended. Use at least eight of the Unit words in the letter.

WRITER'S GUIDE For a sample friendly letter, turn to page 265.

14

Spelling on Your Own

```
            c h o i r
            h
          f a c u l t y
            s
            m
```

UNIT WORDS

Make a "word chain" with the Unit words. Use a letter in one word to write another one of the words. Words may go across or down, as in a puzzle. Make as many chains as necessary to use all the words, or try to fit all the words into one large chain.

MASTERY WORDS

anchor
quit
customer
inquire
ache
quarrel

Finish these exercises using the Mastery words.

1. Write the two words in which the sound /k/ that you hear in *king* is spelled with *ch*.

_____   _____

2. Write the word in which /k/ is spelled with *c*.

_____

3. Write the three words that have the sound /kw/ you hear in *queen*.

_____   _____   _____

Write the Mastery word that is a synonym for each word below.

4. ask _____

5. argue _____

6. pain _____

7. buyer _____

Finish the sentences below using the Mastery words.

"Pull the __8__ into the boat, and we'll head for home."
"We can't __9__ yet. We haven't even caught one fish."
"Let's not __10__ about it. I'm tired and my arms __11__."
"O.K. I'll __12__ at the dock. Maybe we can rent the boat again tomorrow."

8. _____   **9.** _____   **10.** _____

11. _____   **12.** _____

BONUS WORDS

delinquent
consequences
technique
licorice
turquoise
chronic
chaos
masquerade

1. Write the Bonus word in which *qu* may be pronounced either as /k/ or as /kw/. Use your **Spelling Dictionary** if you need help.

2. Write the word that ends with /s/ or /sh/.

3. Write a story title using at least two Bonus words. Then write the story using all the Bonus words.

Review

Follow these steps when you are unsure of how to spell a word.

- **Say** the word. Recall when you have heard the word used. Think about what it means.
- **Look** at the word. Find any prefixes, suffixes, or other word parts you know. Think about other words that are related in meaning and spelling. Try to picture the word in your mind.
- **Spell** the word to yourself. Think about the way each sound is spelled. Notice any unusual spelling.
- **Write** the word while looking at it. Check the way you have formed your letters. If you have not written the word clearly or correctly, write it again.
- **Check** your learning. Cover the word and write it. If you did not spell the word correctly, practice these steps until the word becomes your own.

UNIT 1
southern
campus
jealous
instead
novel
plaid
tongue
symbol
sponge
tremble

UNIT 1 Follow the directions using words from Unit 1.
Write the words that have the same vowel sound as these words. Some words have more than one vowel sound.

1. cast (two words) _____ _____

2. gem (three words) _____

_____ _____

3. fund (four words) _____ _____

_____ _____

4. itch (two words) _____ _____

5. rock _____

6. Write the three words that end with silent letters.

_____ _____ _____

UNIT 2
guarantee
ninety
oppose
complaint
concrete
tyrant
coaxed
senior
inflate
easel

UNIT 2 Follow the directions using words from Unit 2.

7. Write the two words that end with /ē/.

_____ _____

8. Write the four words that have vowel-consonant-e patterns.

_____ _____

_____ _____

9. Write the three words that have consonant clusters.

_____

10. Write the word that has /g/ spelled with two letters. _____

11. Write the word that has /ō/ spelled with two letters. _____

12. Write the two words that have /ē/ spelled with two letters.

_____   _____

13. Write the two words that have /ī/ in the first syllable.

_____   _____

14. Write the word that has /ē/ spelled with one letter in the first syllable.

_____

UNIT 3   **Follow the directions using words from Unit 3.**

15. Write the two words that have /ā/ spelled with four letters.

_____   _____

16. Write the one-syllable word that has /ē/ spelled *ie*. _____

17. Write the word that has /i/ spelled with *ei* in the second syllable.

_____

18. Write the four words that have /ē/ spelled with two letters in the second syllable.

_____   _____

_____   _____

19. Write the two words that may be pronounced two ways.

_____   _____

Finish these sentences.

20. This autumn, we moved to a new _____.

21. In my _____ time, I have been meeting new neighbors.

22. Mr. Lopez, our landlord, gave me tickets to a _____ of plays opening soon.

23. The neighbor across the street has a _____ look, but she's really friendly.

24. The thing I like best, though, is the maple tree in our yard with its

_____ red leaves.

UNIT 3
series
fierce
deceive
fiery
yield
forfeit
eighteen
receipt
leisure
neighborhood

WORDS IN TIME

Today there are standard spellings for almost all English words. This was not always the case.

The word *fire* was written *fire* or *fier*. The first version is now our modern spelling. The second spelling, however, has not been lost. It remains today in the word *fiery*. Why do you think it's important to have standard spellings?

fiery

UNIT 4
region
procedure
soldier
juvenile
foliage
plunge
wedge
gelatin
prejudice
cordial

UNIT 4 Follow the directions using words from Unit 4.
Write the words that have /j/ spelled with the letter or letters below.

25. *dge* _____

26. *j* (two words) _____ _____

27. *ge* (two words) _____ _____

28. *g* (two words) _____ _____

29. *di* (two words) _____ _____

30. *d* before *u* _____

31. Write the word that describes where a person might live.

_____

32. Write the word that describes a young person. _____

33. Write the word that describes a method for doing something.

_____

UNIT 5
character
acquaint
liquid
ridiculous
scheme
choir
auction
sacrifice
squall
quench

UNIT 5 Follow the directions using words from Unit 5.
Complete the sentence using words that have /kw/.

34. The sudden _____ helped to _____

the fire that started on the roof of the _____ loft.

Complete the sentences using words that have /k/.

35. Mai, the main _____ in the play, proposed that the

theater _____ off some stage props.

36. Her _____ seemed _____ at first,
but her efforts earned money for new costumes.

**Write the word that is a synonym for each word below. Then circle the
word that can be used both as a noun and a verb.**

37. inform _____ **38.** fluid _____

39. plot _____ **40.** foolish _____

**Write the words that could be the guide words on a dictionary page
for each group of words below. To answer, find the word from Unit 5
that comes immediately before or after each group in alphabetical
order.**

41. saddle, squad, spinach, scissors

_____ _____

42. rodent, scatter, robot, scenery

_____ _____

Spelling and Reading
A Friendly Letter

Read this friendly letter. Notice the five parts that make up the letter.

178 Highland Lane Elm Cove, New Hampshire 03096 September 21, 19——	**Heading**
Dear Colleen,	**Salutation**
I hope you feel more at home in your new school and neighborhood. Did you decide to join the school choir? You said you were thinking about it in your last letter. I'm sure you miss the fall foliage here in Elm Cove. I'm enclosing a series of photographs that show some of the trees. The region is beautiful now—alive with fiery reds and oranges. My only complaint is that fall doesn't last longer. My big news is that I'm going to plunge into a new activity: I'm going to take an art class! I bought an old easel at an auction, and I'll happily forfeit some of my leisure time to learn to paint. I also started reading a fascinating novel called *The Jealous Tyrant.* It's filled with great characters, and I think you should read it. I guarantee that you'll like it. Write again soon!	**Body**
Your friend, *Tammy*	**Closing** **Signature**

Write the answers to the questions.

1. What question does the writer ask her friend in this letter?

2. What does the writer think Colleen misses about Elm Cove?

3. To what kind of climate has Colleen moved? Which sentence from the letter makes you think as you do?

4. How do you think Tammy and Colleen met?

Underline the review words in your answers. Check to see that you spelled the words correctly.

Spelling and Writing
A Friendly Letter

Words to Help You Write

southern
campus
novel
complaint
neighborhood
character
acquaint
ridiculous
choir
tremble
coaxed
senior

Think and Discuss

A friendly letter is a written chat with a friend. The best way to write a friendly letter is to use a natural, conversational tone, as if you were visiting with your friend in person.

A friendly letter is composed of five parts. Notice the five parts in Tammy's letter on page 27. The first part, the **heading,** includes the address and date. It is followed by the **salutation,** or greeting. What is the only punctuation mark used in these two parts?

The next and most important part of a friendly letter is the **body,** or message of the letter. It should show an interest in your friend. If you are responding to a recent letter from your friend, answer any questions and make comments about the information in the letter. For instance, what does Tammy ask Colleen at the beginning of her letter?

Your friend will be eager to know how you are doing, so be sure to include information about yourself. What new activity does Tammy write about in her letter?

The **closing,** or sign-off word or words, and the **signature** come at the end of the letter. Notice that only the first word of the closing is capitalized. What punctuation mark follows the closing?

Apply

Write a **friendly letter** to a friend or relative who lives in another city or town. Follow the writing guidelines on the next page.

Prewriting

Choose the person you want to write to and think about what you would like to say.

- If you keep a journal, refer to it for ideas.
- If your letter is in response to one you have received, list questions and comments about the information in the letter.
- List any of your own activities or thoughts that you want to write about.

 THESAURUS If you need help finding the exact words you need to describe your activities, turn to page 205.

Composing

Use the lists you made to write the first draft of your friendly letter.

- Make sure you include information about what you have been doing.
- Comment on any activity your friend or relative has mentioned in the last letter.
- Look over your prewriting lists. Do you want to add any comments or information to your draft?

Revising

Read your letter and show it to a classmate. Follow these guidelines to improve your work. Use the editing and proofreading symbols on this page to indicate corrections.

 WRITER'S GUIDE For help revising your letter, see the checklist on page 265.

Editing

- Make sure you have included the five parts of a letter.
- Make sure the tone of your letter is friendly and conversational and is appropriate for the person to whom it's being sent.

Proofreading

- Check your spelling and correct any mistakes.
- Check your capitalization and punctuation.

Copy your letter neatly onto clean paper.

Publishing

Address an envelope and mail it to your friend.

	Editing and Proofreading Marks
≡	capitalize
⊙	make a period
∧	add something
⋀	add a comma
ᵛ ᵛ	add quotation marks
⌵	take something away
◯	spell correctly
¶	indent the paragraph
/	make a lowercase letter
∿ tr	transpose

7 Words with Shifting Accents

UNIT WORDS

1. competition
2. compete
3. sign
4. signature
5. muscle
6. muscular
7. bomb
8. bombard
9. original
10. originality
11. popular
12. popularity
13. relative
14. relation
15. history
16. historical
17. major
18. majority
19. democratic
20. democracy

REL·a·tive
re·LA·tion

The Unit Words

Many English words are spelled with letters that are not pronounced. Often these "silent" letters are present because they were once sounded. *Sign* was once spelled *signe* and pronounced /sig′nə/.

Related words sometimes keep these older pronunciations. We no longer pronounce the letter *g* in *sign,* but we do in *signature.* To remember "silent" letters, think of a related word.

bomb   bom**b**ard

You can use the same method to remember vowel letters. Schwa /ə/ is a weak vowel sound. You can hear it at the beginning of *alone* /ə·lōn′/. The schwa sound can be written with any vowel letter. To spell a word with schwa, think of another word with the same root. You can often hear the strong vowel sound. Look at this pair of words, for example.

rel /ə/ tive   rel /ā/ tion

The sound /ā/ in *relation* tells you that /ə/ in *relative* is spelled with *a.*

Spelling Practice

A. Write the two Unit words that have the same root word as each word below. Underline the letter that is not pronounced in the shorter Unit word.

1. signal _____ _____

2. bombardier _____ _____

3. musculature _____ _____

B. Write the spelling for each pronunciation below. Then write the Unit word that helps you identify the spelling of /ə/ in each pronunciation.

4. /dem'ə·krat'ik/ _____ _____

5. /pop'yə·lər/ _____ _____

6. /his'tə·rē/ _____ _____

7. /rel'ə·tiv/ _____ _____

8. /mā'jər/ _____ _____

9. /kom'pə·tish'ən/ _____ _____

10. /ə·rij'ə·nəl/ _____ _____

C. Complete the paragraphs below using Unit words.

Every four years, amateur athletes from around the world gather to __11__ in the Olympic Games. The opening ceremonies of these games are truly spectacular. A runner bearing a flaming torch relayed from the __12__ site of the games in Greece enters the stadium. The Olympic flame is lit. A __13__ is given, and a parade of athletes, marching behind their national flags, begins.

The __14__ of these games can be traced back to 776 B.C. Foot races were held on the plains of Olympia to honor the god Zeus. These races became so __15__ that soon the __16__ of the Greek city-states took part in the __17__.

11. _____   12. _____   13. _____

14. _____   15. _____   16. _____

17. _____

D. Write the Unit word that rhymes with each word below.

18. calm _____   19. mystery _____

20. line _____   21. bustle _____

22. sensation _____

Using the Dictionary to Spell and Write •
Multiple Definitions

Sometimes you need to look up a word in the dictionary to make sure you used it correctly in your writing. Many entry words in the dictionary have more than one definition. Each definition is numbered. When you look up an unfamiliar word, you must decide which definition best fits the context—that is, the rest of the sentence.

A. Look up the word *major* in the **Spelling Dictionary.** Write the number of the definition that matches the meaning of *major* in each sentence.

_____ **1.** Beethoven's Sixth Symphony is in the key of F *major.*

_____ **2.** Water is a *major* substance in the human body.

_____ **3.** The *major* studied the updated reports of the battle.

_____ **4.** Emily Dickinson was a *major* American poet.

B. Look up the word *original* in the **Spelling Dictionary.** Write the number of the definition that matches the meaning of *original* in each sentence.

_____ **5.** I left the *original* in the copy machine.

_____ **6.** That was a very *original* essay you wrote.

_____ **7.** The *original* inhabitants of North America probably arrived more than twenty thousand years ago.

C. Look up the word *relative.* Notice that *relative* is both a noun and an adjective. Write *N* if *relative* is a noun in the sentence or *A* if it is an *adjective.*

_____ **8.** We argued the *relative* merits of owning a dog or a cat.

_____ **9.** I have *relatives* living across the entire United States.

_____ **10.** *Loud* is really a *relative* term.

D. The dictionary often provides an illustrative example after the definition of a difficult word or concept. The **illustrative example** gives you a further clue to the meaning of the word. Look up *sign* in the **Spelling Dictionary.** Read the illustrative example after each definition. Now write your own illustrative examples for definitions **1** and **3**.

11. Definition **1** _____

12. Definition **3** _____

Emily Dickinson

Writing on Your Own

Imagine that it is Family History Week in your school. Write a short biography of an older relative for a class booklet. If possible, interview your subject and some other family members before you begin. Use as many of the Unit words as you can.

 WRITER'S GUIDE For a sample biography, turn to page 271.

Spelling on Your Own

UNIT WORDS

Copy this chart on a separate piece of paper. Then write each Unit word under the correct heading to complete the chart. You will have to write some words more than once. An example has been done for you.

Nouns	Verbs	Adjectives
sign	sign	

MASTERY WORDS

crumb
limb
comedy
colony
definition
necessary

Some words are hard to spell because not all of the letters are heard clearly. Sometimes thinking of a word that is based on the same root word helps you spell the difficult word. Write the Mastery word that is based on the same root word as each word below.

1. colonial _____
2. comedian _____
3. crumble _____
4. define _____
5. limber _____
6. necessity _____

Finish each sentence using a Mastery word.

7. The dictionary tells you the _____ of a word.

8. You will find the word _____ under *N* in the dictionary.

9. The words *tragedy* and _____ have opposite meanings.

10. A _____ is a tiny piece of bread or cracker.

The word *limb* has two meanings. Look up *limb* in the **Spelling Dictionary.** Write the number of the definition that matches the meaning of *limb* in each sentence.

_____ 11. Your arm is a <u>limb</u> of your body.

_____ 12. The tree <u>limb</u> fell on the roof.

BONUS WORDS

exhibition
exhibit
civilization
civilize
neutral
neutrality
composition
compose

Complete each sentence using a pair of Bonus words that are based on the same root word.

1. She began to ____ signs of fatigue while preparing for the art ____.
2. Many an ancient ____ attempted to ____ the barbarians.
3. The musician will ____ an original ____ for the festival.
4. Switzerland, historically a ____ nation, maintained its ____ through two world wars.

8 Foods from Many Nations

UNIT WORDS

1. parfait
2. omelet
3. mousse
4. tortilla
5. chili con carne
6. enchilada
7. tacos
8. lasagna
9. pizza
10. ravioli
11. wonton
12. chow mein
13. teriyaki
14. sauerkraut
15. pretzel
16. hamburger
17. yogurt
18. sherbet
19. gumbo
20. okra

The Unit Words

You have probably heard the expression "as American as apple pie." What do you think it means?

Every nation has foods that are commonly associated with its culture and traditions. The United States is unusual in that many of the foods we think of as American actually came from other countries. All the groups of immigrants who settled here brought with them their own national dishes. This variety of tastes and textures has become standard American fare.

The names of such foods as *omelet* and *chow mein* were given English pronunciations or spellings when they entered our language. Other names, such as *lasagna, pizza,* and *tortilla,* have kept their original pronunciations and spellings. Since languages differ in the way a sound is spelled, you should know some rules for other languages.

- In Spanish, the sound /y/ as in *yet* is spelled with *ll*. *Tortilla* is pronounced /tôr·tē'yə/.
- In Italian, the letters *gn* before a vowel are pronounced /ny/ as in *onion. Lasagna* is pronounced /lə·zän'yə/. The letter *z* is sometimes pronounced /ts/ as in *cats. Pizza* is pronounced /pēt'sə/.

Spelling Practice

A. Complete the following exercises using the Unit words.

1. Write the five food names that end with /ə/.

_____   _____   _____

_____   _____

2. Write the three food names that end with /ē/.

_____   _____   _____

3. Write the four food names that end with /t/. Then look up the words in the **Spelling Dictionary.** Circle the two words that have alternate spellings.

_____   _____

_____   _____

4. Write the two food names that contain /ā/.

_____   _____

5. Write the five food names that contain /ō/.

_____   _____   _____

_____   _____

6. Write the food name in which both syllables contain /ä/ as in *father.*

_____

7. Write the food name that begins with a consonant cluster.

_____

8. Write the food name that sounds the same as *moose.*

_____

9. Write the food name that was named after a German city.

_____

B. We are accustomed to reading about people who break world records, but here are some astounding records set by foods. Write a Unit word to complete each entry below.

Did you know that . . .

10. it required 2,859 pounds of ground beef to make the largest

_____ patty in the world?

11. a 30-foot pan was needed to cook the 12,440 eggs used in the world's

largest _____?

12. the largest tomato and cheese _____ on record was cut into 60,318 slices? It measured 80 feet 1 inch in diameter.

Proofreading • A Letter of Invitation

Debbie typed this invitation for the school's parent-student dinner. Before typing the final copy, Debbie proofread the letter. She found nine spelling mistakes and five mistakes in using commas. Read the letter carefully.

1. Find Debbie's spelling mistakes. Then circle the misspelled words.

2. Use this symbol ⌀ to delete the commas that are used incorrectly. Use this symbol ∧ to insert any missing commas.

UNIT WORDS

- parfait
- omelet
- mousse
- tortilla
- chili con carne
- enchilada
- tacos
- lasagna
- pizza
- ravioli
- wonton
- chow mein
- teriyaki
- sauerkraut
- pretzel
- hamburger
- yogurt
- sherbet
- gumbo
- okra

---

350 Main Street
Ogden, Utah, 84404
September 30, 19--

Dear Parents

The students in Room 301 would like to invite you to our annual parent-student dinner. The dinner will be held on Thursday October 10, at 7:30 P.M.

The theme of this year's dinner will be "Foods with an International Flavor." You may look forward to a mouth-watering meal that will begin with delicious won ton soup. For dessert you may choose an elegant parfet, made with ice cream and rainbow sherbert, or creamy chocolate moose. In between, we will tempt you with spicy tortilas, lasanya raveoli, and firey chili con carni.

We hope you will attend our dinner.

Yours truly
Room 301

---

3. Write the nine misspelled words correctly.

_____   _____   _____

_____   _____   _____

_____   _____   _____

Writing on Your Own

Pretend you are a reporter for your school newspaper. Your editor has asked you to describe an international food fair given by several neighborhood restaurants. Write a two-paragraph article comparing the restaurants and their foods. Use some of the Unit words. Write an attention-getting headline for your story.

 WRITER'S GUIDE For a sample comparison paragraph, turn to page 263.

Spelling on Your Own

UNIT WORDS

Write each Unit word. Then next to each word, write the country or area of the world in which the food originated. Use the **Spelling Dictionary** for help.

MASTERY WORDS

cocoa
chocolate
sausage
tomato
pickle
chowder

Finish these exercises using the Mastery words. Some words are used more than once.

1. Write the two words that have /ō/.

_____   _____

2. Write the word that has /j/. Then underline the letters that spell /j/.

_____

3. Write the three words that have /k/. Then underline the letters that spell /k/.

_____   _____   _____

4. Write the two words that begin with the consonant digraph in *peach*.

_____   _____

5. Write a lunch menu using the Mastery words.

_____

_____

_____

A Rhyme Styme is a riddle with two rhyming words for the answer. Use a Mastery word and another word to answer this Rhyme Styme.

6. What do you call a preserved cucumber that costs 5¢?

A _____   _____!

BONUS WORDS

minestrone
gazpacho
cruller
shish kebab
sukiyaki
meringue
pumpernickel
smorgasbord

What do you get if you follow these directions? The answers are Bonus words.

1. Place meat and vegetable pieces on skewers. Broil.
2. Beat egg whites and sugar until stiff. Spread on pie and bake.
3. Liquefy vegetables in a blender. Chill. Serve as soup.
4. Fry beef and vegetables quickly in a pan. Serve with rice.
5. Make a soup with vegetables, beans, and pasta.
6. Arrange salads, fish, and meats on a buffet table.
7. Mix rye and whole wheat flours with yeast. Knead. Bake bread one hour.
8. Make dough with flour, sugar, milk, and eggs. Fry in deep fat. Sprinkle with sugar.

9 Plurals

UNIT WORDS

1. sunglasses
2. carloads
3. tune-ups
4. sisters-in-law
5. drive-ins
6. standbys
7. runners-up
8. leftovers
9. cupfuls
10. handfuls
11. spoonfuls
12. mouthfuls
13. passers-by
14. shears
15. scissors
16. shorts
17. politics
18. clothes
19. headquarters
20. slacks

ALL SUNGLASSES ON SALE

Lost
One pair of
green sunglasses.

The Unit Words

Look at the signs. Does the word *sunglasses* itself tell you how many pairs are being talked about? The words *all* and *one pair* give you the clues you need to understand each sign. Some words such as *sunglasses* and *shorts* have only a plural form. You must see the word in context to know its meaning.

When a compound word is written as one word, the plural is formed by adding *s* or *es*.

carload   carloads

The plural of a hyphenated compound word is usually formed by adding *s* to the end of the word.

tune-up   tune-ups

However, if the first word in a hyphenated compound is a noun, the plural is formed by adding *s* to the first word.

sister-in-law   sisters-in-law

The word *standbys* is irregular because you do not change the *y* to *i* and add *es* to form the plural; you just add *s*. Notice also that *standbys* is not a hyphenated compound word.

REMEMBER THIS

To remember the spelling of /ə/ in the word *politics* /pol'ə·tiks/, think of the related word *political*. The strong sound /i/ in the second syllable of *political* /pə·lit'i·kəl/ tells you that *politics* is also spelled with *i*.

POL·i·tics
po·LIT·i·cal

Spelling Practice

A. Write the plural form of each compound word below.

1. carload _____ **2.** tune-up _____

3. drive-in _____ **4.** leftover _____

5. standby _____ **6.** runner-up _____

7. passer-by _____ **8.** sister-in-law _____

B. Complete the recipe below using the plural form of each word in ( ).

Add 1½ (spoonful) __9__ of salt to 1 cup of lukewarm water. Stir in 1 package of yeast. Add 1 tablespoon of shortening. Stir in 3½ (cupful) __10__ of sifted flour. Continue adding (handful) __11__ of flour until dough is stiff. Knead. Let dough rise. Then punch down, shape, and bake until golden brown.

A few (mouthful) __12__ will confirm that this is the best French bread in town!

9. _____ **10.** _____

11. _____ **12.** _____

C. Complete the letter below using the Unit words that have only a plural form.

42 Elm Street
Oneonta, New York 13820
Dear Charlene,   June 20, 19--

   I've packed all of my summer __13__ for our vacation at the beach. I cut off my old jeans to make a new pair of __14__. I couldn't find my mother's pinking __15__, so I had to use my sister's little nail __16__. You can imagine the results. I also packed my good pair of navy __17__ to wear with a jacket for dress-up occasions. I spent my whole allowance on a pair of mirrored __18__. That ought to make me shine on the beach.

   Representative Barbara Jackson has opened her campaign __19__ around the corner from my school. Since I'm really interested in __20__, I think I'll volunteer to work for her reelection.

                    Love,
                    Anita

13. _____ **14.** _____ **15.** _____

16. _____ **17.** _____ **18.** _____

19. _____ **20.** _____

Spelling and Language • Agreement of Subject and Verb

UNIT WORDS

sunglasses
carloads
tune-ups
sisters-in-law
drive-ins
standbys
runners-up
leftovers
cupfuls
handfuls
spoonfuls
mouthfuls
passers-by
shears
scissors
shorts
politics
clothes
headquarters
slacks

A verb must agree with its subject in number. If the subject of a sentence is singular, use a singular verb. If the subject is plural, use a plural verb. Look at the example below.

This pizza <u>is</u> delicious.
These pizzas <u>are</u> delicious.

Use a Unit word or its singular form to complete each sentence below.

1. The _____ are still in the dish on the table.

2. A _____ of bleach is all you need in the wash.

3. Do you know what movie the _____ is showing tonight?

4. There were two _____ in the essay contest.

5. Frequent _____ prolong the life of a car.

6. Do _____ notice the sign in the store window?

7. The _____ are waiting for seats on the next flight.

8. One _____ of my uncle's chili is enough to set your tongue on fire.

9. At her wedding, her _____ were introduced to her.

10. Two _____ of volunteers parked by Joe's house.

As you know, some nouns, such as *politics* and *headquarters,* may be singular in meaning although plural in form. These words take a singular or plural verb depending on their meaning in the sentence. Other words, such as *sunglasses* and *slacks,* always take a plural verb no matter what their meaning is in context. The word *clothes* has only a plural meaning, and it always takes a plural verb.

Writing on Your Own

Imagine this scene. A customer is talking to a travel agent. The customer wants to go on a very unusual vacation. Write the conversation between the customer and the travel agent. Use as many plurals and as many Unit words as you can.

 WRITER'S GUIDE For a sample conversation, turn to page 269.

Spelling on Your Own

UNIT WORDS

Complete this chart by writing the Unit words that fit into each category.

People (4 words)	Objects (7 words)	Places (2 words)

Five Unit words describe measurements or amounts of things. Write these words in alphabetical order. Then write the two remaining words and use each in a sentence.

MASTERY WORDS

wives
bunches
taxes
pants
measles
athletics

Write the plural form for each word below.

1. tax _____
2. bunch _____
3. wife _____

Finish each sentence using a Mastery word.

4. Mr. Osaka bought a suit with an extra pair of _____ .

5. Dr. Johnson gives a _____ shot to each of her patients.

6. Our town has a good after-school _____ program.

Write the word in ( ) that belongs in each sentence below.

7. Is there a sales (tax, taxes) on orange juice? _____

8. A (bunch, bunches) of grapes is a good snack. _____

9. (Athletic, Athletics) is my favorite subject. _____

Write the Mastery word that fits each group of words below.

10. mumps, chicken pox, polio _____

11. jackets, shirts, shoes _____

12. children, parents, husbands _____

BONUS WORDS

men-of-war
lilies of the valley
mathematics
proceedings
shrimp
trout
stand-ins
salesclerks

Write the singular form for each Bonus word that has one. Then complete the sentences using the Bonus words.

1. The chairperson interrupted the ___ of the meeting.
2. Does that actor use ___ for his stunt scenes?
3. How many ___ sailed with the Spanish Armada?
4. ___ is my fifth-period class.
5. Lobster and ___ are edible shellfish.
6. The ___ were asked to check the store's inventory.
7. The florist used ___ in the flower arrangement.
8. No one may catch more than three ___ a day.

10 Homophones

UNIT WORDS

1. principle
2. principal
3. stationery
4. stationary
5. pore
6. pour
7. idle
8. idol
9. dying
10. dyeing
11. alter
12. altar
13. cereal
14. serial
15. naval
16. navel
17. patients
18. patience
19. overdo
20. overdue

It's the principal who counts.

It's the principle that counts.

The Unit Words

The words *principal* and *principle* sound the same, but they are spelled differently and have different meanings. Words like these are called **homophones**. The word *homophone* comes from two Greek word parts: *homo,* meaning "same," and *phone,* meaning "sound."

To help you remember the spelling of a homophone, you may find it helpful to use a mnemonic /ni·män′ik/ device. A **mnemonic device** assists the memory. Here are four mnemonic devices.

The princip<u>al</u> is your p<u>al</u>.
A princip<u>le</u> can become a <u>le</u>gal document.
You write <u>le</u>tters on station<u>e</u>ry.
A st<u>a</u>tue is station<u>a</u>ry.

REMEMBER THIS

To remember which spelling to use for the homophone *serial,* meaning "a story or play in installments," think of the related word *series.*

A <u>seri</u>al is a <u>seri</u>es of TV shows.

Spelling Practice

A. Complete the following exercises using the Unit words. Remember, you will find /ə/ only in an unaccented syllable.

1. Write the five words in which /ən/ is spelled *on*.

_____   _____   _____

_____   _____

2. Write the two words in which /ən/ is spelled with *an*.

_____   _____

3. Write the four words in which /əm/ is spelled with *um*.

_____   _____

_____   _____

4. Write the four words in which /əm/ is spelled with *om*.

_____   _____

_____   _____

5. Write the two words in which /əm/ is spelled with *em*.

_____   _____

6. Write the word in which /əm/ is spelled in a different way.

_____

A **malapropism** /mal'ə·prop'is'əm/ is a mix-up in the use of words that is often quite funny. A word that has a similar sound is used instead of the correct word. These verbal slips are named after Mrs. Malaprop, a comic character in a play called *The Rivals.* Here is an example of a malapropism: "I love to eat synonym toast for breakfast." Of course, the writer meant to use *cinnamon* for *synonym*.

B. Each underlined word below is an example of malapropism. Write the Unit word that should be used.

The great detective realized that the Case of the (**7**) <u>Fanfare</u> Thief was solved. He now knew the identity of the (**8**) <u>village</u> who had stolen the crested (**9**) <u>album</u> from above the castle door. Soon, he would (**10**) <u>summer</u> the suspects into the (**11**) <u>auditory</u> and force the criminal to (**12**) <u>a bandit</u> his disguise. In the (**13**) <u>opossum</u> of the detective, his part of the (**14**) <u>barge-in</u> was complete.

7. _____   **8.** _____

9. _____   **10.** _____   **11.** _____

12. _____   **13.** _____   **14.** _____

Spelling and Language • Synonyms

English is a language that is rich in synonyms. Words borrowed from other languages, invented words, and variations of words all add color and variety to our speech and writing. In English, we are usually not limited to one particular word to express a thought.

A. Write the Unit word that belongs in each group of synonyms.

1. belief, feeling, view   _____

2. rascal, wrongdoer, bully   _____

3. desert, quit, leave   _____

4. haggle, barter, trade   _____

5. insignia, badge, decoration _____

6. indication, sign, evidence   _____

Look at the groups of words above. Although the words in each group are synonyms, their meanings are not identical. When you write, choose the synonym that clearly expresses just what you mean.

B. The underlined word in each sentence below is a synonym for a Unit word, but its meaning in the context is vague. Rewrite each sentence and sharpen its meaning by substituting the more precise Unit word.

7. The students assembled in the <u>hall</u>.

_____

8. They wondered why the principal would <u>call</u> them together today.

_____

9. He asked them to create a <u>phrase</u> to launch the school fund raiser.

_____

10. The funds would go toward a new <u>tile</u> floor for the cafeteria.

_____

11. The new floor would be a colorful <u>red</u> and white.

_____

Writing on Your Own

Imagine that you are running for president of your class. Write the campaign speech that you will deliver at a class meeting. Convince students to vote for you by telling them why you are a good leader and what your goals are for the class. Use at least five of the Unit words.

 WRITER'S GUIDE For help revising your speech, see the checklist on page 257.

Spelling on Your Own

UNIT WORDS

Fourteen of the Unit words below are misspelled. Write these words correctly.

1. opinon	**2.** linolium	**3.** emblum	**4.** venim
5. summon	**6.** phantam	**7.** bargain	**8.** denem
9. antham	**10.** million	**11.** pendulem	**12.** slogin
13. premium	**14.** crimsun	**15.** villan	**16.** abandon
17. symtom	**18.** accustumed	**19.** auditorium	**20.** pelicen

MASTERY WORDS

Finish these exercises using the Mastery words.

1. Write two words that have /ən/ spelled with *ain.*

_____   _____

2. Write the word that has /ən/ spelled with *on.* _____

3. Write the two words that have /əm/ spelled with *um.*

_____   _____

4. Write the word that has /əm/ spelled with *om.* _____

Write the Mastery word that is a synonym for each word below.

5. sure _____   **6.** liberty _____

7. drape _____   **8.** record_____

Finish each sentence using a Mastery word.

9. Gail wanted an _____ to wear while she cooked.

10. The store had them in small, _____, and large.

11. The color matched that of the _____ in her kitchen.

12. Gail was _____ she had made the right choice.

Mastery Words:
apron
certain
curtain
freedom
medium
album

BONUS WORDS

1. Write each Bonus word. Next to each Bonus word, write any other word that has the same spelling for /ən/ or /əm/.

2. Write a paragraph using all the Bonus words.

3. The words *siphon* and *phantom* are derived from ancient Greek words that were spelled with the letter *phi* (Φ). In English, *phi* has become *ph* and is pronounced /f/. Write five more words that have /f/ spelled with *ph.* Check a dictionary to find out if the words you wrote come from Greek.

Bonus Words:
veteran
gruesome
abdomen
comedian
siphon
tantrum
stadium
planetarium

14 The Sounds /ər/ and /əl/

UNIT WORDS

1. laser
2. calendar
3. donor
4. parcel
5. baffle
6. universal
7. civil
8. moderator
9. indicator
10. commuter
11. triangular
12. classical
13. operator
14. peril
15. caterpillar
16. vessel
17. muffle
18. narrator
19. trample
20. panel

The Unit Words

The photograph above shows laser beams. A laser produces light that travels in a narrow beam of parallel waves. Laser beams are used in science, medicine, communications, and industry. *Laser* is a fairly new word in the English language. *Calendar* and *donor,* on the other hand, are words that come from Latin and have been part of our language for hundreds of years. Yet each word, old or new, presents the same spelling problem: What letter spells the weak vowel sound /ə/?

In the Unit words, /ər/ is spelled with these letters.

er as in *laser*
ar as in *calendar*
or as in *donor*

In the Unit words, /əl/ is spelled with these letters.

el as in *parcel*
le as in *baffle*
al as in *universal*
il as in *civil*

REMEMBER THIS

To help you spell *laser,* think of what each letter in the word stands for. Laser is formed from the initials of the words <u>l</u>ight <u>a</u>mplification by <u>s</u>timulated <u>e</u>mission of <u>r</u>adiation.

Spelling Practice

A. Complete these exercises using the Unit words.

1. Write the two words in which /ər/ is spelled with *er*.

_____ _____

2. Write the three words in which /ər/ is spelled with *ar*.

_____ _____ _____

3. Write the three words in which /əl/ is spelled with *el*.

_____ _____ _____

4. Write the three words in which /əl/ is spelled with *le*.

_____ _____ _____

5. Write the four words in which /əl/ is spelled in different ways.

_____ _____

_____ _____

The /ər/ at the end of a word is often spelled with *or* if the suffix *-ion* or *-ation* can be added to the base word or root. For example, direct<u>ion</u>—direct<u>or</u>.

B. Write the Unit word that has the same root as each word below.

6. moderation _____ **7.** donation _____

8. operation _____ **9.** narration _____

10. indication _____

C. The suffix *-er* or *-or* sometimes means "one who does." Use the Unit words to complete these exercises.

11. Write the word that means "one who commutes."

_____

12. Write the word that means "one who gives." _____

13. Write the word that means "the person or thing that points out."

_____

14. Write the word that means "one who narrates." _____

D. Write some more words that mean "one who does."

15. Add *-er* to a Unit word to make a new word that means "a person or thing that quiets noise."

_____

16. Add *-ist* to a Unit word to make a new word that means "one who participates in a panel discussion."

_____

Using the Dictionary to Spell and Write •
Multiple Definitions

UNIT WORDS

laser
calendar
donor
parcel
baffle
universal
civil
moderator
indicator
commuter
triangular
classical
operator
peril
caterpillar
vessel
muffle
narrator
trample
panel

Remember that many entry words in the dictionary have more than one meaning. You can use the different meanings to check if you used a word correctly in your writing. Most dictionaries arrange the definitions so that the most common meaning is given first. But the most common meaning may not be the one that fits the context of the sentence you are reading. So you must keep searching until you find the correct meaning.

A. Look up the word *civil* in the **Spelling Dictionary.** Write the number of the definition that matches the meaning of *civil* in each sentence.

_____ **1.** Please act in a *civil* way toward your brother.

_____ **2.** The *Civil* War began with a shot fired at Fort Sumter.

_____ **3.** Martin Luther King, Jr., led the *civil* rights movement.

_____ **4.** Judge Gomez was appointed to the *civil* court.

B. Look up the word *panel* in the **Spelling Dictionary.** Notice that *panel* is both a noun and a verb. For each sentence below, write *N* if *panel* is used as a noun and *V* if it is used as a verb.

_____ **5.** The *panel* rated each exhibit on a scale from 1 to 10.

_____ **6.** Mr. Tallchief asked Mary to help him *panel* the wall.

_____ **7.** Lights on the control *panel* flashed on and off.

_____ **8.** You can turn jeans into a skirt by adding a fabric *panel*.

C. Look up the word *parcel* in the **Spelling Dictionary.**

9. Write a sentence using *parcel* as a noun.

_____

10. Write a sentence using *parcel* as a verb.

_____

Writing on Your Own

Write a letter to the manager of a local radio station asking to hear more of the music you like. In a few paragraphs, compare and contrast the music you prefer with other kinds of music—country, rock, or opera, for example. Explain why your music deserves more time on the air. End your letter with a specific request. The following Unit words may be useful: *universal, indicator, classical, baffle.*

 WRITER'S GUIDE For a sample paragraph of contrast, turn to page 263.

Spelling on Your Own

Write the Unit words. Underline the verbs and circle the adjectives. Then write the nouns in alphabetical order. A word may be written more than once.

MASTERY WORDS

Write the Mastery word that has the same /ər/ spelling as each word below.

1. thunder _____   **2.** anchor _____

3. collar _____

Write the Mastery word that has the same /əl/ spelling as each word below.

4. pencil _____   **5.** juggle _____

6. pedal _____

The suffixes *-er* and *-or* sometimes mean "one who does." A juggler is a person who juggles.

Write the word that matches each of these definitions.

7. a person who jogs _____

8. a person who invents _____

9. a person who whistles _____

Homophones are words that sound alike but are spelled differently and have different meanings.

10. Write the word that means "a person who sells."

_____

11. Write the Mastery word that is a homophone for the word you wrote for **10**.

_____

12. Write a sentence using the words you wrote for **10** and **11**.

_____

cellar
pupil
medal
whistle
jogger
inventor

BONUS WORDS

Write the Bonus word that is a synonym for each word.

1. clothes   **2.** observer   **3.** attempt   **4.** watch

5. romantic   **6.** antenna   **7.** rival   **8.** trespasser

The word *spectator* comes from the Latin root *spect,* meaning "see." List at least five other words that contain the root *spect.* Then write sentences for five of the words you listed.

endeavor
vigil
sentimental
spectator
aerial
apparel
competitor
intruder

15 Words from Spanish

UNIT WORDS

1. alligator
2. mosquito
3. coyote
4. vanilla
5. lasso
6. stampede
7. corral
8. mustang
9. mesa
10. bronco
11. hammock
12. bonanza
13. patio
14. canyon
15. cafeteria
16. burro
17. rodeo
18. fiesta
19. pueblo
20. adobe

The Unit Words

The map of the United States has not always looked as it does today. Until the middle of the nineteenth century, vast sections of the country belonged to other nations. For centuries, for example, the states named on the map were part of New Spain. Later, Mexico governed the western territories.

The words in this unit are of Spanish origin. Words such as *mosquito* and *alligator* have been part of English since the early days of the Spanish explorers. However, most of the words we have borrowed from Spanish came into our language after 1800. At that time, English-speaking settlers began moving westward and encountered the Spanish in the Southwest and California. Today, people in this area continue to use more names and words derived from Spanish than people in other regions of the nation do.

Spelling Practice

A. Complete the following exercises using the Unit words.

1. Write the six words in which /k/ is spelled with c or *qu.*

_____   _____   _____

_____   _____   _____

2. Write the other word that contains /k/. _____

3. Write the three words that have vowel-consonant-e spellings.

_____   _____   _____

4. Write the word that has /ən/ spelled with *on* and the word that has /ər/ spelled with *or.*

_____   _____

B. Below is a list of Spanish words and their definitions. Write the Unit word that comes from each word. Use the **Spelling Dictionary** if you need help.

5. *lazo,* "a snare"

6. *mestengo,* "a stray"

7. *borrico,* "donkey"

_____   _____   _____

8. *el lagarto,* "the lizard"

9. *vainilla,* "a pod"

10. *estampida,* "stamping"

_____   _____   _____

C. Some Unit words are the same in both Spanish and English. Write the word that fits each definition below.

11. festival _____

12. flat-topped hill _____

13. courtyard _____

14. a rich find _____

15. brick _____

16. a competition _____

D. Complete each sentence using the Unit words.

17. A Hopi _____ was usually built on top of a

_____ as a defense against attack.

18. Houses made of _____ have stood for centuries.

19. A sturdy _____ and yards of

_____ netting are all you need to sleep comfortably

in the jungle.

Proofreading • A Current Events Report

UNIT WORDS

alligator
mosquito
coyote
vanilla
lasso
stampede
corral
mustang
mesa
bronco
hammock
bonanza
patio
canyon
cafeteria
burro
rodeo
fiesta
pueblo
adobe

Jennifer wrote this current events report. Now she must correct her work. Jennifer made six spelling mistakes and six capitalization errors. Read the report carefully.

1. Find Jennifer's spelling mistakes. Then circle the misspelled words.

2. Use these proofreading marks to correct Jennifer's capitalization errors. Draw three small lines under each letter that should be capitalized. Draw a slanting line through each letter that should not be capitalized. For example: my Dog's name is sandy.

A burro Bananaza

An amazing rescue mission took place in the Grand canyon one summer. Hundreds of wild burrows were airlifted to safety and a new life. The National Park service planned to destroy the floppy-eared animals if they remained in the Park. The burros eat the plants needed by the deer in the canyonlands.

Dave Ericsson, an experienced donkey herder, was hired by the Fund for Animals to save the little burros. Earlier attempts to capture the donkeys had failed. Even after being tranquilized with darts, many had stampeeded. In their panic, they often ran over the rocky ledges in the canyon. The burros were lasoed by mr. Ericsson, strapped into hammicks, and flown by helicopters to a nearby coral. They were then shipped to a farm in texas. There, they will be tamed so that they may be adopted as pets.

---

3. Write the six misspelled words correctly.

_____   _____   _____

_____   _____   _____

 WRITER'S GUIDE See the editing and proofreading marks on page 258.

Writing on Your Own

Write a short news story about an important event for a current events bulletin-board display. Choose an event that occurred within the last month. Read several newspaper and magazine articles to gather your facts. Then put your ideas in order. Finally title your story with a clear summary of its main idea. Use some Unit words.

 WRITER'S GUIDE For a sample news story, turn to page 270.

Spelling on Your Own

UNIT WORDS

Write sentences including all of the Unit words. Use as many of the words as you can in one sentence and underline each Unit word. See how few sentences you can write.

MASTERY WORDS

**ranch
potato
tuna
barbecue
tornado
cargo**

1. Write the three words that have the sound /ō/ you hear at the beginning of *open*.

_____   _____   _____

2. Write the word that ends with the sound /ə/ you hear at the beginning of *alone*.

_____

3. Write the word that you sometimes see written as Bar-B-Q.

_____

4. Write the word that has only one syllable. _____

5. Write the plural form of each Mastery word. Remember to add *es* to words ending in *ch* or words ending in a consonant and *o*.

_____   _____   _____

_____   _____   _____

6. Anna wrote this shopping list. Circle her three spelling errors. Write the misspelled words correctly.

> 1 loaf bread
> a jar barbeque sauce
> 3 lb. potatoe salad
>
> 4 cans toona
> 2 lb. hamburger
> 1 qt. milk

BONUS WORDS

**filibuster
vigilante
siesta
plaza
sierra
cinch
avocado
pimiento**

Write the Bonus word that fits each definition.

1. a saddle strap   **2.** delay passage of a law   **3.** a fruit with a pit

4. an afternoon nap   **5.** a mountain range   **6.** a sweet pepper

7. an open square   **8.** a member of a citizens' group that keeps order

The Spanish word *vigilante* comes from the Latin *vigilare*, meaning "to keep watch." Think of two English words that come from *vigilare* and use each in a sentence.

UNIT WORDS

1. friendlier
2. sparkled
3. pitied
4. satisfying
5. conveyed
6. pried
7. dismayed
8. hesitated
9. devoted
10. varied
11. flimsiest
12. pursuing
13. severest
14. wittiest
15. sturdiest
16. horrified
17. struggling
18. identifying
19. eyed
20. eyeing

Maybe they'd be friendlier if they knew we only wanted to shoot their pictures.

The Unit Words

The word *friendlier* means "more friendly." You can change the meaning or add to the meaning of a word by adding the inflectional endings *er, est, s, ed,* and *ing.*

Follow these spelling patterns when you need to add an inflectional ending to a base word.

1. When a word ends in e, drop the final e if the inflectional ending begins with a vowel.

    sparkle   sparkled   sparkling

    ☐ The words *eyeing* and *dyeing* are exceptions to this rule.

    eye   eyed   eyeing

2. When a word ends in a consonant and y, change y to i, unless the ending begins with i.

    pity   pitied   pitying

3. When a word ends in a vowel and y, keep the y.

    convey   conveyed   conveying

REMEMBER THIS

The sound of final /ā/ is usually spelled with *ay,* as in *pay.* Sometimes final /ā/ is spelled with *ey; convey, obey,* and *they* are examples. This sentence will help you remember how to spell *convey.*

Th**ey** conv**ey**ed a message to ob**ey**.

Spelling Practice

A. Add *ed* to each base word and write the word.

1. sparkle _____
2. hesitate _____
3. devote _____
4. eye _____
5. pity _____
6. vary _____
7. horrify _____
8. pry _____
9. convey _____
10. dismay _____

B. Add *ing* to each base word and write the word.

11. struggle _____
12. pursue _____
13. satisfy _____
14. identify _____
15. eye _____
16. dismay _____

C. Add *est* to each base word to form a Unit word.

17. severe _____
18. flimsy _____
19. witty _____
20. sturdy _____

D. Write the following words.

21. friendly + er _____
22. dye + ing _____

E. Write the Unit word that is a synonym for each word.

23. weakest _____
24. strongest _____
25. harshest _____
26. funniest _____
27. shone _____
28. sent _____

F. Write the Unit word that is a homophone for each word.

29. pride _____
30. I'd _____

G. Complete the paragraph using the Unit words.

It was an exciting and __31__ experience for me to observe guide dogs and their owners conscientiously __32__ the task of learning to work together as a team. The dogs had been trained by a professional instructor to guide their owners around obstacles and to stop at all curbs. Even if a "forward" signal is __33__ to the dog by its owner, the dog will not move when a potential danger is present. The new owners soon learned to trust and rely on their well-trained and __34__ dogs.

31. _____
32. _____
33. _____
34. _____

Spelling and Language • Comparison of Adjectives

You often need to compare things or ideas in speech and writing. To compare a quality expressed by an adjective, you can add an inflectional ending to many adjectives. To compare two things, add *er* to form the comparative form of an adjective. To compare three or more things, add *est* to form the superlative form. Look at the sentences below.

> Consuela is tall.
> Alberto is tall<u>er</u> than Consuela.
> Manuel is the tall<u>est</u> in the family.

A. Write the comparative and superlative forms.

	COMPARATIVE	SUPERLATIVE
1. friendly	_____	_____
2. flimsy	_____	_____
3. witty	_____	_____
4. sturdy	_____	_____
5. severe	_____	_____

B. Complete the sentences below using the words you wrote for **1–5**.

6. Last winter we had the _____ storm that I can recall.

7. Did you think Jane's skit was _____ than Joan's was?

8. That's the _____ excuse I've heard in years.

Some adjectives of two syllables and most adjectives of three or more syllables use the words *more* and *most* to form their comparative and superlative forms. If you are uncertain which form to use, check a dictionary. Look at these sentences.

> This hat looks ridiculous.
> That hat looks even <u>more</u> ridiculous.
> The third hat looks the <u>most</u> ridiculous of all.

Writing on Your Own

Imagine that you are the movie critic for a community newspaper. Write a short review comparing the best and the worst films you have seen recently. Describe some of the details of each film to support your opinions. Use as many of the Unit words as you can. You may also want to use the comparative forms of some adjectives.

WRITER'S GUIDE For help revising your movie review, use the editing and proofreading marks on page 258.

Spelling on Your Own

The chart below has been started for you. Copy and complete the chart using all the remaining Unit words.

VERB	+ed	+ing		ADJ	+er	+est
eye	eyed	eyeing		witty	wittier	wittiest

MASTERY WORDS

promised
noticed
applying
lying
lied
prettiest

Write each word below with *ed* added.

1. promise _____
2. notice _____
3. lie _____

Write each word below with *ing* added.

4. apply _____
5. lie _____

Finish each sentence using a Mastery word.

6. Lin had been thinking about _____ for a job.

7. Buying the _____ clothes she could find had cut into her budget.

8. She _____ her Dad she would start looking today.

The verbs *lie* and *lay* are often confused. *Lie* means "be in a flat position." *Lay* means "place."

The past form of *lie* is *lay*: For years, Sleeping Beauty <u>lay</u> asleep.
The past form of *lay* is *laid*: She <u>laid</u> the vase down gently.

Be careful not to mix up either word with the verb *lie,* meaning "tell a falsehood." The past form of *lie* is *lied.* For example, "She <u>lied</u> to me."

Use the past form of *lie, lay,* or *lie* to finish these sentences.

9. Nancy _____ in bed too late this morning.

10. She was glad she had _____ out clothes last night.

11. She hoped her friend hadn't _____ about meeting her.

BONUS WORDS

mystified
justified
drowsier
terrifying
contaminated
clarifying
concentrated
evaluated

Write the Bonus word that is related to each word.

1. value
2. clarity
3. mystery
4. contamination
5. terror
6. central
7. justice
8. drowsily

Write a short mystery story using the Bonus words.

17 Music and Art Words

UNIT WORDS

1. realistic
2. abstract
3. guitar
4. sketch
5. landscape
6. portrait
7. sculpture
8. sculptor
9. woodcut
10. ceramics
11. batik
12. chorus
13. rehearsal
14. orchestra
15. symphony
16. lyrics
17. composer
18. concert
19. waltz
20. polka

Pablo Picasso. *Man with a Guitar.* 1913. Oil on canvas. Collection. The Museum of Modern Art, NY. Andre Meyer Bequest.

Edgar Degas, *Degas's Father Listening to Pagans.* c. 1869. Oil on canvas. Musée du Louvre, Paris.

The Unit Words

The two paintings of guitar players are examples of realistic and abstract art. An artist who has a realistic style tries to give you a "true-to-life" feeling, while an artist who has an abstract style feels free to vary or change nature in order to create a more imaginative work.

Art and music play an important part in our lives. Every civilization has its own history of the arts. The history of Western art goes back to ancient Greek culture. Many of the words we use in speaking or writing about the arts—words such as *chorus, orchestra, symphony, ceramics, guitar,* and *lyrics*—come from Greek words.

REMEMBER THIS

The letters *gu* in the word *guitar* have the sound /g/. This sentence may help you remember the silent *u* in *guitar*.
"Gee, U can play the guitar!"

Spelling Practice

A. Complete the following exercises using the Unit words.

1. Write the six words that come from Greek.

_____   _____   _____

_____   _____   _____

2. Which two words you wrote for **1** have /i/ spelled with *y*?

_____   _____

3. Which two words you wrote for **1** have /k/ spelled with *ch*?

_____   _____

4. Which word you wrote for **1** has /f/ spelled with *ph*?

_____

5. Write the two Unit words that have /ch/.

_____   _____

6. Write the word that means "true to life."

_____

7. What long vowel sound do you hear in the first syllable of the word you wrote for **6**?

_____

8. Write the word that describes a type of art that is not "true to life."

_____

9. Write the word that means "a practice session."

_____

10. Write the two words that name dances.

_____   _____

11. Write the word you wrote for **10** that has /ō/. _____

12. Write the two words that end with a suffix that means "one who does."

_____   _____

B. Write the Unit word that goes with each definition below.

13. cloth colored using wax and dye   _____

14. likeness of a person   _____

15. picture of scenery   _____

16. program of music   _____

17. print made from carved wood block   _____

Proofreading • A News Story

Sally wrote this article for the school newspaper. She must now proofread her work before handing it in. Sally made twelve spelling mistakes and forgot to use a period in four places. Read the news story.

1. Find Sally's spelling mistakes. Then circle the misspelled words.
2. Insert the four missing periods and circle them.

UNIT WORDS

realistic
abstract
guitar
sketch
landscape
portrait
sculpture
sculptor
woodcut
ceramics
batik
chorus
rehearsal
orchestra
symphony
lyrics
composer
concert
waltz
polka

> The Hillside J.H.S auditoriom was crowded last Thursday evening at 8 PM. as the audience waited pateintly for the spring consert to begin. Finally, with a wave of Mr Kodner's baton, the opening strains of the national anthem floated through the air.
>
> The program opened with Saint-Saëns's Symfony for Piano and Orcestra "The Blue Danube" walts by Strauss and a Beethoven sonata followed.
>
> After the intermission, Alan Jenkins, who has studied classical guiter for several years, performed two sonatas by Scarlatti. The school choros ended the evening's selections with a medley of songs from West Side Story, the musical written by the American composor Leonard Bernstein, with lirics by Steven Sondheim.
>
> Refreshments were served in the cafateria after the performance.

3. Write the twelve misspelled words correctly.

_____ _____ _____

_____ _____ _____

_____ _____ _____

_____

4. Write Sally's first paragraph correctly. Be sure you include the missing periods.

_____

_____

_____

_____

_____

Writing on Your Own

Pretend that you have been asked to plan the publicity for a concert at school. Write a letter to an artist giving directions for the kind of poster you want. Tell the exact words you want to appear on the poster and set a deadline for the artist's sketch. Use as many of the Unit words as you can.

WRITER'S GUIDE For a sample business letter, turn to page 266.

Spelling on Your Own

UNIT WORDS

Write in alphabetical order the fifteen Unit words that have /k/. Underline the letters that spell /k/. Then alphabetize the other words.

MASTERY WORDS

musical
artist
performance
instrument
painting
museum

Finish these exercises using the Mastery words.

1. Write the two words that have /yo͞o/ as in *unit.*

_____   _____

2. Which letter in the words you wrote for **1** spells /yo͞o/? _____

3. Write the two words in which the letter *u* spells /ə/.

_____   _____

4. Write the word that has /ā/. _____

5. Write the word that has the sounds /är/ heard in *farmer.*_____

6. Write the word that has the sounds /ôr/ heard in *fork.* _____

Joy wrote this note. Find her six spelling mistakes. Circle them.

> I'm having a great time at camp. The girls in my cabin took a ten-mile hike. In the evenings, I can learn to play any musicel instrament I want. I chose the guitar. I'll give a performance when I get home.
>
> We also took a trip to Boston. We went to the art museem. The panting I liked best was by an artest named Mary Cassatt.

7. Write the six misspelled words correctly.

_____   _____   _____

_____   _____   _____

BONUS WORDS

percussion
piccolo
saxophone
xylophone
acrylics
kiln
graphics
lithograph

Complete the sentences below using the Bonus words.

1. The ____ is a small flute.

2. Laura used ____ to paint her self-portrait.

3. We glazed our pots and put them in the ____.

4. Mrs. Campbell sells drawings, posters, and other kinds of ____.

5. Some artists destroy the lithography stone after they print a ____.

6. Joann likes to play jazz music on her ____.

7. The drum and the ____ are both ____ instruments.

Review

UNIT 13

bargain
auditorium
accustomed
million
symptom
pelican
villain
linoleum
phantom
opinion

UNIT 13 Follow the directions using words from Unit 13.

Complete each of these words with the letters that spell /ən/ or /əm/. Write the word.

1. sympt_____ _____   2. milli_____ _____

3. accust_____ed _____   4. barg_____ _____

5. auditori_____ _____   6. vill_____ _____

7. linole_____ _____   8. pelic_____ _____

9. phant_____ _____   10. opini_____ _____

UNIT 14

calendar
peril
parcel
operator
commuter
laser
civil
universal
triangular
baffle

UNIT 14 Write the word or words from Unit 14 that have /ər/ or /əl/ spelled with the same letters as each word below.

11. error _____   12. label _____

13. pupil (two words) _____ _____

14. saucer (two words) _____ _____

15. cellar (two words) _____ _____

16. pedal _____   17. title _____

WORDS IN TIME

Villain comes from *villa,* the Latin word for farm. *Villains* were originally farm servants, or peasants, who worked for a feudal lord. The word *villain* has come down to us meaning "a wicked person." What might this say about the attitudes of the feudal lords toward the peasants?

UNIT 15 Follow the directions using words from Unit 15.

18. Write the four words that have /k/.

_____ _____

_____ _____

19. Write the four words that have /ō/.

_____ _____

_____ _____

20. Write the four words that end in /ə/.

_____ _____

_____ _____

UNIT 15

mosquito
cafeteria
rodeo
canyon
vanilla
fiesta
mesa
alligator
patio
coyote

Complete the paragraph.

Dennis dreamed he was hiking to the bottom of a __21__. He could hear the lonely howl of a __22__. Somehow, an __23__ from the swamps crawled into his dream. He was glad when he woke up safe, sitting on his own __24__. The only creature attacking him there was a pesky __25__.

21. _____ **22.** _____ **23.** _____

24. _____ **25.** _____

UNIT 16 Follow the directions using words from Unit 16.
Add *ed* to each of these base words.

26. hesitate _____ **27.** vary _____

28. convey _____ **29.** pity _____

30. dismay _____

UNIT 16

varied
hesitated
satisfying
eyeing
friendlier
conveyed
pitied
dismayed
pursuing
wittiest

Add *ing* to each of these base words.

31. satisfy _____ **32.** eye _____

33. pursue _____

Write the words that are synonyms for these words.

34. paused _____ **35.** alarmed _____

36. chasing _____ **37.** fulfilling _____

38. different _____ **39.** carried _____

40. observing _____ **41.** funniest _____

42. nicer _____

rehearsal
orchestra
sculptor
guitar
sketch
chorus
lyrics
ceramics
sculpture
symphony

UNIT 17   Follow the directions using words from Unit 17.
Write the word that fits each description.

43. a group of people who sing together _____

44. the art of making pottery from clay _____

45. a practice session _____

46. a large group of musicians performing together _____

47. a quickly made or rough drawing _____

48. the words to a song _____

49. a musical composition _____

50. a person who creates sculpture _____

51. a musical instrument _____

52. the art of carving or shaping figures _____

**Six of the nine words below are spelled incorrectly. Circle the
misspelled words and write them correctly.**

rehaersal	lyrics	chorus
ceramics	gitar	orkestra
simphony	sculpchure	sculpter

53. _____   **54.** _____   **55.** _____

56. _____   **57.** _____   **58.** _____

Finish these two sentences. You will use each word from Unit 17 once.

59. At today's dress _____, the _____

played the Brahms _____ beautifully, but the singers

in the _____ did not know all the

_____ to their song.

60. The _____ drew a _____ of a man

playing a _____ before she molded a

_____ of him in the _____ shop.

Spelling Practice

A. Add *ed* or *ing* to each one-syllable or compound word below to form a Unit word.

1. hum _____ **2.** dim _____

3. stun _____ **4.** quiz _____

5. outfit _____

B. The final syllable is accented in each of these words. Add *ed* or *ing* to each one to form a Unit word.

6. omit _____ **7.** commit _____

8. permit _____ **9.** submit _____

10. regret _____ **11.** upset _____

12. forget _____ **13.** forbid _____

C. The final syllable is not accented in these words. Add *ed* or *ing* to each word to form a Unit word.

14. credit _____ **15.** limit _____

16. deposit _____ **17.** benefit _____

D. Add *ed* or *ing* to each word below to form a Unit word.

18. respond _____ **19.** succeed _____

20. braid _____

E. Complete each sentence using a Unit word.

21. Are we _____ about solar energy when we build houses?

22. The archaeologist spent days _____ the expedition with suitable clothing.

23. Roger Bannister _____ in breaking the record for the four-minute mile.

24. Hurry! We have only a _____ time for lunch.

25. The sound you hear is the _____ of the bees' wings.

26. Adele is _____ her savings in the bank.

27. You will be _____ on this material on Friday.

28. Losing her wallet was an _____ experience for Ann.

29. The lights are _____; the play will soon begin.

Proofreading • An English Report

UNIT WORDS

depositing
dimming
regretted
credited
quizzed
committed
benefited
omitting
stunned
limited
permitting
forbidding
succeeded
submitting
upsetting
braiding
responding
humming
outfitting
forgetting

Curtis joined the Tribute to Sports committee. He wrote his report on the Harlem Globetrotters. Now he must proofread his work. Curtis made twelve spelling errors and six capitalization mistakes. Read the report carefully.

1. Find Curtis's spelling mistakes. Then circle the misspelled words.

2. Correct Curtis's capitalization errors. Draw three lines under each letter that he should capitalize. Draw this mark / through a capital letter that he should make lowercase.

The Harlem Globetrotters

The Harlem Globetrotters can be creditted with making basketball a world-famous game. Audiences in more than ninty countries have respondded with laughter and delight to the antics of the fabulous five.

In 1927, abe Saperstein recruited five players from chicago and preceeded to turn them into a team. The team soon suceeded in winning so many games that offers to play other teams were limitted. That's when the comedy routines were introduced into the trotters' game. The sports fans were at first stuned and then amused to see a Globetrotter hiding a ball beneath his jersey or forgeting about depositting the ball in the basket as he dribbled his way into the stands. When adviced by a Referee that a foul had been comited a player might jump into the referee's arms or beg for mercy.

Reece "Goose" Tatum and Meadowlark Lemon are two famous Globetrotter comedians. bringing new vitality to the team is the addition of the first woman Globetrotter, Lynette woodard. Basketball has certainly benefitted from the popularity of the skillful Harlem Globetrotters.

---

3. Write the twelve misspelled words correctly.

_____   _____   _____

_____   _____   _____

_____   _____   _____

_____   _____

Writing on Your Own

Imagine that it's Sports Week at your school. Write a two-paragraph report for your classmates to read. Compare two sports events you participated in or watched and tell why you enjoyed them. You may wish to add *ed* or *ing* endings to some of these words and use them in your report: *regret, commit, benefit, stun, permit, succeed, upset, respond.*

 SPELLING DICTIONARY For help with spelling, turn to page 161.

Spelling on Your Own

UNIT WORDS

Write sentences using all of the Unit words. Use as many of the words as you can in each sentence. See how few sentences you can write.

MASTERY WORDS

swapped
trotting
wrapped
elected
pointed
planning

Add *ed* to each word to form a Mastery word.

1. wrap _____

2. swap _____

3. point _____

4. elect _____

Add *ing* to each word to form a Mastery word.

5. plan _____

6. trot _____

Look at the words you wrote for **1–6.** Then follow these directions.

7. Circle the two words you wrote in which you did not double the final consonant.

8. Both words you circled end with two _____.

Write the Mastery word that fits each description below.

9. voted into office _____

10. traded _____

11. thinking ahead _____

12. running _____

Finish these exercises using the Mastery words.

The word *pointed* has two meanings. Look at these sentences.

> The fence has *pointed* slats.
> Marjorie *pointed* at the fence.

13. Write a sentence using each meaning of *pointed.*

_____

_____

14. Write the word that is a homophone for *rapped.* _____

15. Write a sentence using the homophones in **14.**

_____

BONUS WORDS

rebelling
patrolling
compelled
repelled
appealed
sprawling
rivaled
crammed

1. Use each Bonus word in a sentence.

2. The Latin root *pel,* which you find in *compel* and *repel,* means "drive." To repel an attack is to drive it away. Another form of this root is *puls,* as in *repulse.* Write as many *pel/puls* words as you can. You may use a dictionary for help. Write a sentence using two of the words you wrote.

20 Synonyms and Antonyms

UNIT WORDS

1. exterior
2. interior
3. cautious
4. colossal
5. confidence
6. corridor
7. crafty
8. cunning
9. essential
10. expedition
11. frequently
12. fundamental
13. hallway
14. interfere
15. meddle
16. minute
17. rarely
18. reckless
19. trek
20. uncertainty

The Unit Words

This painter has confused the meanings of *interior* and *exterior*. The two words mean the opposite of each other. *Interior* and *exterior* are **antonyms.**

Words that mean the same or nearly the same thing are called **synonyms.** *Interior* and *inside* are synonyms. You can often substitute one synonym for another in a sentence, but the meanings of the words usually vary slightly. These slight differences are called **shades of meaning.** For example, *meddle* and *interfere* are synonyms. But read these two sentences. Do they really say exactly the same thing?

Please don't <u>meddle</u> with my work.
Please don't <u>interfere</u> with my work.

When you write, try to choose the synonym that has the exact shade of meaning you want to convey.

REMEMBER THIS

You won't forget the spelling of /ə/ in the final syllable of *confidence* /kon'fə•dəns/ if you think of the related word *confidential* /kon'fə•den'shəl/. You can hear the sound /e/ clearly in *confidential*. It reminds you that *confidence* is also spelled with e.

CON·fi·dence
con·fi·DEN·tial

Spelling Practice

A. Write the two Unit words that are synonyms for each of these words.

1. basic   _____   _____

2. hinder   _____   _____

3. passageway _____   _____

4. sly   _____   _____

5. journey   _____   _____

B. Write the Unit word that is the synonym for each of these words. Then write the Unit word that is an antonym for the word.

6. outside _____   _____

7. often _____   _____

8. huge _____   _____

9. careful _____   _____

10. sureness _____   _____

An **analogy** shows a similarity between two sets of ideas. "*Hot* is to *cold* as *on* is to *off*" is an analogy. *Hot* and *cold* are antonyms. They have the same relationship to each other as *on* and *off* do.

C. Complete the following analogies using the Unit words. Think of the relationship between the first pair of words to help you choose the correct word to complete the analogy.

11. *Anxiously* is to *calmly* as *frequently* is to _____.

12. *Incredible* is to *believable* as *colossal* is to _____.

13. *Permit* is to *allow* as *interfere* is to _____.

14. *Friendly* is to *hostile* as *cautious* is to _____.

15. *Peril* is to *danger* as *hallway* is to _____.

16. *Ally* is to *foe* as *exterior* is to _____.

17. *Devoted* is to *loving* as *crafty* is to _____.

18. *Venom* is to *poison* as *trek* is to _____.

D. Complete each sentence using a Unit word.

19. Amy was making plans for an _____ to the zoo.

20. Jane and Sarah wanted to go, but they didn't want to

_____ with Amy's plans.

21. Jane started to _____ home and had an idea.

22. If she offered to drive, maybe it wouldn't seem like she was trying to

_____.

Using the Dictionary to Spell and Write • Usage Notes

UNIT WORDS

exterior
interior
cautious
colossal
confidence
corridor
crafty
cunning
essential
expedition
frequently
fundamental
hallway
interfere
meddle
minute
rarely
reckless
trek
uncertainty

There are several ways a dictionary can help you write and speak correctly. Besides giving you the spelling and pronunciation of a word, the dictionary can also help you use a word correctly. The dictionary indicates if a word is slang. Most people believe that slang should only be used in informal writing or speaking. The dictionary shows how the meanings of some words have changed over the years. The dictionary also tells if a word has a special meaning in a particular subject area, such as music or sports. Often the dictionary will indicate an unusual regional definition as well.

These dictionary aids are called **usage notes** or **usage labels.** In the **Spelling Dictionary,** a blue circle signals a usage note. The usage note usually appears at the end of the main entry.

Look up the words *crafty, cunning, interfere,* and *trek* in the **Spelling Dictionary.** Use these words to complete the following exercises.

1. Write the two words that used to have a positive meaning but now have a negative meaning.

_____   _____

2. Each sentence below illustrates the current meaning or the original meaning of one of the two words you wrote for **1.** Write C if the sentence illustrates the current meaning or O if it illustrates the original meaning.

_____ The crafty fox stole the meat.

_____ The crafty tailor made excellent clothes.

_____ The tailor is cunning with her hands.

_____ The burglar was cunning in entering the house.

3. Write the word that may be used humorously. _____

4. Write a sentence to show the humorous usage of the word you wrote for **3.**

_____

5. Write the word whose usage note tells you how the word may be used in a positive way. _____

6. Write a sentence using the word you wrote for **5** in a positive way.

_____

Writing on Your Own

Pretend you have been hired to write a guide to your school building for new students. Describe the general layout of your school and all of its special features. Use as many Unit words as possible.

 THESAURUS For help finding clear, positive words, turn to page 205.

Spelling on Your Own

UNIT WORDS

Write each Unit word. Then write a sentence for as many Unit words as you can using both the Unit word and an antonym for the word. Here's an example: "Sturdy shoes are *essential* for this hike, but rock climbing gear is *unnecessary*." The antonyms you use need not be Unit words.

MASTERY WORDS

victory
defeat
decrease
increase
sorrow
sadness

Use the Mastery words to finish these exercises.

1. Write the word that means "a loss." _____

2. Write the word that is an antonym for the word you wrote for **1**.

_____

3. Write the word that means "grow larger."

_____

4. Write the word that is an antonym for the word you wrote for **3**.

_____

5. Write the two words that mean "unhappiness."

_____   _____

Finish these sentences using the Mastery words.

6. There was great _____ and _____ in Mudville the day Casey struck out at bat.

7. The fans had been rooting for a _____.

8. The _____ was very hard to bear.

9. Do you think Casey will get an _____ or a _____ in salary next spring?

Write the plural form of each noun.

10. victory _____   **11.** defeat _____

12. sorrow _____   **13.** sadness _____

BONUS WORDS

hindrance
enthusiastic
inexact
evident
obstacle
precise
apparent
indifferent

1. Write the Bonus words that are synonym pairs.
2. Write the Bonus words that are antonym pairs.
3. The Latin prefix *in-* sometimes means "not." Look through the **Spelling Dictionary.** List at least ten words that have the prefix *in-* meaning "not." Then write an antonym for five of the words. Remember that *in-* may also appear in a word as *im-, il-,* or *ir-.*

21 Double-Letter Spellings

UNIT WORDS

1. occasion
2. opportunity
3. vacuum
4. correspond
5. possession
6. affectionate
7. bazaar
8. committee
9. attitude
10. accompanied
11. boycott
12. occupational
13. recommend
14. unnecessary
15. embarrass
16. immense
17. successful
18. intelligent
19. anniversary
20. mayonnaise

The Unit Words

All the words in this unit have double letters that spell one sound. For example, you hear only one /p/ in *opportunity* /op′ər•t(y)o͞o′nə•tē/, but it is spelled with two *p*'s.

The double *u* in *vacuum* and the double *a* in *bazaar* are not very common, but double consonant letters appear often in words you need to write. It may be helpful to remember that double consonant letters often follow a short vowel sound, as in *anniversary*. Double consonant letters also occur when a prefix that ends with a consonant is added to a base word that begins with the same consonant letter.

un + necessary = unnecessary

90

Spelling Practice

A. Complete these exercises using the Unit words.

1. Write the word that has a double *c* and a double *s*.

_____

2. Write the three other words that have a double *c*.

_____ _____ _____

3. Write the three other words that have a double *s*. Then circle the word that has a double *s* twice.

_____ _____ _____

4. Write the three words that have a double *t*.

_____ _____ _____

5. Circle the word you wrote for **4** that has three pairs of double letters.

6. Write the two words that have a double *r*.

_____ _____

7. Write the two words that have double vowels. Circle the word that can be pronounced with either two or three syllables.

_____ _____

B. Complete the following sentence using the Unit words.

8. If you will _____ the living room, I will have the

_____ to spread these crackers with

_____ before the _____ party for

Mom and Dad begins.

C. Words are often divided into syllables between double consonant letters. These three-syllable words have one syllable division marked for you. Write each word. Then draw lines to divide the word into three syllables.

9. may|onnaise _____ **10.** rec|ommend _____

D. Write these words. Then draw lines to divide each word into three syllables.

11. committee _____ **12.** possession _____

E. Write the Unit word that is a synonym for each word.

13. bright _____ **14.** huge _____

15. chance _____ **16.** fair _____

17. loving _____ **18.** event _____

Proofreading • A Laboratory Report

Jim wrote this lab report. Now he must proofread it. Jim made nine spelling mistakes. Read the report carefully.

1. Find Jim's spelling mistakes. Then circle the misspelled words.

UNIT WORDS
occasion
opportunity
vacuum
correspond
possession
affectionate
bazaar
committee
attitude
accompanied
boycott
occupational
recommend
unnecessary
embarrass
immense
successful
intelligent
anniversary
mayonnaise

Purpose:
To determine whether there are more molecules in motion in water or in air.

Materials:
2 wide-necked vaccum bottles of equal size
2 cupsful of water to fill one bottle
2 ice cubes

Proceedure:
1. Our commitee pored water into one bottle. It was then allowed to stand until the water reached room temperature. No water was placed in the coresponding bottle.
2. An ice cube was depositted into each bottle, and the bottles were immediately sealed. The time was recorded.
3. Each bottle was opened frequantly to see if the ice cube had melted. We proceded to record the exact time that each ice cube had completely melted.

Observation:
The ice cube in water melted at a faster rate than the ice cube in air.

Conclusion:
Ice cubes melt as they absorb heat energy. Heat is caused by the motion of molecules. Therefore, since the ice cube melted faster in water than in air, we can conclude that there must be more molecules in motion in water than in air.

2. Write the nine misspelled words correctly.

_____ _____ _____

_____ _____ _____

_____ _____ _____

Writing on Your Own

Imagine that your school will soon be celebrating its twenty-fifth anniversary. You are on the invitation committee. Write a letter that will go to the students who have graduated from your school. Tell them about the celebration and convince them that they should attend. Use as many of the Unit words as you can.

 WRITER'S GUIDE For a sample persuasive paragraph, turn to page 264.

Spelling on Your Own

Write the Unit words. Write a synonym or an antonym after as many words as you can. Label the synonyms *S* and the antonyms *A*.

| MASTERY WORDS |

occur
pressure
sheriff
squirrel
surround
appoint

Write the Mastery words that have these double letters.

1. cc _____ **2.** ff _____

3. pp _____ **4.** ss _____

5. rr (two words) _____ _____

Write the Mastery word that is a synonym for each word.

6. force _____ **7.** happen _____

8. nominate _____ **9.** encircle _____

Write the Mastery word that belongs with each group.

10. deputy, horse, badge _____

11. chipmunk, mouse, rabbit _____

Add *ed* to each verb. Remember the rules you have learned.

12. pressure _____ **13.** surround _____

14. appoint _____ **15.** occur _____

Find the two misspelled words in each sentence and write them correctly.

16. Did it ever ocurr to you that the sherif always captures the bad guys in old-time westerns?

_____ _____

17. As soon as he hears the news, the sheriff apoints some deputies, and quick as a wink, they suround the bandits.

_____ _____

| BONUS WORDS |

accommodate
aggravate
exaggerate
approximately
appropriate
exceed
aggressive
bizarre

Complete each sentence using the Bonus words.

1. Slippers are not ____ for mountain climbing.
2. New York City has ____ eight million residents.
3. The male robin is ____ when defending its territory.
4. Will your car trunk ____ my cello?
5. Save gas. Don't ____ the speed limit.
6. Scratching a rash will only ____ the condition.
7. Cartoonists ____ the features of their characters.

Write a story entitled "The Bizarre Bazaar." Use as many Bonus words as you can.

22 Prefixes

UNIT WORDS

1. *insomnia*
2. *invalid*
3. *informal*
4. *inability*
5. *incapable*
6. *inaccurate*
7. *illegal*
8. *imperfect*
9. *irregular*
10. *nonsense*
11. *nonessential*
12. *nonprofit*
13. *nonexistent*
14. *nonflammable*
15. *disarmament*
16. *distract*
17. *dissimilar*
18. *discouraged*
19. *disinfectant*
20. *disconnect*

in·FOR·mal
in·for·MAL·i·ty

The Unit Words

Look at the movie marquee /mär·kē′/. If you attend the preview, you will *view* the movie *before* the official opening. When a word starts with *pre-*, "before" is part of the meaning of the word. A **prefix** is a word part added (or fixed) to the beginning of a word to make a new word. A prefix comes *before* the base word.

Pre- is a prefix. *In-*, *non-*, and *dis-* are also prefixes. Each of the last three adds the meaning "not" to a word. For example, *non* + *sense* means "something without sense, or absurd."

When the prefix *in-* is added to base words that begin with *b*, *m*, or *p*, the *n* is changed to *m*, as in *imperfect*. When *in-* is added to words beginning with *l*, the *n* is changed to *l*, as in *illegal*. When *in-* is added to words beginning with *r*, the *n* is changed to *r*, as in *irregular*.

REMEMBER THIS

You won't forget the spelling of words with /ə/ in the final syllable if you think of a related word. Look at these words: *informal*, *informality*. The vowel sound /a/ that you hear clearly in *informality* /in′fôr·mal′ə·tē/ tells you that *informal* is also spelled with *a*.

Spelling Practice

A. Add a prefix to each of these words to form its antonym.

1. connect _____

2. essential _____

3. perfect _____

4. legal _____

5. formal _____

6. regular _____

7. similar _____

8. capable _____

B. Write the Unit word that fits each meaning below.

9. sleeplessness _____

10. without hope _____

11. not correct _____

12. not for gain _____

_____

13. foolishness _____

14. failure _____

C. Complete the following exercises using the Unit words.

15. Write the word that means "doesn't exist." _____

16. The Latin root *tract* means "draw or pull." Write the word that means "draw someone's attention away."

_____

17. Which word names a product that kills germs? It makes things not infectious or infected.

_____

18. Write the word that means "a reduction of a nation's armed forces."

_____

19. The word *valid* means "sound": "Give me a *valid* reason for your absence." *Invalid* has two meanings, both of which mean "not sound." Write a sentence using one of the two meanings of *invalid*.

_____

20. *Flammable* and *inflammable* are synonyms. They mean "able to burn." Write the word that is the antonym of *flammable*.

_____

D. Complete these sentences using the Unit words.

Scientists are __21__ by their __22__ to prove the existence of the Loch Ness monster. The beast appears only at __23__ intervals, and all descriptions of sightings seem vague and __24__.

21. _____

22. _____

23. _____

24. _____

Spelling and Language • Adding -ly

UNIT WORDS

insomnia
invalid
informal
inability
incapable
inaccurate
illegal
imperfect
irregular
nonsense
nonessential
nonprofit
nonexistent
nonflammable
disarmament
distract
dissimilar
discouraged
disinfectant
disconnect

Adverbs are used to modify verbs. An **adverb** tells how, when, or where. You can often form an adverb by adding -ly to the end of an adjective. Look at these sentences.

ADJECTIVE Madeline gets frequent colds.
ADVERB Madeline gets colds frequently.

When you add -ly to most words, do not change the spelling of the base word. Here's an example: *rare + ly = rarely.*

A. Write each word adding -ly.

1. informal _____

2. inaccurate _____

3. illegal _____

4. imperfect _____

5. irregular _____

6. dissimilar _____

Look at the sentences about Madeline and her colds at the top of the page. Notice how adding -ly to the adjective and moving the new adverb to another position changes the structure of the sentence. When you want to add variety to your writing, this is a good technique to remember.

B. The adjective in each of these sentences is written in italics. Change each sentence by adding -ly to the adjective. You will also need to change the word order of the sentence.

7. The *cunning* raccoon pried open the garbage pail.

_____

8. The *reckless* driver raced down the street.

_____

9. The *affectionate* dog nuzzled its owner.

_____

10. The *intelligent* child solved the puzzle.

_____

Writing on Your Own

Write a letter to a manufacturer about a defective product. It may be a bicycle, a TV, a piece of clothing, or something else. Tell when you purchased the product and when and in what way you found it unsatisfactory. Decide how you want the manufacturer to solve the problem and end your letter with a specific request. Use at least five of the Unit words or their adverb forms in your letter.

 WRITER'S GUIDE For help revising your letter, use the checklist on page 257.

Spelling on Your Own

UNIT WORDS

Write the Unit words in alphabetical order. Circle the words that have double consonant letters. Use each of the circled words in a sentence or try to use all of them in one or two sentences.

MASTERY WORDS

Write the Mastery word that is the antonym for each of these words. Then underline the prefix in each word you wrote.

disagree
impolite
unpleasant
incorrect
dishonest
uncertain

1. certain _____
2. pleasant _____
3. agree _____
4. honest _____
5. polite _____
6. correct _____

Finish these exercises using the Mastery words.

7. Write the two words that have double letters.

_____ _____

8. Write the word in which /ən/ is spelled with *ain*. _____

9. Write the word that has a "silent" *h*. _____

Add the suffix -*ly* to the word in ( ) to finish each sentence.

10. Terry approached Mrs. Johnson's desk (uncertain)

_____.

11. She knew she had spoken (impolite) _____ during

class yesterday and she wanted to apologize.

12. Terry had answered the teacher's question (incorrect)

_____.

13. Embarrassed, she had (dishonest) _____ blamed

another student for her error.

BONUS WORDS

inconvenience
disqualified
irresistible
disadvantage
immortal
immobile
nontoxic
irrational

1. Write the five Bonus words that have a form of the prefix *in-*.

2. If you are not qualified for a job, you are unqualified. What does the word *disqualified* mean?

3. Use each Bonus word in a sentence.

4. The word *mobile* means "able to move," as in *mobile home*. The sculptor Alexander Calder called some of his works *mobiles*. Find this definition in a dictionary or encyclopedia and write a short paragraph about mobiles.

23 More Prefixes

UNIT WORDS

1. unicycle
2. university
3. unison
4. uniform
5. unanimous
6. paraprofessional
7. parasite
8. parallel
9. paramedic
10. monogram
11. monotonous
12. monopoly
13. biweekly
14. bifocals
15. bisect
16. biceps
17. bilingual
18. semiannual
19. semisweet
20. semicircle

The Unit Words

Would you know what a unicycle is if you saw the word without an accompanying picture? You can often figure out the meaning of an unfamiliar word by thinking of the meaning of its parts. *Unicycle* can be divided into the root *cycle* and the prefix *uni-*. You know that a bicycle is a two-wheeled vehicle and that a tricycle has three wheels. So *cycle* must mean "wheel." The words *unit, united,* and *universal* tell you that the prefix *uni-* means "one." In math, the units place is reserved for *one*-digit numbers. When people are united, they act as *one* person. You know, therefore, that *unicycle* must mean "a vehicle with one wheel."

The chart below gives you the meanings of the other prefixes found in the Unit words.

PREFIX	MEANING	EXAMPLE
para-	"alongside of"	*parallel*
mono-	"one"	*monogram*
bi-	"two"	*bilingual*
semi-	"half"	*semicircle*

Spelling Practice

A. The Latin prefix *uni-* and the Greek prefix *mono-* both mean "one." Below is a list of Latin and Greek words and their meanings. Each is the root of a Unit word that begins with *uni-* or *mono-*. Write the Unit word.

1. *animus,* "a mind" _____

2. *polein,* "to sell" _____

3. *forma,* "a shape" _____

4. *cyclum,* " a wheel" _____

5. *gramma,* "a letter" _____

6. *universitas,* "the whole" _____

7. *tonos,* "a tone" _____

8. *sonus,* "a sound" _____

B. The prefix *para-* means "alongside of." Use a Unit word with the prefix *para-* to complete each sentence.

9. Frank practices gymnastics on the _____ bars.

10. The _____ gave the patient oxygen until the ambulance reached the hospital.

11. A tapeworm is an example of a _____.

12. The _____ worked with a small group of students in the back of the classroom.

C. The prefix *bi-* means "two." The prefix *semi-* means "half." Use a Unit word to complete the first sentence in each pair. Then write a new word using *bi-* or *semi-* to complete the second sentence.

13. Rosa's doctor told her to return in six months for her

    _____ checkup.

    Dawn's doctor told her to return in two years for her

    _____ checkup.

14. Dan receives a _____ magazine every two weeks.

    Adam receives a _____ newspaper twice a week.

D. Write the Unit word that fits each description.

15. able to speak two languages _____

16. half a circle _____

17. eyeglasses with a two-part lens _____

18. the muscles in the upper arm _____

19. somewhat bitter _____

20. to cut into two equal parts _____

UNIT WORDS

unicycle
university
unison
uniform
unanimous
paraprofessional
parasite
parallel
paramedic
monogram
monotonous
monopoly
biweekly
bifocals
bisect
biceps
bilingual
semiannual
semisweet
semicircle

The prefix *in-* sometimes means "not." However, if you try to figure out the meaning of the word *inflate* using that meaning, you will find that it doesn't apply. *Inflate* doesn't mean "not flated."

The dictionary lists prefixes as separate entries. This will help you check if you used a word with a prefix correctly in your writing. Look up *in-* in the **Spelling Dictionary.** Notice that *in-* also means "in, into, within, or on." These definitions will help you understand the meaning of *inflate.* When you inflate a balloon, you blow *into* it.

A. Look up *semi-* in the **Spelling Dictionary.** Write the number of the definition for *semi-* that fits each word.

_____ **1.** semiannual   _____ **2.** semicircle   _____ **3.** semisweet

B. Look up *in-* in the **Spelling Dictionary.** Notice the small number after each entry. The number tells you that you will find more than one entry for the prefix. Decide which entry for *in-* would best help you understand the meaning of each word below. Write the number of the entry for each word. Think of the meaning of the word to help you.

_____ **4.** inflate   _____ **5.** incapable   _____ **6.** indicator   _____ **7.** interior

C. Homographs are words that are spelled alike but have different meanings and sometimes different word histories. The prefixes *in-* and *in-* are homographs. Homographs may also be pronounced differently.

8. Look up *minute* in the **Spelling Dictionary.** Notice that *minute* has a homograph. Use each homograph in a sentence that shows its meaning.

_____

_____

min·ute[1] /min′it/ *n.* A measure of time; 1/60 of an hour.
mi·nute[2] /mī·n(y)o͞ot′/ *adj.* Very tiny.

9. The words *rare* and *rare* are also homographs. Think of the two different meanings of *rare.* Use the **Spelling Dictionary** if you need help. Write a sentence to show each meaning you thought of.

_____

_____

Writing on Your Own

Newspaper writers sometimes use alliteration, or the repetition of the first sounds in words, to create catchy headlines. Use some of the Unit words that start with the same sounds to make up some silly headlines to share with your friends. Here's an example: *Uniformed Unicorns Unicycle in Unison.* You may need to change some of the Unit words slightly or add other words to complete each headline. Make up at least five.

Spelling Practice

A. Complete the following exercises using the Unit words.

1. Write the four words that have the prefix meaning "over or above."

_____   _____

_____   _____

2. Write the four words that have the prefix meaning "around."

_____   _____

_____   _____

B. Write the Unit word that is a synonym for each word below.

3. block _____   **4.** clear _____

5. change _____   **6.** in the middle _____

7. pause _____   **8.** interpret _____

C. Use a Unit word with the prefix *inter-* or *intra-* to complete each sentence.

9. If you move from Arkansas to Nebraska, you are making an

_____ move.

10. However, if you move from Los Angeles to San Francisco, you are

making an _____ move.

11. When a school's seventh-grade team plays the eighth-grade team, it is

an _____ game.

D. Use Unit words with the prefix *trans-* to complete the sentences below.

12. Dr. Barnard performed the first heart

_____ in South Africa.

13. After the operation, the patient needed a blood

_____.

14. In the middle of the intersection, my car's

_____ broke down.

15. Christine's job at the United Nations is to

_____ the Chinese
delegates' speeches into English.

16. Andrew protected his pastel sketch with

_____ wrap.

Spelling and Language • Word Families

When you add a prefix to a root, you create a new word. For example, the Latin root *port* means "carry." Notice how a new meaning is added to the root *port* when a prefix is added to each word below. However, the basic meaning "carry" remains in each word.

> *transport*, "carry across"
> *report*, "carry back news"
> *import*, "carry goods into the country"
> *export*, "carry goods out of the country"

UNIT WORDS

superstition
supernatural
circumstances
circumference
intercept
interstate
intrastate
transplant
translate
intramural
circuit
supervision
transparent
intermediate
transmission
circumnavigate
superintendent
transform
interval
transfusion

A. Complete these exercises.

1. Write the Unit word that has the root *cept,* meaning "take."

_____

2. Add the prefix *ac-* to *cept* to form a word that means "receive."

_____

3. Now add the prefix *ex-* to *cept* to form a different word.

_____

4. Write the Unit word that has the Latin root *form,* which means "shape."

_____

5. Add the Latin prefix meaning "one" to *form* to create another word.

_____

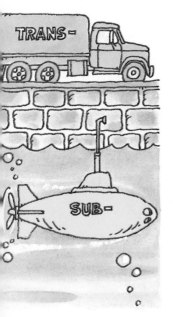

B. Look at the prefixes below. Write the four words that may be formed by adding these prefixes to the root *mit,* meaning "send."

   trans-   com-   per-   sub-

6. _____   **7.** _____

8. _____   **9.** _____

Writing on Your Own

Write a science-fiction story to read to your class. Begin with a character who is solving a mystery on a distant planet or who is escaping danger by traveling into the future. Start your story at its most exciting point and use as many of the Unit words as you can.

WRITER'S GUIDE For a sample narrative paragraph, turn to page 261.

Spelling on Your Own

UNIT WORDS

Write the Unit word that would come next in alphabetical order after each word below. The first word has been done for you.

1. circle—circuit
2. circulation
3. circumflex
4. circumscribe
5. intercede
6. intermarry
7. interpret
8. interurban
9. intractable
10. intransitive
11. superhuman
12. supermarket
13. supersonic
14. superstructure
15. transfer
16. transformer
17. transit
18. translucent
19. transmit
20. transpire

MASTERY WORDS

transportation
circular
interest
rebuild
rewind
transfer

1. Write the two Mastery words with the prefix that means "across."

_____   _____

2. The prefix *re-* means "again." Write the two words that begin with *re-*.

_____   _____

3. Use each word you wrote for **2** in a sentence.

_____

_____

4. The prefix *circum-* means "around." Write the word that means "round."

_____

5. Sometimes you drop a syllable when you say a word. Write the word that is often pronounced /in'trist/.

_____

6. Look up *interest* in the **Spelling Dictionary**. Write sentences for two of its meanings.

_____

_____

BONUS WORDS

circumstantial
interruption
interpretation
transistor
superficial
superfluous
superlative
transaction

Write the Bonus word that has the same Latin root as each of these words.
1. active   2. disrupt   3. fluid   4. instance
Complete these exercises using the Bonus words.
5. Sometimes a new word is formed by blending together two existing words. The word *motel* is a blend of the words *motor* and *hotel.* Write the Bonus word that is a blend of *transfer* and *resistor.* Then write two other blends.
6. Write sentences using all of the Bonus words.

UNIT WORDS

1. society
2. inflation
3. income
4. irrigation
5. manufacturing
6. management
7. labor
8. agricultural
9. industrial
10. production
11. assembly
12. technology
13. economy
14. corporation
15. stockholder
16. rural
17. urban
18. global
19. commerce
20. surplus

AGRICULTURE   COMMERCE   MANUFACTURING

The Unit Words

Social studies is the study of society, how people live and work together. The words *social* and *society* come from the Latin word *socius,* which means "companion." Our system of government originated in Greece and Rome. The words we use to name this system are Greek *(democracy)* and Latin *(republic).* Many other words used in social studies also come from these languages.

Look at the Unit words. You will find some familiar prefixes and base words. The words *inflation, income,* and *irrigation,* for example, have the Latin prefix *in-,* meaning "not," "in," "into," "within," and "on." It can also mean "to or toward." Can you figure out what *irrigation* means?

e·CON·o·my
ec·o·NOM·i·cal

REMEMBER THIS

To help you remember the spelling of /ə/ in *economy* /i·kon′ə·mē/, think of the related word *economical* /ek′ə·nom′i·kəl/. The strong vowel sound /o/ that you hear in *economical* tells you that *economy* is also spelled with o.

Spelling Practice

A. Complete the following exercises using the Unit words.

1. Write the Unit word in which /k/ is spelled with *ch*. _____

2. Write the word in which /k/ is spelled with *ck*. _____

3. Write the seven words in which /k/ is spelled with *c*.

_____ _____ _____

_____ _____ _____

_____

4. Write the two words in which *c* or *ce* spell the sound /s/.

_____ _____

5. Write the two words in which /s/ is heard twice.

_____ _____

6. Write the word in which the sound /j/ is spelled with *ge*.

_____

7. Write the three words that have double consonant letters.

_____ _____

_____

8. Write the four words that end with the sounds /əl/.

_____ _____

_____ _____

9. Write the two words that end with the sounds /ər/.

_____ _____

10. Write the four words that have the vowel sound heard in *play*.

_____ _____

_____ _____

11. Write the two words that have the vowel sound heard in *burn*.

_____ _____

B. Each sentence contains a word that is misspelled. Circle the misspelled word and write the correct Unit word.

12. Joan prefers urben life to country life. _____

13. She is part of the labur force working in the city. _____

14. During her leisure time, she enjoys globel travel. _____

15. Her trips have been limited, however, due to the high rate of inflashun.

_____

Proofreading • A Social Studies Report

UNIT WORDS

society
inflation
income
irrigation
manufacturing
management
labor
agricultural
industrial
production
assembly
technology
economy
corporation
stockholder
rural
urban
global
commerce
surplus

Isabella wrote this report for her social studies class, but she forgot to proofread her work. There are nine spelling mistakes and six mistakes in capitalization. Read the report carefully.

1. Find Isabella's spelling mistakes. Then circle the misspelled words.

2. Correct Isabella's capitalization mistakes using three lines under those letters that should be capitalized and a slanting line through each letter that should not be capitalized.

---

mexico

Mexico is a rapidly developing nation. Since the Mexican Revolution in 1910, its econamy has been improving steadily.

Mexico had always been an agriculturel country. Huge estates called *haciendas* were owned by wealthy landlords. After the revolution, the government divided these estates to provide farmland for the rurul population. The government also built large irigation projects to supply water to the land.

Mexico is self-sufficient agriculturally. Surpluss crops, such as Coffee, Cotton, and Sugar, are exported to other nations. Petroleum is Mexico's leading export.

Manufactoring has recently been developed in Mexico. Mexico City is its major industral center. Industry is also expanding in other cities, such as Monterrey and guadalajara. The government hopes that Mexico's greater use of teknology will help decrease its dependence on imported finished goods. In the meantime, Mexico relies heavily on foreign investments and the large incom it receives from Tourism.

---

3. Write the nine misspelled words correctly.

_____   _____   _____

_____   _____   _____

_____   _____   _____

 WRITER'S GUIDE See the editing and proofreading marks on page 258.

Writing on Your Own

Write a report to present to the class comparing the economies of two of the fifty states. Base your report on facts you find in almanacs, atlases, or encyclopedias. Use as many of the Unit words as you can.

 WRITER'S GUIDE For a sample research report, turn to page 272.

Spelling on Your Own

Use each Unit word in a sentence, or if you prefer, write a paragraph or two using as many Unit words as you can.

MASTERY WORDS

government
election
frontier
tariff
treaty
explorer

Finish the exercises using the Mastery words.

1. Write the two words that have /u/ spelled with o.

_____   _____

2. Write the word that has /ē/ twice. _____

3. Write the word that has double consonant letters.

_____

4. Write the word that has /k/ spelled with c. _____

5. Write the word that ends with the suffix that means "one who does."

_____

6. Write a sentence using *treaty, frontier,* or *explorer.*

_____

Write the Mastery words that fit in alphabetical order in these lists.

7. glide

goose

_____

grand

8. tape

_____

traffic

_____

9. _____

_____

fuel

Finish each sentence using the Mastery words.

10. The federal _____ holds a Presidential

_____ every four years.

11. When the British added a _____ on tea, the American colonists became angry.

BONUS WORDS

productivity
municipal
industrialization
legislation
financier
inauguration
unconstitutional
dictatorship

1. Write each Bonus word. Then write another word that has the same root.
2. Start with *industry.* Add three suffixes, one at a time, to build a Bonus word. Write the three words.
3. Write a sentence using each Bonus word.
4. The suffix *-ier* as in *financier* occurs in words borrowed from French. List at least three other words that end with *-ier.* Use each word in a sentence.

27 Words from French

UNIT WORDS

1. collage
2. ballet
3. league
4. unique
5. chef
6. rouge
7. picturesque
8. brochure
9. vague
10. sabotage
11. antique
12. beret
13. parachute
14. boutique
15. bouquet
16. chandelier
17. beige
18. dialogue
19. gourmet
20. depot

The Unit Words

The picture at the top of this page is a collage. A **collage** is a work of art made of many materials, such as paper, wood, and fabric, which are pasted onto a flat surface. *Collage* comes from the French word *colle,* meaning "glue."

Many words in English come from French. In 1066, England was conquered by the Normans, who spoke French. French, therefore, became the official language of the land. After several hundred years, English again became the standard language of England. But hundreds of French words remained part of the English language and are still part of our everyday vocabulary.

French words in English usually keep their French spellings. The chart below shows some French spellings that occur in the Unit words.

SPELLING	SOUND	EXAMPLE
et	/ā/	ballet
gue	/g/	league
que	/k/	unique
ch	/sh/	chef
ge	/zh/	rouge

In many French words, such as *depot* /dē'pō/, the final consonant is not pronounced.

Spelling Practice

A. Complete the following exercises using the Unit words.

1. Write the word that ends with /ō/. _____

2. Write the four words that end with /ā/.

_____   _____

_____   _____

3. Write the four words that end with /zh/.

_____   _____

_____   _____

4. Write the four words that have /sh/.

_____   _____

_____   _____

5. Write the four words that end with /k/.

_____   _____

_____   _____

6. Write the two other words that have /k/.

_____   _____

Edgar Degas, *Classe de Danse*

7. Write the three words that end with /g/.

_____   _____   _____

B. Complete the following paragraph using four Unit words.

Edgar Degas /də·gä′/ was a French painter who, along with other famous artists, developed a __8__ style of painting called Impressionism. The Impressionists were not interested in creating detailed historical pictures. They wanted to show scenes from modern life. Degas chose not to paint a __9__ rural setting or a beautiful __10__ of flowers as the other Impressionists did. He preferred to paint people doing ordinary things, such as __11__ dancers at a rehearsal or a dancing class.

8. _____   **9.** _____

10. _____   **11.** _____

C. Write the Unit word that best fits each description below.

12. a station _____   **13.** something old _____

14. not clear _____   **15.** a pamphlet _____

16. a shop _____   **17.** a light fixture _____

Using the Dictionary to Spell and Write
Locating Unfamiliar Words

Even if you do not know how a word is spelled, you can find it in a dictionary. Here is a good method to use.

Suppose you want to look up the word *symphony*. Start by thinking of the spellings you know for /s/: *c, s, sc, ss, ce,* and *se*. Since *s* is the most frequent spelling for /s/, turn first to the *S* section in the dictionary. The next sound in *symphony* is /i/. The sound /i/ may also be spelled in several ways: *i, e, y,* and *ui*. Check these letters and you will soon find *symphony*.

Words that come from other languages often keep their original spellings. *Symphony* is borrowed from ancient Greek. Many words from Greek have /i/ spelled with *y*. Knowing the common foreign spellings can help you choose the most likely spelling for a word. Then you can locate it more quickly in the dictionary.

A. Think of the spellings you know for /sh/. Then write the spelling for each pronunciation. In each exercise, the answer is a Unit word or a word from an earlier unit.

1. /shef/ _____   **2.** /shirz/ _____

3. /shôrts/ _____   **4.** /shan′də•lir′/ _____

B. Think of the spellings you know for /ā/. Then write the spelling for each pronunciation.

5. /vāg/ _____   **6.** /bāzh/ _____

7. mā′sə/ _____   **8.** /mā′ə•nāz′/ _____

C. Write the spelling for the pronunciation in each sentence.

9. We gave Mrs. Stein a /bō•kā′/ after the play. _____

10. Michelle works in her mother's /boo•tēk′/ on Saturdays. _____

act, āte, cåre, ärt;	egg, ēven;	if, īce;	on, ōver, ôr;	boŏk, foōd;	up, tûrn;
ə=a in *ago,* e in *listen,* i in *giraffe,* o in *pilot,* u in *circus;*		yoo=u in *music;*	oil;		out;
chair; sing; shop; thank; that; zh in *treasure.*					

 SPELLING DICTIONARY Remember to use your **Spelling Dictionary** when you write.

Writing on Your Own

Imagine that you own a hotel. It might be a lodge in a national park, a resort on a tropical island, a peaceful country inn, or a busy hotel in the heart of an exciting city. Write a brochure that tells travelers all about the attractions of your hotel and its location. Convince potential visitors that your hotel is the best one in the area. Use as many of the Unit words as you can.

 WRITER'S GUIDE For help revising your brochure, use the checklist on page 257.

Spelling on Your Own

UNIT WORDS

Write the Unit words in alphabetical order. Then group the words into ten pairs, beginning with the first two alphabetized words. Write a sentence using each pair of words. Here's an example: "The <u>ballet</u> dancer wore an <u>antique</u> cloak for the opening performance."

MASTERY WORDS

Finish these exercises using the Mastery words.

1. Write the three words that have /j/ spelled with *ge*.

_____ _____ _____

2. Write the word that has /sh/ spelled with *ss*. _____

3. Write the word that has the sound /yo͞o/ that you hear in *use*.

_____

4. Write the word that ends with /ch/. _____

5. The word *view* has several meanings. Look up *view* in the **Spelling Dictionary**. Write one sentence using *view* as a verb. Then write a sentence using *view* as a noun.

_____

_____

Finish each sentence using the Mastery words.

6. Keep our city clean. Keep _____ in a covered can.

7. We wrapped Keith's present in colored _____ paper.

8. Green leafy vegetables, such as _____, give you a large amount of vitamins and iron.

9. A homing _____ can find its home from far away.

10. On his first _____, Columbus sighted San Salvador.

pigeon
garbage
spinach
view
voyage
tissue

BONUS WORDS

Write the word for each pronunciation. How is /ē/ spelled in these French words?

1. /kam′ə·fläzh/   **2.** /də·brē′/   **3.** /sin′ə·mə/   **4.** /ō·pāk′/
5. /fə·tēg′/   **6.** /klēk/   **7.** /in·trēg′/   **8.** /byo͝or′ō/

Use the Bonus words to complete these exercises.

9. Look up each word in the **Spelling Dictionary**. Then write the three words that have alternate pronunciations.

10. Write a short story. Use as many Bonus words as you can.

fatigue
camouflage
opaque
bureau
debris
clique
intrigue
cinema

28 Adjective Suffixes

UNIT WORDS

1. flexible
2. valuable
3. nervous
4. noticeable
5. lovable
6. excusable
7. believable
8. reasonable
9. considerable
10. desirable
11. permissible
12. responsible
13. legible
14. sensible
15. incredible
16. marvelous
17. mysterious
18. industrious
19. anxious
20. numerous

The Unit Words

A healthy body is very flexible. It is able to bend with ease. The word *flexible* is made up of two parts: the root *flex*, "bend," and the suffix *-ible*, "able to."

Flexible is an adjective. It can be used to describe a noun. The suffixes *-ible*, *-able*, and *-ous* are adjective-forming suffixes. When you add one of these suffixes to the end of a base word, you make the word into an adjective.

Here are some rules for adding *-ible*, *-able*, and *-ous*.

1. If a word ends with *e*, drop the final *e* before adding a suffix that begins with a vowel letter. However, if a word ends with *ce* or *ge*, keep the final *e*.

      value   valuable   notice   noticeable

2. When a word ends with a consonant and *y*, change the *y* to *i* before adding a suffix.

          mystery   mysterious

☐ The words *anxious* and *numerous* do not fit these rules. *Anxious* is related to the noun *anxiety*. The *b* in *number* is dropped when *-ous* is added to form *numerous*.

Spelling Practice

A. Add *-able* or *-ible* to each of these verbs to form a Unit word.

1. believe _____

2. desire _____

3. flex _____

4. notice _____

5. reason _____

6. sense _____

7. love _____

8. excuse _____

9. value _____

10. consider _____

B. Change these nouns into adjectives that end with *-ous.*

11. mystery _____

12. industry _____

13. anxiety _____

14. nerve _____

C. Write the Unit word that belongs with each group of words. The suffix in ( ) is a clue to the correct word. Then complete the exercise.

15. amazing, wonderful *(-ous)* _____

16. unbelievable, absurd *(-ible)* _____

17. many, plentiful *(-ous)* _____

18. allowable, acceptable *(-ible)* _____

19. reliable, trustworthy *(-ible)* _____

20. readable, clear *(-ible)* _____

21. Write a sentence using the word *incredible.*

_____

Usually when you add the suffix *-ly* to a word, you don't change the spelling of the base word. However, when a word ends with *le,* drop the *le* before adding *-ly: legible, legibly.*

D. Add *-ly* to each adjective in ( ) to complete the story.

Jay waited (anxious) __22__ for the ski lift to reach the top of the slope. It was (noticeable) __23__ windier up there, and even though he was (sensible) __24__ dressed, Jay shivered slightly. Looking around (nervous) __25__, Jay noticed how (incredible) __26__ steep the trail looked. Today was his first time on the intermediate slope, and Jay wondered whether he should think twice about skiing it. Maybe he should wait until he had (considerable) __27__ more experience. "Well, I guess it's now or never," Jay thought. "So here goes. . . ."

22. _____

23. _____

24. _____

25. _____

26. _____

27. _____

Spelling and Language • Antonyms

flexible
valuable
nervous
noticeable
lovable
excusable
believable
reasonable
considerable
desirable
permissible
responsible
legible
sensible
incredible
marvelous
mysterious
industrious
anxious
numerous

Words that mean the opposite of each other are called **antonyms.** *Vague* and *specific* are antonyms.

A. Write the Unit word that is an antonym for each of these words. Then answer the question.

1. lazy _____

2. forbidden _____

3. explainable _____

4. hidden _____

5. Which two Unit words are antonyms for each other?

_____   _____

B. Some of the Unit words mean the same or nearly the same thing. Write two Unit words that are both antonyms for each word below.

6. calm _____ _____

7. hateful _____ _____

Some prefixes, such as *in-, un-, non-,* and *dis-,* have negative meanings. These prefixes can change a word into its antonym.

C. Each word below is the base of a Unit word. Add *un-* and an adjective-forming suffix to each word to form the antonym of the Unit word. Here is an example: *un + notice + able = unnoticeable.*

8. believe _____

9. reason _____

D. Add *in-* to each of these Unit words to form an antonym. Remember that *in-* changes to *il-* before *l* and to *ir-* before *r.*

10. excusable _____

11. responsible _____

12. flexible _____

13. legible _____

E. Write the word from an earlier unit that is the antonym for each of these words. Each word you will write begins with a negative prefix.

14. capable _____

15. burnable _____

Writing on Your Own

Pretend you are looking for someone to care for your pet while you are away. Write an ad for the "Help Wanted" section of your local newspaper. Describe your pet, the kind of care it needs, and the dates of your vacation. Also describe the kind of person you want to do the work. Include some way for job hunters to contact you. Use some of the Unit words or their antonyms in your ad.

 WRITER'S GUIDE For a sample descriptive paragraph, turn to page 260.

Spelling on Your Own

UNIT WORDS

Arrange the Unit words in vertical columns so that a word or message can be read horizontally. Look at the example. Create as many puzzles as you can.

MASTERY WORDS

breakable
terrible
enjoyable
enormous
serious
impossible

Finish these exercises using the Mastery words.

1. Write the two words that end with *-able*.

_____   _____

2. Write the two words that end with *-ible*.

_____   _____

3. Write the two words that end with *-ous.* _____   _____

Write the Mastery word that is the antonym for each word.

4. funny _____   **5.** tiny _____

The prefixes *in-*, *im-*, and *un-* mean "not." Add a prefix to each of these words to make it mean the opposite.

6. possible _____   **7.** breakable _____

8. enjoyable _____

Two Mastery words mean the opposite of each other.

9. Use one of these words to finish the sentence below.

Anna had a(n) _____ time at the park.

10. Now change the meaning of the sentence by using the second word.

Anna had a(n) _____ time at the park.

BONUS WORDS

convertible
advisable
accessible
traceable
conspicuous
contagious
reliable
reversible

Complete each sentence using a Bonus word.

1. Flu is a very ____ disease.
2. It is ____ to drink liquids when you have a fever.
3. Lost objects whose owners are not ____ are put up for public auction.
4. Erika's pink coat will be very ____ in a crowd.
5. Reporters must get their facts from ____ sources.
6. Canyon de Chelly is not easily ____ by car.

Both *convertible* and *reversible* have the Latin root *vert/vers,* "to turn."

7. Use each word in a sentence.
8. Write five other words that also have the root *vert/vers.*

123

29 Noun Suffixes

UNIT WORDS

1. *enlargement*
2. *retirement*
3. *announcement*
4. *judgment*
5. *sincerity*
6. *probability*
7. *historian*
8. *nationality*
9. *encouragement*
10. *guardian*
11. *responsibility*
12. *pedestrian*
13. *tournament*
14. *immunity*
15. *adjustment*
16. *civilian*
17. *acknowledgment*
18. *librarian*
19. *argument*
20. *vegetarian*

The Unit Words

Nouns are often formed by adding noun endings to another part of speech. The suffix *-ment,* for example, is added to a verb to form a noun: *retire + ment = retirement.* Notice that the final *e* is dropped before *-ment* is added to *argue, acknowledge,* and *judge.*

The suffix *-ity* is added to an adjective to form a noun: *sincere + ity = sincerity.* Notice that when you add *-ity* to words that end in *ble,* you must insert an *i* between *b* and *l: probable, probability.*

The suffix *-an* or *-ian,* however, is added to a word that is already a noun. It adds the meaning "a specialist." A *historian* is a specialist in history. □ The word *vegetarian* is formed from the noun *vegetable* and the suffix *-arian,* which means "a believer."

Pedestrian and *tournament* were formed many years ago. The base words from which these words were formed are no longer used without the suffixes.

Spelling Practice

A. Write the Unit word that is formed by adding the suffix -ment to each of these verbs.

1. argue _____

2. enlarge _____

3. encourage _____

4. announce _____

5. acknowledge _____

6. judge _____

7. adjust _____

8. retire _____

B. Write the Unit word that best fits each description.

9. a person who studies history _____

10. a person who doesn't eat meat _____

11. a person who works in a library _____

12. a person who watches over _____

13. a person not in the military _____

14. a series of games _____

Dr. Jonas Salk

C. Complete these sentences using Unit words that end with -ity.

15. Dr. Jonas Salk developed a vaccine that provides

_____ against polio.

16. The president has a great deal of _____.

17. The candidate for the school board spoke with _____ about education.

18. Your passport gives your description, age, and _____.

19. In all_____, if we destroy forests and jungles, many animal and plant species alive today will be extinct by the year 2000.

D. Each Unit word below was formed by adding -ity to an adjective. Write the adjective.

20. immunity _____

21. sincerity _____

22. probability _____

23. nationality _____

24. responsibility _____

E. Complete the paragraph using Unit words that end with -ment.

Mrs. Li made an __25__ that her __26__ from the company will take place next month. Mrs. Li has never needed any urging or __27__ to start new activities, so making the __28__ to a new life will be easy for her.

25. _____

26. _____

27. _____

28. _____

Proofreading • An English Report

Chuck wrote this report. Now he must proofread it. Chuck made twelve spelling mistakes. He also used three punctuation marks incorrectly. Read the report carefully.

1. Find Chuck's spelling mistakes. Then circle the misspelled words.

2. Use editing and proofreading marks to correct the punctuation.

UNIT WORDS

enlargement
retirement
announcement
judgment
sincerity
probability
historian
nationality
encouragement
guardian
responsibility
pedestrian
tournament
immunity
adjustment
civilian
acknowledgment
librarian
argument
vegetarian

> Writers of many nationilities have written great works of literature. In some people's judjment, however, a Spaniard named Miguel de Cervantes /ser·van′tēz/ created the greatest novel of all time. The name of the novel is Don Quixote /kē·(h)ōt′ē./
>
> Born in 1547, Cervantes did not begin to write Don Quixote until he was fifty-eight years old. Historiens know little about Cervantes's early life. However, it is known that he was a soldier for many years. Later, he was captured by pirates and spent five years as a slave. These experiences provided valueable material for his novel?
>
> Don Quixote is the story of a Spanish landowner who becomes bored with his retirment. To bring excitement into his monotonus life, he reads books about knights. With the encouragment of his servant Sancho, the landowner imagines that he is the knight Don Quixote. Don Quixote feels that it is his responsibilety to perform hearoic deeds and to become the guardan of the helpless. He wishes to conquer evil, However, despite his great sincerety, Quixote often cannot separate the real from the imaginary. A country inn becomes a castle and a windmill turns into a four-armed giant. Cervantes is able safely to poke fun at the soceity of his time through the mad deeds of his character Don Quixote.

3. Write the twelve misspelled words correctly.

_____   _____   _____

_____   _____   _____

_____   _____   _____

_____   _____   _____

Pablo Picasso, *Don Quixote,* 1955.

Writing on Your Own

Pretend the editor of your school yearbook has asked you to write a short essay about a classmate. Choose someone you want to get to know better to interview. Take notes or tape-record your conversation. Then summarize what you learn in your essay. Use at least five of the Unit words.

 WRITER'S GUIDE Learn about interviews on page 270.

Spelling on Your Own

UNIT WORDS

Write the plural form of each Unit word. Then use either the singular or plural form of each word in a sentence.

MASTERY WORDS

musician
department
activity
community
refreshment
amusement

Finish these exercises using the Mastery words.

1. Write the three words that end with -ment.

_____ _____ _____

2. Write the two words that end with -ity.

_____ _____

3. Write the word that ends with -ian. _____

4. Write the plural form of each word.

_____ _____ _____

_____ _____ _____

Ben wrote this announcement for the school bulletin board. Before he hangs it up, Ben must check his work. Ben made five spelling mistakes. Read the announcement carefully.

5. Find Ben's spelling mistakes. Circle the misspelled words.

> As a special after-school activety, the music departmint is giving a jazz concert on Friday at 3 P.M. Other musisians in the comunity are invited to play, too.
>
> After the concert, rafreshments will be served. Everyone will have a chance to get together and talk about jazz.

6. Write the five misspelled words correctly.

_____ _____ _____

_____ _____

BONUS WORDS

achievement
supplement
contentment
regularity
gaiety
politician
physician
legality

1. Write each Bonus word. Next to each word, write at least one other word that has the same root.

2. Use each Bonus word in a sentence. If you can, use another word with the same root in the sentence as well.

3. When the suffix -ity is added to gay, the y in gay becomes i and the i in -ity becomes e. List as many other words as you can that end with ety. Use a dictionary if you need help.

Review

Follow these steps when you are unsure of how to spell a word.
- **Say** the word. Recall when you have heard the word used. Think about what it means.
- **Look** at the word. Find any prefixes, suffixes, or other word parts you know. Think about other words that are related in meaning and spelling. Try to picture the word in your mind.
- **Spell** the word to yourself. Think about the way each sound is spelled. Notice any unusual spelling.
- **Write** the word while looking at it. Check the way you have formed your letters. If you have not written the word clearly or correctly, write it again.
- **Check** your learning. Cover the word and write it. If you did not spell the word correctly, practice these steps until the word becomes your own.

UNIT 25

interval
intramural
transparent
circuit
superstition
circumstances
circumference
supervision
interstate
transform

UNIT 26

manufacturing
society
industrial
economy
production
technology
irrigation
corporation
rural
agricultural

UNIT 25 **Follow the directions using words from Unit 25.**
Write the word or words that have prefixes with these meanings.

1. above, over (two words) _____ _____

2. across, through (two words) _____ _____

3. around (three words) _____ _____

   _____

**Complete each sentence with a word that has the prefix *inter-*
or *intra-*.**

4. We knew our class would win the _____ soccer
   competition at our school.

5. During the _____ between games we started
   planning for the next step in our tournament.

6. We would be using the _____ highway to get to our
   new challengers in the adjoining state.

UNIT 26 **Follow the directions using words from Unit 26.**

7. Write the six words that have /k/. Circle the word that spells /k/ with a *ch*.

   _____ _____ _____

   _____ _____ _____

8. Write the three words that end with /əl/.

   _____ _____ _____

9. Write the word that has double consonant letters. _____

10. Write the three words that end with /ē/.

_____ _____ _____

UNIT 27 Follow the directions using words from Unit 27.
Write the word or words that have each of these sounds.

11. /sh/ _____

12. /ō/ _____

13. /g/ (two words) _____ _____

14. /zh/ (two words) _____ _____

15. /k/ (three words) _____ _____

_____

Write the word that best fits each description.

16. a master cook _____ **17.** old _____

18. a type of dance _____ **19.** rare _____

20. a conversation _____ **21.** not clear _____

22. a damaging act _____ **23.** charming_____

24. a light color _____ **25.** a station _____

UNIT 27

ballet
antique
depot
dialogue
chef
picturesque
unique
vague
beige
sabotage

UNIT 28 Follow the directions using words from Unit 28.
**Write the word that belongs with each group of words. The suffix in ( )
is a clue to the correct word.**

26. creditable, true, *(-able)* _____

27. worried, uneasy, *(-ous)* _____

28. apparent, observable, *(-able)* _____

UNIT 28

anxious
believable
incredible
sensible
noticeable
considerable
numerous
permissible
industrious
legible

Write the words ending in these suffixes.

-ible (four words) *-able* (three words) *-ous* (three words)

_____ _____ _____

_____ _____ _____

_____ _____ _____

_____

129

vegetarian
argument
nationality
responsibility
judgment
pedestrian
announcement
acknowledgment
librarian
guardian

UNIT 29 Follow the directions using words from Unit 29.
Change these words into nouns.

39. national _____   40. judge _____

41. responsible _____   42. argue _____

43. acknowledge _____   44. guard _____

45. library _____   46. announce _____

Write the word that best fits each group of words.

47. fight, dispute, quarrel _____

48. fish, fruit, grain _____

49. notice, declaration, advertisement _____

50. sidewalk, person, foot _____

51. opinion, decision, conclusion _____

52. author, shelf, book _____

53. mother, adult, father _____

54. job, obligation, duty _____

55. reply, recognition, answer _____

Six of the words below contain spelling errors. Circle the words that are misspelled. Then write them correctly.

vegatarian   librarian   arguement

pedestrian   nationality   acknowledgement

guardiun   anouncement   judgmunt

56. _____   57. _____   58. _____

59. _____   60. _____   61. _____

WORDS IN TIME

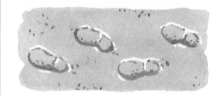

A pedestrian is a person who moves around by foot. The word *pedestrian* comes from the Latin words *ped,* meaning "foot," and *ire,* meaning "to go." The root *ped* is found in many other English words. Can you think of some?

Spelling and Reading
A How-to Article

Read the following how-to article. Notice what materials are needed and what steps are involved in the making of a piñata.*

The tradition of the piñata comes from Latin American society. Originally, piñatas were decorated containers filled with treats. On holidays and birthdays, children wearing blindfolds tried to break open the animal-shaped piñatas to get the treats inside. Piñatas are still used for this purpose, but they are also used as picturesque decorations all year round. Here's how you can make a piñata of your own design.

To begin manufacturing a piñata, you must gather numerous materials. You will need a balloon, masking tape, paper towels, paint, shellac, newspaper, flour, water, and a set of art scraps.

First blow up the balloon to the circumference you desire for your piñata. Then mix flour with water to form a paste. Add shredded newspaper to this mixture to make papier-mâché.** Complete one circuit around the balloon with the papier-mâché, making a vague outline of your soon-to-be piñata animal.

Next add features to the shape by attaching art scraps with masking tape. You can make incredible feet, ears, beaks, and so forth out of pieces of cardboard and cloth. Cover these features with more of the papier-mâché. After a brief interval, press a layer of paper towels over the whole production.

Now cut a thin hole in the top of your piñata and insert some small treats. Smooth over the hole and allow the piñata to dry. Use your paint and art scraps to add more details to your creation. Finally apply a layer of shellac to harden and protect the piñata.

Write your answers to the questions.

1. According to the writer, where does the piñata tradition come from?

2. What materials must you combine to make the papier-mâché?

3. What purpose does the balloon serve in making a piñata?

4. What other materials might be used to add additional touches to your piñata?

Underline the review words in your answers. Check to see that you spelled the words correctly.

*The word *piñata* is pronounced /pēn·yä′tə/.
**The word *papier-mâché* is pronounced /pā′pər·mə·shā′/.

Spelling and Writing
A How-to Article

Words to Help You Write

circumstances
chef
agricultural
believable
incredible
permissible
vegetarian
nationality

Think and Discuss

A how-to article explains how to make something or how to do something. In the first paragraph of a how-to article, the writer tells what the reader will learn how to make or do. What can the reader learn from the how-to article on page 131?

In the body of a how-to article, the writer provides a list of the materials that will be needed for the project. What materials does the writer list as necessary for making a piñata?

In addition to listing the materials in the body of a how-to article, the writer explains the steps involved in the how-to process. In an efficient, well-organized how-to article, the writer describes these steps completely, clearly, and in the correct time order. What might the result be if the steps in a how-to article were incomplete, unclear, or listed in the wrong sequence? Look at the how-to article on page 131. What does the writer list as the third step in making a piñata? What would happen if the reader performed the third step without performing the second step?

One way a writer can help a reader understand the sequence of steps in a how-to article is to use transitional words (or expressions). Transitional words are signals to the reader that the writer is about to move to a new step in the process. Some transitional words are *first, later,* and *as soon as possible.* What transitional words or expressions can you find in this how-to article? What effect would it have on the article if all of these words were removed?

Apply

Now it's your turn to write a **how-to article.** Pick something that you know how to make or do, and explain it to a younger person who is not familiar with the process. Follow the writing guidelines on the next page.

Prewriting

Decide what you will write about and whom you will write it for. Choose a topic that interests both of you and that you can explain.

- List the materials the reader will need.
- List the steps the reader should follow. Visualize yourself demonstrating the process to someone. Each time you mention a new material, check your materials list to make sure you have included it.

 THESAURUS For help finding exact words to describe the process you are explaining, turn to page 205.

Composing

Use your lists to write your how-to article.

- Write a sentence or two to introduce the process you are explaining.
- Write a paragraph in which you list the materials needed. Describe each item clearly.
- Describe the steps of the process in time order. Add transitional words that make the sequence of steps easier to understand.
- Look back over your prewriting lists to make sure you have not left out any materials or steps.

Revising

Read your how-to article and show it to a classmate. Follow these guidelines to improve your work. Use the editing and proofreading marks on this page to indicate corrections.

Editing

- Make sure you have included all the materials.
- Make sure your steps are clear and in sequence.
- Make sure your words are simple enough so a younger person will understand the process.

Proofreading

- Check your spelling, capitalization, and punctuation.

Copy your news story neatly onto clean paper.

Publishing

Give your how-to article to the person you had in mind as your audience or to a classmate who wants to learn the process you have explained. Find out if your reader found your article easy to follow.

Editing and Proofreading Marks

☰	capitalize
⊙	make a period
∧	add something
⋀	add a comma
⸉⸊	add quotation marks
⟋	take something away
◯	spell correctly
⍭	indent the paragraph
/	make a lowercase letter
∿tr	transpose

UNIT WORDS

1. recital
2. arrival
3. dismissal
4. proposal
5. permission
6. confession
7. admission
8. extension
9. provision
10. profession
11. impression
12. instruction
13. suspicion
14. appreciation
15. generation
16. participation
17. imagination
18. examination
19. consideration
20. organization

The Unit Words

The words in this unit are all nouns. You can often recognize a noun by looking at the final letters. You know that *-ment, -ity,* and *-ian* are noun suffixes. The final letters *-al* and *-ion* can also identify a noun. These suffixes may be added to verbs to form nouns.

recite + al = recital
instruct + ion = instruction

With some verbs you must do more than just add *-ion* to form the noun. To make the noun form of *admit,* you change the final *t* to *s* and add *-sion.* To make the noun form of *examine,* you must add *-ation.*

REMEMBER THIS

Sometimes riddles or tongue-twisters can help you remember the spelling of a word. To help you remember the c in the word *suspicion,* think of the tongue-twister below.

"I see what I see," said Inspector McGee.
"What I see is a <u>c</u> in suspicion."

Spelling Practice

A. Write the Unit word that is formed by adding a noun-forming suffix to each of these verbs.

1. arrive _____
2. instruct _____
3. impress _____
4. dismiss _____
5. examine _____
6. propose _____
7. organize _____
8. profess _____
9. confess _____
10. consider _____
11. imagine _____
12. generate _____
13. recite _____
14. appreciate _____
15. participate _____

Some verbs in Latin have different spellings for the present and past tenses. However, the meaning of the root does not change. For example, *mit* and *mis* are different spellings for the Latin root that means "send." This accounts for the different spellings of the verb *omit* and the noun *omission.*

B. Write the Unit word that is related to each of these groups of words.

16. permit, permissible _____
17. admit, admittance _____
18. extend, extensive _____
19. suspect, suspicious _____
20. provide, provisional _____

omit
omission

C. These verbs are the base words for some of the Unit words. Add a suffix to each word and write a Unit word. Then write the verb with *ing* added.

21. recite _____ _____
22. arrive _____ _____
23. propose _____ _____
24. appreciate _____ _____
25. generate _____ _____
26. imagine _____ _____
27. examine _____ _____
28. organize _____ _____
29. participate _____ _____

Using the Dictionary to Spell and Write •
Multiple Definitions

UNIT WORDS

recital
arrival
dismissal
proposal
permission
confession
admission
extension
provision
profession
impression
instruction
suspicion
appreciation
generation
participation
imagination
examination
consideration
organization

Knowing the different meanings of a word can help you when you write. Do you know the meanings of the words below? Each word actually has several meanings. You cannot accurately give a meaning for a word that has more than one definition unless you see the word used in a sentence. The context will tell you which meaning to choose. For example, the words *Jason's proposal* alone do not tell you whether Jason is proposing marriage or a trip to the bowling alley.

proposal	organization	admission
arrival	consideration	examination

A. Look up the word *impression* in the **Spelling Dictionary.** Write the number of the definition that fits the word as it is used in each sentence.

_____ **1.** Columbus was under the *impression* that the world is round.

_____ **2.** Columbus made a good *impression* on Queen Isabella.

_____ **3.** Columbus's foot made a deep *impression* on the beach.

_____ **4.** Columbus had the *impression* that he was in India.

B. Sometimes the plural form of a word has a particular meaning that is different from its other meanings. Look up the word *provision* in the **Spelling Dictionary.** Write the number of the definition that fits the word as it is used in each sentence.

_____ **5.** A new *provision* was written into the will.

_____ **6.** Was any *provision* made to feed the hamster during the vacation?

_____ **7.** We carried extra *provisions* for the journey.

C. Look up *organization* and *arrival* in the **Spelling Dictionary.** Write the number of the definition that fits the word as it is used in each sentence.

8. The *organization* of the group is based on democratic principles. _____.

9. She joined an *organization* to help animals. _____

10. The new *arrival* quickly became accustomed to the town. _____

11. We prepared for the *arrival* of our guest. _____

Writing on Your Own

Pretend that your friend Jeff is coming to your house for the first time. He wants to make a good impression on your family and has written a letter asking you what he needs to do. Send him a list of tips on how to make an excellent first impression. You may want to use these and some other Unit words in your letter: *arrival, impression, appreciation, generation, participation, imagination, consideration.*

SPELLING DICTIONARY To make sure you are correctly using words with multiple definitions, turn to page 161.

Spelling on Your Own

UNIT WORDS

Each Unit word below is incomplete. Think of the missing suffix in each word. Then write the word.

1. impres_____
2. arriv_____
3. instruct_____
4. generat_____
5. exten_____
6. recit_____
7. imagin_____
8. profes_____
9. admis_____
10. appreciat_____
11. permis_____
12. dismiss_____
13. confes_____
14. participat_____
15. propos_____
16. suspic_____
17. consider_____
18. provis_____
19. examin_____
20. organiz_____

MASTERY WORDS

**discussion
expression
location
survival
suggestion
terminal**

Finish these exercises using the Mastery words.

1. Write the four words that end with -ion.

_____   _____

_____   _____

2. Write the two words that end with -al.

_____   _____

3. Write the word in which an e was dropped before adding -ion.

_____

4. Write the word in which an e was dropped before adding -al.

_____

Finish each sentence with a Mastery word. The underlined word in each sentence is a clue.

5. Try to <u>locate</u> our present _____ on the map.

6. The actor <u>expressed</u> his feelings by the _____ on his face.

7. We <u>discuss</u> many interesting topics in our _____ group.

8. My _____ is that you ask the librarian to <u>suggest</u> a book for your report.

BONUS WORDS

**betrayal
denial
tension
disposition
distribution
collision
petition
excursion**

Write the Bonus word that has the same Latin root as each of these words.

1. tense
2. betray
3. dispose
4. deny
5. distribute
6. collide
7. current

Write the Bonus word that is a synonym for each word below.

8. refusal
9. strain
10. temperament
11. crash
12. appeal
13. a trip

UNIT WORDS

1. pattern
2. textile
3. fiber
4. logic
5. linen
6. molar
7. dial
8. fuel
9. luggage
10. silent
11. legend
12. riot
13. gravel
14. spiral
15. college
16. pliers
17. fabric
18. basis
19. liar
20. clinic

The Unit Words

Sometimes you need to divide a word at the end of a line. The rules below will help you do this, but check a dictionary if you are not sure how the word is divided. Remember that you never divide a one-syllable word or separate a one-letter syllable from the rest of the word.

1. When a word has two consonant letters between vowel letters, divide between the consonants except in the case of a consonant digraph.

pat·tern   tex·tile   rath·er

2. When a word has two vowel sounds between consonant sounds, divide between the vowel letters. The words *dial* and *fuel* are often pronounced as one-syllable words, but they still follow the same pattern as *liar*.

li·ar   di·al   fu·el

3. When a word has one consonant letter between two vowel letters:
   a. divide *before* the consonant if the first vowel sound is long.

fi·ber

   b. divide *after* the consonant if the first vowel sound is short and the first syllable is accented.

lin·en

Spelling Practice

A. Complete these exercises using the Unit words.

1. Write the five words that have two vowel sounds between two consonant sounds. Then draw a line between the syllables in each word.

_____   _____   _____

_____   _____

2. Write the five words that have two consonant letters between two vowel sounds. Then draw a line between the syllables in each word.

_____   _____   _____

_____   _____

3. Find the words in which one consonant letter comes between two vowel letters. Write the five words in which the first vowel sound is short and the first syllable is accented.

_____   _____   _____

_____   _____

4. Draw a line between the syllables in each word you wrote for **3.**

5. Write the five words in which one consonant comes between two vowel sounds and the first vowel sound is long.

_____   _____   _____

_____   _____

6. Draw a line between the syllables in each word you wrote for **5.**

B. Write the Unit word that is a synonym for each word below.

7. reason _____   **8.** fibber _____

9. design _____   **10.** quiet _____

11. suitcases _____   **12.** thread _____

13. cloth (two words)

_____   _____

C. A Rhyme Styme is a riddle that has two rhyming words for the answer. Complete these Rhyme Stymes. One of the Unit words is part of both answers.

14. What do you call oil that is used to heat a junior high?

_____   _____

15. What do you call the hay eaten by a type of pack animal?

_____   _____

Proofreading • A Reading Log Entry

Jean wrote this in her weekly reading log. Now she must proofread her entry. Jean made twelve spelling mistakes. She also omitted three quotation marks and made two other punctuation errors. Read the entry carefully.

1. Circle the misspelled words and insert the missing punctuation marks.

Our school librarion suggested that I read "Cemetery Path" by Leo Rosten. It was marvelus. A man named Ivan lived in a small town in Russia many years ago. Every evening the men of the town gathered at a tavern. Although the shortest way home was through the cemetery, Ivan was too frightened to go home this way. One night, a lieutenant made Ivan a proposel. If Ivan would walk through the cemetery, the lieutenant would give him five rubles. The only provition was that Ivan must plant a sword in front of a large tomb as proof that he had been there. Ivan agreed to the dare.

The wind spiriled the snow around Ivan's head as he began to walk along the cemetery path. All was silant except for the crunch of the grevel beneath his feet. I must be sensable. Its only earth Ivan said to himself, trying to boost his courage with logec. "I must not let my imaganation run away with itself.

At last, Ivan reached the tomb. Every fibber in his body shook with terror. He drew the sword and quickly plunged it into the hard ground, pounding it in as deep as possible. It was over. The money was his. Ivan tried to stand up, but something gripped him. He couldn't move.

The next morning they found Ivan frozen to death, an expression of incredable horror on his face. The sword was deep in the ground where Ivan had pounded it—through the fabric of his own coat.

2. Write the twelve misspelled words correctly.

_____ _____ _____

_____ _____ _____

_____ _____ _____

_____ _____ _____

Writing on Your Own

Write a book entry for a class reading log. Choose a book you felt strongly about, summarize it, and explain why you felt as you did. Support your opinion with reasons and examples. Your entry should help a classmate decide whether to read the book. Use some Unit words.

 WRITER'S GUIDE For a sample book report, turn to page 268.

Spelling on Your Own

UNIT WORDS

Write a paragraph using the Unit words to describe a walk past the stores in your town. Then write each word you didn't use in a separate sentence.

MASTERY WORDS

Finish these exercises using the Mastery words.

1. Write the two words that have /ō/ in the first syllable.

_____   _____

2. Draw a line between the syllables in each word you wrote for **1.**

3. Write the two other words that have one consonant letter between two vowel sounds.

_____   _____

4. Write each word you wrote for **3** again. Then draw a line between the syllables in each word.

_____   _____

5. Draw a line under the accented syllables in each word you wrote for **3.**

Finish this sentence with two Mastery words. Then draw a line between the syllables in each word you wrote.

When I __**6**__, I feel a great __**7**__ on the first day.

6. _____   **7.** _____

Don't confuse the word *petal,* a part of a flower, with *pedal,* a part of a bicycle. Finish these sentences using the words *petal* and *pedal.*

8. A _____ dropped to the ground as I picked the daisy.

9. Johnny tried to fix the broken _____ on his bike.

10. Will you be able to _____ your bike up the hill?

Mastery Words box:
hunger
total
robot
petal
diet
limit

BONUS WORDS

Write the Bonus word that is a synonym for each word below. Then draw a line between the syllables in each word you wrote.

1. a crack	**2.** wild	**3.** turn	**4.** prejudice
5. a splinter	**6.** scoundrel	**7.** double	**8.** concentrate

Write each Bonus word in a sentence, or write a paragraph including all the Bonus words.

Bonus Words box:
frantic
rascal
sliver
crevice
rotate
focus
bias
dual

33 Words from Latin

/ə·kwâr′ē·əm/

The Unit Words

Did you know that there are more than one million words in the English language? Of course, a large number of these are technical words that are seldom used. Scholars estimate that the average adult's vocabulary actually consists of 30,000 to 60,000 words. To build its million-word vocabulary, English borrowed many words from other languages. The majority of English words were borrowed from Latin or have Latin roots.

Latin words have come into English in several ways. In A.D. 43, Roman armies marched into Britain; they stayed for four hundred years. Latin, of course, was the language used during this period. Later, tribes speaking a language similar to German invaded Britain. Modern English is based on this language. Many Latin words, however, remained.

In 1066 the Normans brought the French language to England. Many more Latin words entered English through French. As the years passed, new words with Latin origins were borrowed from Italian and Spanish as well.

In modern times scientists often use a Latin word to name a new discovery. *Virus* came into English in this way.

Spelling Practice

A. Write the Unit word that belongs in each group of words.

1. House of Representatives, Assembly _____

2. terrarium, cage _____

3. entrance, doorway _____

4. stadium, arena _____

5. germ, bacteria _____

6. kidney, liver _____

7. excuse, explanation _____

8. a sign, warning _____

B. Complete each sentence using a Unit word.

9. Geraldo Muñoz, a _____ for political office, took time out to evaluate his campaign.

10. Posters and other _____ had been put up in town.

11. His speech discussing the Smith _____ Jones legal case was written.

12. He hoped the President's _____ of the tax cut would help boost his votes.

13. An added _____ to his campaign was the support of the Nobel Peace Prize winner.

14. Special agent Jim Guthrie was considered to be a

_____ by his peers.

15. Jim had developed a way to identify people by testing

_____ from their mouths.

16. He was known for his skills in the jungle, where he used the

_____ on trees to find his way.

17. Newer agents felt _____ to the experienced agent.

18. But Agent Guthrie, who used the _____ Jim Smith, always made everyone feel important.

C. Complete these exercises using Unit words.

19. Write the two words that end with /ər/.

_____   _____

20. Write the three words that end with /əm/.

_____   _____   _____

Using the Dictionary to Spell and Write • Etymologies

UNIT WORDS

aquarium
virus
propaganda
genius
appendix
alibi
item
inferior
coliseum
bonus
senate
omen
veto
saliva
candidate
superior
exit
alias
versus
fungus

An **etymology** is a word history. It explains how a word came into our language. An etymology also tells how the meaning of a word has changed and developed. This information can be helpful when you write. The **Words in Time** features in this book give you the etymologies of many words. You can also find etymologies in dictionaries. Some dictionaries provide etymologies for most of the words. Others give only the etymologies of words with particularly interesting histories.

Look at the etymologies below for the word *senate.*

sen·ate /'sen·ət/ *n* [ME *senat,* fr. OF, fr. L *senatus,* lit., council of elders, fr. *sen-, senex* old, old man—more at SENIOR] **1** : an assembly or council usu. possessing high deliberative and legislative functions: as **a** : the supreme council of the ancient Roman republic and empire **b** : the second chamber in the bicameral legislature of a major political unit (as a nation, state, or province) **2** : the hall or chamber in which a senate meets **3** : a governing body of some universities charged with maintaining academic standards and regulations and usu. composed of the principal or representative members of the faculty

sen·ate (sen'it), *n.* **1.** an assembly or council having the highest deliberative functions. **2.** *(cap.)* the upper house of the legislature of certain countries, as the United States, France, etc. **3.** the room or building in which such a group meets. **4.** *Rom. Hist.* the supreme council of the Roman state. **5.** a governing, advisory, or disciplinary body, as in certain universities. [ME *senat* < L *senāt(us)* council of elders = *sen(ex)* old + *ātus* -ATE³]

Both dictionaries agree on the etymology of *senate,* but they present the information differently. The abbreviation *fr.* and the symbol < both mean "from." If you are not sure of the meaning of an abbreviation or symbol, look in the front of the dictionary for an explanation.

Look up the underlined words in your **Spelling Dictionary.** Then answer the questions.

1. What is the Latin root word of <u>aquarium</u>? _____

What is another word that has the same root?

_____

2. What does <u>veto</u> mean in Latin? _____

3. What does <u>exit</u> mean in Latin? _____

4. What does <u>virus</u> mean in Latin? _____

Writing on Your Own

Prepare notes for an oral report to present to your class on the etymology of four words. Choose two Unit words and two other words that interest you. Look them up in a library dictionary.

Spelling on Your Own

Write the Unit words in alphabetical order. Then use as many of the words as you can in a story.

MASTERY WORDS

republic
junior
extra
senator
lunar
volcano

Finish these exercises using the Mastery words.

1. Write the three words that end with /ər/.

_____   _____   _____

2. Write the word that ends with /ə/. _____

3. Write the two words that have the sound /k/.

_____   _____

4. Write the three words that have two syllables.

_____   _____   _____

5. Write the three words that have three syllables.

_____   _____   _____

Finish each sentence using a Mastery word.

6. In 1980, Mt. St. Helens, a _____ in the state of Washington, erupted.

7. Do you think you'll need an _____ blanket tonight?

8. Margaret Chase Smith was a _____ from Maine.

9. When the moon passes through the earth's shadow, a

_____ eclipse takes place.

BONUS WORDS

nucleus
dexterity
ultimatum
sinister
apparatus
stamina
forum
insignia

1. Use each Bonus word in a sentence that clearly shows its meaning. Use the **Spelling Dictionary** if you are not sure of a word's meaning.

2. *Ultimatum* comes from the Latin word *ultimatus,* meaning "final." *Insignia* comes from Latin *in-,* meaning "upon," and *signum,* meaning "a mark." Write a few sentences explaining how the Latin meanings of *ultimatum* and *insignia* relate to their modern meanings.

34 Multisyllabic Words

UNIT WORDS

1. pantomime
2. institution
3. convention
4. ignition
5. subscription
6. adviser
7. independent
8. traditional
9. triumphant
10. ceremony
11. revolution
12. interference
13. narration
14. administer
15. experimentation
16. questionnaire
17. desolate
18. satisfaction
19. explanation
20. eliminate

Marcel Marceau, pantomimist

The Unit Words

Pantomime is an ancient form of drama. It comes from the Greek words *panto*, meaning "all," and *mimos*, meaning "imitating." Pantomime is acting without words.

Is *pantomime* a new word for you? Your vocabulary is expanding every day. You are finding new words all the time—in the books you read, in the programs you watch on television, and in the conversations you have with others. You will want to include these new words in your written vocabulary as well. Many of these new words will be multisyllabic (*multi*, "many," + *syllable*). Multisyllabic words have many syllables. Don't be afraid of multisyllabic words. Divide them into word parts. Think of the meanings of the smaller parts. Think of the pronunciations and the spellings of the smaller parts. If you are still in doubt, use a dictionary. Remember that a dictionary is your most valuable reference tool.

REMEMBER THIS

Think of an elephant when you want to remember the spelling of *triumphant.* Elephants were often part of the triumphant parades through the streets of Rome. *Elephant* and *triumphant* both end with *-phant.*

Spelling Practice

A. Write the Unit word that is related to each word below.

1. advise _____

2. satisfy _____

3. explain _____

4. subscribe _____

5. ignite _____

6. administration _____

7. revolt _____

8. mimic _____

B. Finish each sentence using a Unit word.

9. The desert seemed to be a _____ place to the pioneers.

10. Their _____ spirit helped them survive the hostile environment.

11. They felt _____ when they reached their destination.

12. The students at Oak Park Junior High School host a mock political _____ every year.

13. It has become _____ for the students to make posters and give speeches for their candidates.

14. At the closing _____ this year, the principal congratulated them on a successful meeting.

15. The principal feels that this type of _____ helps students become responsible citizens.

16. Each year the students fill out a _____ checking the topics in which they are interested.

17. Then the teachers _____ the topics with the fewest votes.

18. The school counselor gave a _____ with the film about the college.

19. The college was considered a fine _____ of learning.

20. The _____ from noises outside, however, made it difficult to hear the entire talk.

C. Add the suffix -ly to each adjective below to form an adverb.

21. triumphant _____

22. independent _____

23. desolate _____

24. traditional _____

D. Choose two adjectives and two adverbs from **21–24.** Use the four words in one or two sentences.

_____

_____

_____

147

Proofreading • A Business Letter

Karen wrote this letter to her local newspaper to publicize the work of the Sunshine Club. Karen must proofread her letter before she mails it. She made six spelling mistakes. She also left out two apostrophes.

1. Circle the misspelled words and insert the missing apostrophes.

> 6 Emerald Drive
> Ames, Iowa 50010
> March 14, 19——
>
> *The Bugle-Independent*
> 5 Main Street
> Ames, Iowa 50010
>
> Dear Editor:
>
> We are a group of students who like to entertain after school in hospitals and rest homes. Our clubs advisar, Mrs. Green, thought that your readers might find an explaination of our organisation of interest.
>
> Enclosed is the program from a recent performance. Dan and Mike did the hilarious dilog "Whos on First." Luis and Carol presented a pantamine act that is really unique. Angela sang a medley of popular songs. With a little encouragment, the whole audience happily joined in.
>
> Yours truly,
>
> *Karen Walker*

2. Write the six misspelled words correctly.

_____   _____   _____

_____   _____   _____

Writing on Your Own

Pretend you are the administrator of a hospital in Iowa. Write a letter to Karen Walker inviting the Sunshine Club to perform in your hospital. Suggest a convenient date and time for the performance and describe the age group you would like entertained. Describe other programs that patients have enjoyed. Use at least five of the Unit words in your letter.

 WRITER'S GUIDE For help revising your letter, turn to the checklist on page 257.

Spelling on Your Own

UNIT WORDS

Write each Unit word. Then rewrite each word showing where it can be divided at the end of a line. Use a hyphen to mark all the syllable divisions. Use the **Spelling Dictionary** to help you.

MASTERY WORDS

Write the Mastery word that best completes each of these sentences.

1. *North, east, south,* and *west* each name a _____.

2. Radios, lamps, and clocks all run on _____ current.

3. Drawing, dancing, and acting are all _____ activities.

4. My book, my pen, and my sweater are my own _____.

Some words are said differently in different parts of the country. Write the words that have these pronunciations.

5. /en′və·lōp/ or /än′və·lōp/ _____

6. /hang′kər·chif/ or /hang′kər·chēf/ _____

Write the plural form of each word below.

7. direction _____   8. envelope _____

9. property _____   10. handkerchief _____

Complete these exercises using Mastery words.

11. Look up each Mastery word in the **Spelling Dictionary.** Then write the word showing where it can be divided at the end of a line. Use a hyphen to mark the syllable divisions.

_____   _____   _____

_____   _____   _____

12. The word *directions* has a meaning that is different from *direction.* Write a sentence using *directions.*

_____

| electric |
| direction |
| property |
| handkerchief |
| envelope |
| artistic |

SPELLING DICTIONARY
If you need help, use the pronunciation key on page 162.

BONUS WORDS

Write the Bonus word that has the same Latin root as each of these words. Then complete the exercise.

1. heredity   2. extravaganza   3. commission   4. respond
5. respiratory   6. signify   7. precipitate   8. use

9. Write the three words with prefixes that have negative meanings. Write an antonym for each word.

| extravagant |
| insignificant |
| precipitation |
| commitment |
| inheritance |
| unusually |
| irresponsible |
| conspiracy |

UNIT WORDS

1. photographer
2. illustrator
3. dentist
4. veterinarian
5. oceanographer
6. pharmacist
7. psychologist
8. engineer
9. chemist
10. electrician
11. accountant
12. technician
13. therapist
14. dietitian
15. surgeon
16. secretary
17. mechanic
18. cashier
19. lawyer
20. computer programmer

BASIC FOODS

The Unit Words

Most of the pictures in this book were created by photographers or illustrators. A photographer captures images with a camera. An illustrator draws pictures for books, newspapers, and other publications.

The Unit words are all words that name people who work at specialized jobs. Notice that most of the words end with one of these noun-forming suffixes: *-er, -or, -ian,* or *-ist.* These suffixes mean "one who does" or "one who specializes in."

A dentist is someone who works with teeth. The Latin word for tooth is *dens.* A veterinarian specializes in the treatment of animals. The Latin adjective *veterinus* was used to describe animals old enough to carry burdens. An oceanographer is someone who studies and describes the oceans. The Greek root *graph* means "write (about)."

REMEMBER THIS

Think of this sentence to help you remember that the word *dietitian* has *t* twice.

The dietitian said,
"My die_t suits me to a _T_."

Spelling Practice

A. Complete these exercises using the Unit words.

1. Write the five words that end with the suffix *-ist.*

_____ _____ _____

_____ _____

2. Write the four words that end with the suffix *-ian.* Then circle the word in which *-ian* is pronounced as two syllables.

_____ _____

_____ _____

3. Write the only word ending in the suffix /ən/ not spelled *-ian.*

_____

4. Write the three words in which /f/ is spelled with *ph.*

_____ _____ _____

5. Write the four words in which /k/ is spelled with *ch.*

_____ _____

_____ _____

6. Write the five other job titles that have /k/.

_____ _____ _____

_____ _____

7. Write the three words that have /j/. Then underline the letter that spells /j/ in each word.

_____ _____ _____

8. Write the word that ends with the sounds /yər/ heard in *junior.*

_____

B. Write the job specialist you would go to if you needed

9. drawings for a school paper _____

10. your appendix removed _____

11. a transmission installed _____

12. a letter typed _____

13. a healthful meal plan _____

14. a prescription filled _____

15. to have your picture taken _____

16. to pay for your purchase _____

Spelling and Language • Possessive Nouns

UNIT WORDS

photographer
illustrator
dentist
veterinarian
oceanographer
pharmacist
psychologist
engineer
chemist
electrician
accountant
technician
therapist
dietitian
surgeon
secretary
mechanic
cashier
lawyer
computer
    programmer

The possessive form of a word shows ownership. Nouns and pronouns are the only words that have possessive forms.

Jessica's sweater   her sweater

To form the possessive of a singular noun, you add an apostrophe and *s*.

Lassie's collar   Les's book   the princess's crown

To form the possessive of a plural noun ending with *s*, you add only an apostrophe.

the Williamses' house   the actors' costumes

A. Write the possessive form of each noun below.

1. cashier

2. pharmacist

3. electrician

_____   _____   _____

4. therapist

5. lawyer

6. soldier

_____   _____   _____

B. Write the plural form of each noun below. Then write the plural form again showing possession. The first one has been done for you.

7. guardian   _____   _____

8. secretary   _____   _____

9. veterinarian   _____   _____

10. mosquito   _____   _____

To form the possessive of a hyphenated compound, you add an apostrophe and *s* after the last word.

my father-in-law's hat

C. Write the possessive form of each noun in (   ) in the sentences below.

11. King is my (sister-in-law) _____ dog.

12. The (runner-up) _____ medal is silver.

Writing on Your Own

Pretend you are a reporter for a local newspaper. You have been asked to write an editorial about career education in schools. On Career Day more than fifty working people visited schools and discussed the jobs they do. Decide whether you think this program is worthwhile. Then write an editorial to express your opinion. Use facts and examples to convince your readers that you are right. Use as many Unit words and possessive nouns as you can.

 WRITER'S GUIDE For a sample persuasive paragraph, turn to page 264.

Spelling on Your Own

UNIT WORDS

The final letters of each Unit word have been left out. Think of the missing letters. Then write the word on a separate piece of paper.

1. veter_____
2. techni_____
3. den_____
4. oceanogra_____
5. secret_____
6. mechan_____
7. psychol_____
8. thera_____
9. cash_____
10. electri_____
11. pharma_____
12. law_____
13. account_____
14. engin_____
15. surg_____
16. illustra_____
17. photogra_____
18. chem_____
19. dieti_____
20. compu_____ program_____

MASTERY WORDS

Finish the exercises using the Mastery words.

1. Write the word that has /s/ spelled with *sc*. _____
2. Write the word that has /s/ spelled with *se*. _____
3. Write the word that has the sounds /ər/ spelled with *or*. _____
4. Write the word that has a "silent" *b*. _____
5. Write the word that has the sound /j/. _____
6. Write the word that has the sound /ā/. _____
7. Write the word that has the sound /ī/. _____

Write a sentence telling what a person with each of these jobs does.

8. plumber _____

_____

9. author _____

_____

10. scientist _____

_____

> nurse
> plumber
> author
> manager
> scientist
> baker

BONUS WORDS

1. Write the seven Bonus words that have a suffix meaning "one who does" or "one who specializes in."

2. Write a sentence for each Bonus word. In the sentence, briefly describe what a person with this job does.

3. Write a paragraph describing a job you might like to have either now or in the future.

> architect
> physicist
> cosmetologist
> optician
> pediatrician
> compositor
> astronomer
> statistician

36 Review

ARRIVED

Follow these steps when you are unsure of how to spell a word.

- **Say** the word. Recall when you have heard the word used. Think about what it means.
- **Look** at the word. Find any prefixes, suffixes, or other word parts you know. Think about other words that are related in meaning and spelling. Try to picture the word in your mind.
- **Spell** the word to yourself. Think about the way each sound is spelled. Notice any unusual spelling.
- **Write** the word while looking at it. Check the way you have formed your letters. If you have not written the word clearly or correctly, write it again.
- **Check** your learning. Cover the word and write it. If you did not spell the word correctly, practice these steps until the word becomes your own.

UNIT 31

suspicion
permission
instruction
organization
arrival
dismissal
appreciation
participation
imagination
profession

UNIT 31 Follow the directions using words from Unit 31.
Write the word that is related to each word.

1. arrive _____

2. dismiss _____

3. organize _____

4. appreciate _____

5. Write the eight words that end with /shən/.

_____ _____ _____

_____ _____ _____

_____ _____

6. Write the two words that end with /əl/.

_____ _____

Write the noun form of these verbs.

7. permit _____

8. participate _____

9. suspect _____

10. imagine _____

11. instruct _____

12. profess _____

WORDS IN TIME

The word *suspicion* comes from the Latin verb *suspicere,* which means "to suspect or mistrust." *Suspicere,* in turn, comes from two other Latin words meaning "to look" and "under." When you suspect someone, you look under the surface of his or her actions.

Prewriting

Think of a subject to describe. Decide on the tone you would like to create in describing this subject. Then make a chart to help you organize some details you can use in your description.

- Divide a sheet of paper into six columns. Label the first five columns *see, hear, smell, taste, touch.* Label the last column *feelings.*
- In the first five columns, write vivid words that describe what you might sense if you were in the scene.
- In the column marked *feelings,* list words that tell how you might feel.
- Circle the words that contribute to the tone you would like to create.

 THESAURUS For help finding vivid words that support the tone you want to create, turn to page 205.

Composing

Use your chart to write the first draft of your descriptive paragraphs.

- Write the topic sentence for each paragraph, setting the tone of each.
- Write sentences that support the tone and include vivid sensory details.
- Include details that let readers know your own reactions to and feelings about the subject you are describing.
- Look over your prewriting chart. Do you want to add any details to your draft to sharpen the impression you have given?

Revising

Read your description and show it to a classmate. Follow these guidelines to improve your work. Use the editing and proofreading marks on this page to indicate corrections.

Editing

- Check that your paragraphs describe your scene vividly.
- Make sure your detail sentences support the topic sentences and contribute to the tone you want to set.
- Check that you have given your own feelings about the scene in a way that adds to the tone of your descriptive paragraphs.

Proofreading

- Check your spelling, capitalization, and punctuation.

Copy your description neatly onto clean paper.

Publishing

Read your descriptive paragraphs to your classmates. See if they can tell you the tone of your description. Discuss your use of descriptive details.

Editing and Proofreading Marks

☰	capitalize
⊙	make a period
∧	add something
⌄	add a comma
⌄⌄	add quotation marks
ℯ	take something away
◯	spell correctly
¶	indent the paragraph
/	make a lowercase letter
∼ tr	transpose

SPELLING DICTIONARY

PRONUNCIATION KEY

Remember these things when you read pronunciations:

- Parentheses around a sound symbol show that the sound is not always pronounced. /tûr′k(w)oiz/
- A primary accent mark ′ comes after the syllable that is said with the most force. A secondary accent mark ′ follows the syllable that is said with slighty less force. /fun′də·men′təl/

/a/	act, cat	/m/	mother, room	/u/	up, come
/ā/	ate, rain	/n/	new, can	/û/	early, hurt
/â/	care, bear	/ng/	sing, hang	/yo͞o/	mule, few
/ä/	car, father	/o/	on, stop	/v/	very, five
/b/	bed, rub	/ō/	over, go	/w/	will
/ch/	chair, watch	/ô/	or, saw	/y/	yes
/d/	duck, red	/oi/	oil, toy	/z/	zoo, buzz
/e/	egg, hen	/ou/	out, cow	/zh/	treasure
/ē/	even, see	/o͞o/	food, too	/ə/	The schwa
/f/	fish, off	/o͝o/	book, pull		is the sound
/g/	go, big	/p/	pig, hop		represented by
/h/	hat, hit	/r/	ran, car		these letters:
/i/	if, sit	/s/	see, miss		a in ago
/ī/	ice, time	/sh/	show, wish		e in listen
/j/	jump, bridge	/t/	take, feet		i in giraffe
/k/	cat, look	/th/	thing, tooth		o in pilot
/l/	lost, ball	/t͟h/	that, weather		u in circus

Symbols in the Spelling Dictionary

This symbol ► marks a word history.
This symbol ● indicates a note about the correct use of a word.

---

abandon

A

a·ban·don /ə·ban′dən/ **1** *v.* To give up completely. **2** *v.* To desert or leave behind: We had to *abandon* the car in the snow. **3** *n.* Careless freedom: The children danced with happy *abandon*.

ab·bre·vi·ate /ə·brē′vē·āt/ *v.* **ab·bre·vi·at·ed, ab·bre·vi·at·ing 1** To reduce a word or phrase to a shortened form. **2** To shorten or condense.

ab·do·men /ab′də·mən *or* ab·dō′mən/ *n.* **1** In mammals, the part of the body between

accept

the thorax and the pelvis; belly. **2** In insects, the hindmost section of the body.

-able *suffix* Able to be: *likable*.

ab·stract /ab′strakt/ *adj.* **1** Not dealing with a specific or particular thing: an *abstract* idea. **2** Offering an imaginative form or pattern rather than an actual image of an object: *abstract* art.

ac·cept /ak·sept′/ *v.* **1** To take or receive something offered or given: *accept* an award. **2** To agree to: *accept* an invitation. **3** To welcome; to approve of: *accept* into the family.

ac·cess /ak′ses/ *n.* **1** Permission or ability to approach, enter, or get: *access* to the files. **2** A means of entrance: The tunnel gives *access* to the street.

ac·ces·si·ble /ak·ses′ə·bəl/ *adj.* **1** Capable of being reached; obtainable. **2** Easily reached.

ac·com·mo·date /ə·kom′ə·dāt/ *v.* **ac·com·mo·dat·ed, ac·com·mo·dat·ing** **1** To hold or be suitable for: This room *accommodates* two beds. **2** To provide for: We can always *accommodate* one more at our house. **3** To help or do a favor for: If you need a ride, I'll be happy to *accommodate*.

ac·com·pa·ny /ə·kum′pə·nē/ *v.* **ac·com·pa·nied, ac·com·pa·ny·ing** **1** To go along with; escort. **2** To play a musical instrument while someone sings.

ac·count·ant /ə·koun′tənt/ *n.* A person whose work involves recording and summarizing amounts of money received or paid out.

ac·cus·tomed /ə·kus′təmd/ *adj.* Regular or usual.

ache /āk/ *v.* **ached, ach·ing,** *n.* **1** *v.* To have or suffer a dull, steady pain. **2** *n.* A dull steady pain. **3** *v.* To have pity for: My heart *ached* for her. **4** *v.* To long for: I'm *aching* to take a vacation.

a·chieve·ment /ə·chēv′mənt/ *n.* **1** Something achieved or accomplished. **2** The act of achieving or accomplishing.

ac·knowl·edg·ment /ak·nol′ij·mənt/ *n.* **1** The act of recognizing or giving credit. **2** Something done or given to show receipt of or thanks for something. *Alternate spelling:* **acknowledgement.**

ac·quaint /ə·kwānt′/ *v.* To show or introduce; to help someone get to know something or someone.

a·cryl·ic /ə·kril′ik/ *n.* **1** A synthetic paint that produces clear, bright colors. **2** (*pl.*) An artist's medium for painting.

ac·tiv·i·ty /ak·tiv′ə·tē/ *n., pl.* **ac·tiv·i·ties** **1** The state of being active; movement. **2** Something that is done. **3** Work or pastime.

ad·just·ment /ə·just′mənt/ *n.* The process of changing or fixing something to make it fit or work properly.

ad·min·is·ter /ad·min′is·tər/ *v.* **1** To be in charge of; to manage or direct. **2** To give or supply with, as medicine or first aid.

ad·mis·sion /ad·mish′ən/ *n.* **1** The act of admitting or acknowledging something. **2** The right to enter. **3** A ticket price.

a·do·be /ə·dō′bē/ *n.* **1** Sun-baked bricks. **2** *adj. use:* an *adobe* building. ▸ *Adobe* is a Spanish word meaning "brick."

ad·vice /ad·vīs′/ *n.* A suggestion made or an opinion given.

ad·vis·a·ble /ad·vī′zə·bəl/ *adj.* Fit to be done; sensible; wise.

ad·vise /ad·vīz′/ *v.* **ad·vised, ad·vis·ing** **1** To make suggestions; to give advice. **2** To inform; to communicate information: We *advised* him of the decision.

ad·vis·er /ad·vī′zər/ *n.* **1** A person who gives advice. **2** A teacher who counsels students about courses, careers, etc. *Alternate spelling:* **advisor.**

aer·i·al /âr′ē·əl/ **1** *adj.* Of, from, or in the air. **2** *adj.* Of, by, or for flying. **3** *n.* An antenna used for radio or television reception.

af·fect /ə·fekt′/ *v.* To act upon; to have an influence on: Fear *affects* our behavior.

af·fec·tion·ate /ə·fek′shən·it/ *adj.* Expressing warmth or love. —**af·fec′tion·ate·ly** *adv.*

ag·gra·vate /ag′rə·vāt/ *v.* **ag·gra·vat·ed, ag·gra·vat·ing** **1** To make worse or more severe: Coughing *aggravates* a sore throat. **2** To cause annoyance; to provoke to anger: The children's noise *aggravated* the man.

ag·gres·sive /ə·gres′iv/ *adj.* **1** Quick to fight or attack. **2** Eager; forceful.

ag·ri·cul·tur·al /ag′rə·kul′chər·əl/ *adj.* Of or having to do with agriculture or farming: an *agricultural* school.

-al *suffix* **1** Of or having to do with something: *logical*. **2** The act or process of doing something: *refusal*.

al·bum /al′bəm/ *n.* **1** A book used for keeping stamps, coins, pictures, etc. **2** A long-playing record or set of records.

Abbreviations

n. = noun; *v.* = verb; *adj.* = adjective; *adv.* = adverb; *prep.* = preposition; *conj.* = conjunction

alias

a·li·as /ā′lē·əs/　**1** *n.* A false name taken to conceal one's identity.　**2** *conj.* Otherwise known as.　► *Alias* comes from the Latin word *alius,* "other."

al·i·bi /al′ə·bī/ *n., pl.* **al·i·bis**　**1** The fact or the claim that an individual suspected of a crime was in another place when the crime was committed.　**2** An excuse intended to place blame or fault elsewhere.　► *Alibi* is a Latin word meaning "elsewhere; in another place."

al·le·giance /ə·lē′jəns/ *n.* Loyalty to a ruler or a larger group such as a political party or a country.

al·ley /al′ē/ *n.*　**1** The narrow space between or behind buildings.　**2** A lane or course for bowling.

al·li·ga·tor /al′ə·gā′tər/ *n.* A large reptile found mainly along rivers in the southeastern United States, similar to a crocodile but with a wider snout.　► *Alligator* comes from the Spanish words *el lagarto,* "the lizard."

al·ly /al′ī *or* ə·lī′/ *v.* **al·lied, al·ly·ing,** *n., pl.* **al·lies**　**1** *v.* To join together for a cause or purpose, often for defense.　**2** *n.* A person or country joined with another for a particular purpose; a partner.

al·tar /ôl′tər/ *n.* A raised table used in religious ceremonies.

al·ter /ôl′tər/ *v.* To change or make different in some way.

a·muse·ment /ə·myōōz′mənt/ *n.*　**1** The condition or state of being entertained or amused.　**2** Something that entertains or amuses.

an·chor /ang′kər/　**1** *n.* A heavy object attached to a ship or boat by a cable or rope and cast overboard to hold the ship or boat in place.　**2** *v.* To secure a ship or boat by means of the anchor.　**3** *v.* To fix securely.

an·ni·ver·sa·ry /an′ə·vûr′sə·rē/ *n., pl.* **an·ni·ver·sa·ries**　**1** The day on which something important took place in an earlier year.　**2** *adj. use:* an *anniversary* party.

an·nounce·ment /ə·nouns′mənt/ *n.* A public or formal declaration or notice.

an·them /an′thəm/ *n.* A song or hymn of praise or patriotism: We sang the national *anthem* before the baseball game began.

architect

an·tique /an·tēk′/　**1** *adj.* From early times; old: The *antique* dresser was priceless.　**2** *n.* Something, usually furniture, that is old and often valuable.

anx·ious /angk′shəs/ *adj.*　**1** Eager; desiring very much.　**2** Worried; uneasy; filled with anxiety. —**anx′ious·ly** *adv.*

ap·pa·ra·tus /ap′ə·rat′əs *or* ap′ə·rā′təs/ *n., pl.* **ap·pa·ra·tus** A device or the equipment needed for a particular purpose. *Alternate plural:* **apparatuses.**

ap·par·el /ə·par′əl/ *n.* Clothes; garments.

ap·par·ent /ə·par′ənt/ *adj.*　**1** Obvious; able to be seen by anyone: It was *apparent* that they were lost.　**2** Seeming; only appearing to be.

ap·peal /ə·pēl′/　**1** *v.* To make an earnest plea or request: to *appeal* for help.　**2** *n.* A plea or request.　**3** *v.* To ask someone for a decision in one's favor: The lawyer *appealed* to the judge for a recess.　**4** *v.* To be attractive or pleasing: The idea *appealed* to me.

ap·pen·dix /ə·pen′diks/ *n., pl.* **ap·pen·dix·es**　**1** A section at the end of a book.　**2** A narrow, closed tube in the human body, extending out from the large intestine. *Alternate plural:* **appendices.**　► *Appendix* is a Latin word meaning "an addition."

ap·ply /ə·plī′/ *v.* **ap·plied, ap·ply·ing**　**1** To put on: to *apply* make-up.　**2** To put to a particular use.　**3** To make a request: to *apply* for a job.

ap·point /ə·point′/ *v.*　**1** To choose or select for a position.　**2** To fix or set: Let's *appoint* a time to meet.

ap·pre·ci·a·tion /ə·prē′shē·ā′shən/ *n.*　**1** The act of recognizing the value or quality of something.　**2** Thankfulness; gratitude.

ap·pro·pri·ate /*adj.* ə·prō′prē·it, *v.* ə·prō′prē·āt/ *adj., v.* **ap·pro·pri·at·ed, ap·pro·pri·at·ing**　**1** *adj.* Proper or suitable: *appropriate* behavior.　**2** *v.* To put aside for a specific purpose: to *appropriate* funds.

ap·prox·i·mate·ly /ə·prok′sə·mit·lē/ *adv.* More or less; about.

a·pron /ā′prən/ *n.* A garment worn over clothes to protect them.

a·quar·i·um /ə·kwâr′ē·əm/ *n., pl.* **a·quar·i·ums**　**1** A tank, pond, etc., in which fish, water animals, and water plants are kept.　**2** The place where such a collection is exhibited.　► *Aquarium* comes from the Latin word *aqua,* "water."

ar·chi·tect /är′kə·tekt/ *n.* A person who designs buildings and oversees their construction.

argument

besiege

B

ar·gu·ment /är′gyə·mənt/ *n.* **1** An angry discussion; a quarrel. **2** The reason or reasons for or against something: Mary had a strong *argument* why her parents should let her go to the party.

-arian *suffix* A believer in something: *disciplinarian.*

ar·ri·val /ə·rī′vəl/ *n.* **1** The act of reaching a place: the ship's *arrival.* **2** Someone or something that has just come: the new *arrivals.*

ar·tist /är′tist/ *n.* **1** A person skilled in one of the fine arts, as painting or sculpture. **2** A person who shows exceptional skill.

ar·tis·tic /är·tis′tik/ *adj.* **1** Having to do with art or artists. **2** Demonstrating skill and good design. **3** Possessing a sense of the beautiful.

as·sem·bly /ə·sem′blē/ *n., pl.* **as·sem·blies** **1** A gathering or meeting of people for a specific purpose. **2** A putting together of parts or pieces. **3** Part of the legislature in most states, usually the lower house.

as·tron·o·mer /ə·stron′ə·mər/ *n.* A person skilled in the study of the stars, planets, and other heavenly bodies.

ath·let·ics /ath·let′iks/ *n. pl.* Sports and games, as football, basketball, rowing, etc.

-ation *suffix* **1** The act or process of: *temptation.* **2** The condition or quality of: *consideration.* **3** The result of: *information.*

at·las /at′ləs/ *n.* A book of maps.

at·ti·tude /at′ə·t(y)ōōd/ *n.* A way of feeling or looking at things; a mental view.

auc·tion /ôk′shən/ **1** *n.* A public sale at which things are sold to the highest bidder: Harry went to the *auction* in order to buy a lamp for his living room. **2** *v.* To sell something at an auction.

au·di·to·ri·um /ô′də·tôr′ē·əm/ *n.* A building or large room or hall in which people gather: a school *auditorium.*

au·thor /ô′thər/ *n.* **1** A person who has written something, as a book, story, or article. **2** A person who creates or originates: the *author* of a plan.

av·o·ca·do /av′ə·kä′dō/ *n., pl.* **av·o·ca·dos** A pear-shaped fruit with a dark green skin, soft edible pulp, and a large pit; sometimes called an *alligator pear. Alternate plural:* **avocadoes.** ► *Avocado* comes from the Spanish word *aguacate.*

baf·fle /baf′əl/ *v.* **baf·fled, baf·fling** To confuse completely; to bewilder.

bak·er /bā′kər/ *n.* A person whose job is baking breads, pies, cookies, etc.

bal·let /bal′ā *or* ba·lā′/ *n.* **1** A formalized, graceful, and difficult form of dance. **2** A group that performs this form of dance.

ban·quet /bang′kwit/ *n.* A feast; a large formal meal.

bar·be·cue /bär′bə·kyōō/ *n., v.* **bar·be·cued, bar·be·cu·ing** **1** *n.* In the United States, a social gathering where food is roasted over an open fire. **2** *n.* A grill or pit used for outdoor cooking. **3** *v.* To roast food over an open fire. **4** *n.* Food cooked with a highly seasoned sauce.

bar·gain /bär′gən/ **1** *n.* An agreement made about a trade or payment. **2** *n.* Something sold at a lower price than usual. **3** *v.* To try to get a better price; to haggle about price.

ba·sis /bā′sis/ *n., pl.* **ba·ses** /bā′sēz/ The foundation or essential part of something.

ba·tik /bə·tēk′ *or* bat′ik/ *n.* **1** The process of creating designs on cloth by applying wax and dyeing the cloth. When the wax is removed, the undyed designs are revealed. **2** Cloth painted by this process.

ba·zaar /bə·zär′/ *n.* **1** An Oriental marketplace. **2** A fair to raise money for a certain purpose: a school *bazaar.*

beige /bāzh/ *n., adj.* A grayish tan color. ► *Beige* in French also means "natural color, especially the natural color of wool."

be·liev·a·ble /bi·lēv′ə·bel/ *adj.* Capable of being accepted as true; appearing true.

ben·e·fit /ben′ə·fit/ **1** *n.* Something that is helpful or good. **2** *v.* To be helpful or profitable: The new medical discovery will *benefit* humanity. **3** *v.* To receive benefit or help: A person can always *benefit* from good advice.

be·ret /bə·rā′ *or* ber′ā/ *n.* A soft, flat cap with a tight headband and no visor, usually made of wool.

be·siege /bi·sēj′/ *v.* **be·sieged, be·sieg·ing** **1** To attempt to capture by surrounding and wearing down resistance. **2** To crowd around: The movie star was *besieged* with fans. **3** To annoy or bother: to *besiege* with phone calls.

---

act, āte, câre, ärt;   egg, ēven;   if, īce;   on, ōver, ôr;   bŏŏk, fōōd;   up, tûrn;
ə=a in *ago,* e in *listen,* i in *giraffe,* o in *pilot,* u in *circus;*   yōō=u in *music;*   oil;   out;
   chair;   sing;   shop;   thank;   that;   zh in *treasure.*

betray   bureau

be·tray /bi·trā'/ *v.* **1** To be a traitor to; to fail or desert a trust: to *betray* your country. **2** To reveal: to *betray* a secret. **3** To give away something without meaning to: His voice *betrayed* his nervousness.

be·tray·al /bi·trā'əl/ *n.* The act of betraying a trust or being unfaithful.

bi- *prefix* **1** Twice; two: *bilingual.* **2** Once every two: *biannual.*

bi·as /bī'əs/ *n., pl.* **bi·as·es,** *v.* **bi·ased, bi·as·ing** **1** *n.* The diagonal in the weave of cloth: cut on the *bias.* **2** *n.* A preference; a prejudice. **3** *v.* To prejudice: The newspaper articles *biased* the jury. **4** *adj. use:* a *biased* jury. *Alternate spellings:* **biassed, biassing.**

bi·cen·ten·ni·al /bī'sen·ten'ē·əl/ **1** *adj.* Occurring once every 200 years. **2** *n.* A 200th anniversary or its celebration. ► *Bicentennial* is made up of Latin *bi-,* "two," *cent(um),* "hundred," and *ann(us),* "year."

bi·ceps /bī'seps/ *n., pl.* **bi·ceps** A large muscle in the upper arm between the shoulder and the elbow.

bi·cy·cle /bī'sik·əl/ *n., v.* **bi·cy·cled, bi·cy·cling** **1** *n.* A vehicle with two wheels, pedals, and handlebars. **2** *v.* To ride a bicycle.

bi·fo·cals /bī'fō·kəls/ *n. pl.* Eyeglasses made with two parts to each lens, one for correcting close vision and one for correcting distance vision.

bi·lin·gual /bī·ling'gwəl/ *adj.* Having the ability to use two languages.

bis·cuit /bis'kit/ *n.* A bread baked in small cakes.

bi·sect /bī·sekt'/ *v.* To cut into two equal parts: This line *bisects* the angle.

bi·week·ly /bī·wēk'lē/ **1** *adj.* Happening once every two weeks. **2** *adv.* Once every two weeks.

bi·zarre /bi·zär'/ *adj.* Very different from the usual; fantastic.

bomb /bom/ **1** *n.* A container filled with explosive material that can be set off for destructive purposes. **2** *v.* To destroy or attack with bombs. **3** *n.* A container of liquid under pressure: insecticide *bomb.*

bom·bard /bom·bärd'/ *v.* **1** To attack with shells or bombs. **2** To make many requests or ask many questions.

bo·nan·za /bə·nan'zə/ *n.* **1** A large and rich ore deposit, as a gold mine. **2** Anything that makes one rich: Her business was a real *bonanza.* ► *Bonanza* is a Spanish word meaning "fair weather" or "prosperity."

bo·nus /bō'nəs/ *n.* Something given in addition to what is normally due, as money given in addition to an employee's regular salary. ► *Bonus* is a Latin word meaning "good."

bou·quet /bō·kā' *or* boo·kā'/ *n.* Flowers gathered together in a bunch.

bou·tique /boo·tēk'/ *n.* A small shop that sells stylish items, such as clothes, accessories, or decorative items.

boy·cott /boi'kot/ **1** *v.* To refuse to buy from, sell to, or associate with. **2** *n.* An act of boycotting.

braid /brād/ **1** *v.* To twist three or more strands together. **2** *n.* Anything twisted like this: a *braid* of hair.

break·a·ble /brāk'ə·bəl/ *adj.* Able to be broken easily.

breath /breth/ *n.* **1** Air inhaled and exhaled. **2** Ability to breathe freely: catch my *breath.* **3** A slight movement of air.

breathe /brēth/ *v.* **breathed, breath·ing** **1** To inhale and exhale. **2** To live or be alive.

bro·chure /brō·shoor'/ *n.* A pamphlet or booklet. ► *Brochure* comes from the French word *brocher,* "to sew," probably because the pages were few enough to be stitched together easily.

bron·co /brong'kō/ *n., pl.* **bron·cos** A small wild or not completely tamed horse, usually found in the western United States. *Alternate spelling:* **broncho.** ► *Bronco* is a Mexican-Spanish word meaning "rough or wild."

bunch /bunch/ **1** *n.* A number of things growing together or put together. **2** *n.* A group: a *bunch* of friends. **3** *v.* To gather or form into a bunch.

bu·reau /byoor'ō/ *n., pl.* **bu·reaus** **1** A bedroom dresser or chest of drawers, usually with a mirror. **2** A specialized government department: the Federal *Bureau* of Investigation. **3** An office or division of a business establishment: a travel *bureau.* *Alternate plural:* **bureaux.**

burro   **chemistry**

bur·ro /bûr′ō/ *n., pl.* **bur·ros** A small donkey, usually used to carry packs. ► *Burro* comes from the Spanish word for a small horse or donkey, *borrico.*

c

caf·e·te·ri·a /kaf′ə·tir′ē·ə/ *n.* A restaurant in which customers pick up their own food and carry it to the tables.

cal·en·dar /kal′ən·dər/ *n.* **1** A chart showing dates, days of the week, months of the year, etc., in order. **2** An orderly list; a schedule of things. ► *Calendar* comes from the Latin word *calendae,* "the first day of the Roman month."

cam·ou·flage /kam′ə·fläzh/ *n., v.* **cam·ou·flaged, cam·ou·flag·ing** **1** *n.* A coloring or covering that conceals or protects. **2** *v.* To change the appearance of, in order to conceal.

cam·pus /kam′pəs/ *n.* The grounds and buildings of a school, college, or university.

can·di·date /kan′də·dāt/ *n.* A person who seeks or is nominated for an office or award of some kind: a presidential *candidate;* a *candidate* for a new job.

can·yon /kan′yən/ *n.* A deep, narrow valley with very steep sides, often with water running through it. ► *Canyon* comes from the Spanish word *cañon,* "a large tube."

car·go /kär′gō/ *n., pl.* **car·goes** The freight carried by a ship, train, aircraft, etc. *Alternate plural:* **cargos.**

car·load /kär′lōd′/ *n.* The amount that will fill a car, especially a railroad freight car.

cash·ier /ka·shir′/ *n.* A person whose job is to handle money, as in a store, restaurant, or bank.

cat·er·pil·lar /kat′ər·pil′ər/ *n.* The fuzzy, wormlike form of an insect, especially a butterfly or moth, after it hatches from the egg; larva.

cau·tious /kô′shəs/ *adj.* Very careful or watchful.

cel·lar /sel′ər/ *n.* A room or area partly or completely underground beneath a building: The *cellar* is used for storage.

ce·ram·ics /sə·ram′iks/ *n.* The art of molding and firing clay to make pottery. ► *Ceramics* comes from the Greek word *keramos,* "potter's clay."

ce·re·al /sir′ē·əl/ *n.* **1** Any grain that can be eaten. **2** A breakfast food made from grain: We eat *cereal* every morning.

cer·e·mo·ny /ser′ə·mō′nē/ *n., pl.* **cer·e·mo·nies** A formal service or series of actions performed in a certain manner.

cer·tain /sûr′tən/ *adj.* **1** Entirely sure. **2** Known, but not named or stated: A *certain* person called today. **3** Some: *certain* things to do.

chan·de·lier /shan′də·lir′/ *n.* A decorative lighting fixture that hangs from the ceiling. ► *Chandelier* is the French word for "candlestick."

cha·os /kā′os/ *n.* Complete disorder and confusion: There was total *chaos* when the cheering fans ran onto the field. ► *Chaos* comes from the Greek word *khaos,* "a vast cleft in the earth."

char·ac·ter /kar′ik·tər/ *n.* **1** All the individual traits of mind and personality that make people what they are: a person of good *character.* **2** A person in a story.

chasm /kaz′əm/ *n.* A deep opening in the surface of the earth; a gorge.

chef /shef/ *n.* **1** A highly skilled cook in charge of a staff of cooks or a kitchen. **2** A cook. ► *Chef* is a shortened form of the French *chef de cuisine,* "head of the kitchen."

chem·ist /kem′ist/ *n.* A person trained in the field of chemistry.

chem·is·try /kem′is·trē/ *n., pl.* **chem·is·tries** The science that deals with substances, their structures, and how they react.

---

act, āte, câre, ärt;   egg, ēven;   if, īce;   on, ōver, ôr;   book, food;   up, tûrn;
ə=a in *ago,* e in *listen,* i in *giraffe,* o in *pilot,* u in *circus;*   yoo=u in *music;*   oil;   out;
chair; sing; shop; thank; that; zh in *treasure.*

chest   **classical**

chest /chest/ *n.* **1** The area of the body enclosed by the ribs and breastbone. **2** The front part of this area. **3** A box with a lid used for storing goods. **4** A cabinet with drawers.

chief /chēf/ **1** *n.* A person highest in command or authority. **2** *adj.* Possessing the highest command or authority. **3** *adj.* Main.

chili con car·ne /chil′ē kän′ kär′nē *or* chil′ē kən kär′nē/ *n.* A dish made with meat, tomatoes, chili peppers, and often beans. ▸ *Chili con carne* is a Spanish name meaning "chili with meat." The food itself is of Mexican origin.

choc·o·late /chôk′(ə·)lit *or* chok′(ə·)lit/ **1** *n.* Cacao nuts that have been roasted and ground. **2** *n.* A drink or candy made from this. **3** *adj.* Made or flavored with this.

choir /kwīr/ *n.* A group of people who sing together, especially in a church service.

chor·us /kôr′əs/ *n.* **1** A group of singers or dancers who perform together. **2** The part of a song that is repeated after every verse. ▸ *Chorus* comes from the Greek word *choros,* "a band of dancers or singers" or "a dance."

chow·der /chou′dər/ *n.* A thick soup or stew, made with vegetables, clams or fish, and often milk.

chow mein /chou′ mān′/ *n.* A Chinese-American dish made from small pieces of meat and vegetables cooked together and served with crisp fried noodles. ▸ *Chow mein* comes from two Chinese words: *ch'ao,* "fry," and *mein,* "dough." The dish itself is of American origin.

chrome /krōm/ *n.* Chromium; a shiny, grayish-white metal that does not rust or change color easily.

chron·ic /kron′ik/ *adj.* **1** Continuing over a long period; constant: a *chronic* complainer. **2** Lasting or recurring: a *chronic* illness.

cinch /sinch/ **1** *n.* A strong strap that holds a pack or saddle on an animal. **2** *v.* To tighten, as a cinch. **3** *n.* Something that is easy or certain. ▸ *Cinch* comes from the Spanish word *cinchar,* "to fasten or encircle."

cin·e·ma /sin′ə·mə/ *n.* **1** The art or craft of making motion pictures. **2** A movie theater. **3** Movies and films in general.

cir·cuit /sûr′kit/ *n.* **1** A route that returns to where it began. **2** The various wires, outlets, and switches in an electrical system. ▸ *Circuit* comes from Latin *circum,* "around," and *ire,* "to go."

cir·cu·lar /sûr′kyə·lər/ **1** *adj.* Having the shape of or moving in a circle. **2** *n.* A notice or advertisement sent to many people.

circum- *prefix* Around: *circumnavigation.*

cir·cum·fer·ence /sər·kum′fər·əns/ *n.* **1** The outer rim of a circle. **2** The distance around a circle. ▸ *Circumference* comes from Latin *circum,* "around," and *ferre,* "to carry."

cir·cum·nav·i·gate /sûr′kəm·nav′ə·gāt/ *v.* **cir·cum·nav·i·gat·ed, cir·cum·nav·i·gat·ing** To go completely around, especially by water. ▸ *Circumnavigate* comes from Latin *circum,* "around," and *navigare,* "to sail."

cir·cum·stance /sûr′kəm·stans/ *n.* **1** The facts or details surrounding or connected with an act or event. **2** (*pl.*) Condition in life. ▸ *Circumstance* comes from Latin *circum,* "around," and *stare,* "to stand."

cir·cum·stan·tial /sûr′kəm·stan′shəl/ *adj.* Having to do with the circumstances or conditions surrounding an action or incident: *circumstantial* evidence.

civ·il /siv′əl/ *adj.* **1** Having to do with being a citizen: *civil* rights. **2** Having to do with legal problems that do not involve a crime: Divorces and inheritance cases are handled in a *civil* court. **3** Within a country or nation: a *civil* war. **4** Polite: a *civil* answer.

ci·vil·ian /sə·vil′yən/ *n.* A person who is not actively serving in the military. ▸ *Civilian* comes from the Latin word *civilis,* "a good citizen."

civ·i·li·za·tion /siv′ə·lə·zā′shən/ *n.* **1** The condition of human society in which culture and science are highly developed. **2** The society and culture of a people, place, or time: modern *civilization.* ▸ *Civilization* comes from the Latin word *civitas,* "a state."

civ·i·lize /siv′ə·līz/ *v.* **civ·i·lized, civ·i·liz·ing** **1** *v.* To order or change so as to make fit for society. **2** *adj. use:* a *civilized* person.

clar·i·fy /klar′ə·fī/ *v.* **clar·i·fied, clar·i·fy·ing** **1** To make understandable: to *clarify* the problem. **2** To make clear or pure, as a liquid: We *clarified* the soup by straining it.

clas·si·cal /klas′i·kəl/ *adj.* **1** Characteristic of ancient Greek and Roman culture. **2** Following an established or traditional form.

clinic   complementary

clin·ic /klin′ik/ *n.* **1** A facility, sometimes attached to a hospital, where medical or psychological treatment is provided. **2** A meeting held to analyze problems and develop solutions or to improve specific skills or knowledge.

clique /klēk *or* klik/ *n.* A small exclusive group of individuals who stick together and keep others out.

clothes /klō(th)z/ *n., pl.* Garments worn by people to cover the body, such as skirts, pants, etc.

coast /kōst/ **1** *n.* Land by or near the ocean. **2** *v.* To ride or slide down a slope with little or no effort.

coax /kōks/ *v.* To persuade gently and sweetly.

co·coa /kō′kō/ *n.* **1** A powder made from the seeds of the cacao tree; chocolate. **2** A hot chocolate-flavored drink.

col·i·se·um /kol′ə·sē′əm/ *n.* **1** A large building or stadium used for public entertainment, such as exhibitions, sports events, etc. **2** (*written* **Coliseum**) A spelling of *Colosseum*, a stadium in Rome built in A.D. 69–80. ► *Coliseum* comes from the Latin word *colosseus*, "gigantic."

col·lage /kə·läzh′/ *n.* A decorative or artistic piece made by pasting or gluing bits of paper, cloth, string, etc., on a surface.

col·lege /kol′ij/ *n.* **1** A school of higher learning in which the course of study leads to a bachelor's degree. **2** The building or buildings used for this educational purpose. **3** A professional school usually part of a large university: a *college* of law.

col·li·sion /kə·lizh′ən/ *n.* A violent coming together; a crash.

col·o·ny /kol′ə·nē/ *n., pl.* **col·o·nies** **1** A group of people who leave their own country to settle somewhere else. **2** A land that is ruled by another country. **3** A group of plants or animals.

co·los·sal /kə·los′əl/ *adj.* Huge; enormous.

com- *prefix* **1** With: *companion*. **2** Together: *compound*.

co·me·di·an /kə·mē′dē·ən/ *n.* An actor or entertainer who makes people laugh.

com·e·dy /kom′ə·dē/ *n., pl.* **com·e·dies** **1** A play, movie, or TV show that is humorous or has a happy ending. **2** Any experience that is amusing or humorous.

com·merce /kom′ərs/ *n.* The exchange or buying and selling of goods, especially on a large scale, as between nations; trade. ► *Commerce* comes from Latin *com-*, "together," and *merx*, "merchandise."

com·mit /kə·mit′/ *v.* **com·mit·ted, com·mit·ting** **1** To do or perform. **2** To pledge or devote yourself to something.

com·mit·ment /kə·mit′mənt/ *n.* **1** The act or state of promising, pledging, or devoting. **2** A pledge or promise.

com·mit·tee /kə·mit′ē/ *n.* A group of people who volunteer or are chosen to do specific things.

com·mu·ni·ty /kə·myoo′nə·tē/ *n., pl.* **com·mu·ni·ties** **1** A group of people living together in one area. **2** A group of people who share a common interest. **3** The public.

com·mut·er /kə·myoo′tər/ *n.* A person who travels a long distance to and from work.

com·pel /kəm·pel′/ *v.* **com·pelled, com·pel·ling** To force; to demand.

com·pete /kəm·pēt′/ *v.* **com·pet·ed, com·pet·ing** To strive to do better than another; to take part in a contest.

com·pe·ti·tion /kom′pə·tish′ən/ *n.* **1** The effort to do better than others. **2** A contest between two or more people.

com·pet·i·tor /kəm·pet′ə·tor/ *n.* A person who competes, as in games or business; a rival.

com·plaint /kəm·plānt′/ *n.* **1** Expression of dissatisfaction. **2** The cause of protest or source of dissatisfaction. **3** A charge against someone or something: She filed a *complaint* against the store.

com·ple·men·ta·ry /kom′plə·men′tər·ē/ *adj.* **1** Serving to fill up, contrast, or complete: Pieces of a puzzle are *complementary*. **2** Of two angles that together form a right angle.

---

act, āte, câre, ärt;   egg, ēven;   if, īce;   on, ōver, ôr;   book, food;   up, tûrn;
ə=a in *ago*, e in *listen*, i in *giraffe*, o in *pilot*, u in *circus;*   yoo=u in *music;*   oil;   out;
chair; sing; shop; thank; that; zh in *treasure.*

complimentary

cordial

com·pli·men·ta·ry /kom′plə·men′tər·ē/ *adj.* **1** Paying a compliment; expressing praise or admiration. **2** Given away free: a *complimentary* ticket.

com·pose /kəm·pōz′/ *v.* **com·posed, com·pos·ing** **1** To make up; to form: Coral is *composed* of the tiny skeletons of sea animals. **2** To create or write: to *compose* a poem. **3** To make calm or relaxed: I took a moment to *compose* myself before I answered. **4** *adj. use:* a *composed* manner.

com·po·ser /kəm·pō′zər/ *n.* A person who writes music.

com·po·si·tion /kom′pə·zish′ən/ *n.* **1** What something is made of; the parts of a whole: The *composition* of water is one part oxygen to two parts hydrogen. **2** A thing that is put together or created: a musical *composition*. **3** A short essay.

com·pos·i·tor /kəm·poz′ə·tər/ *n.* A person who sets printing type.

com·put·er pro·gram·mer /kəm·pyōō′tər prō′gram·ər/ *n.* A person who specializes in the preparation of computer programs or coded instructions.

con·ceit·ed /kən·sē′tid/ *adj.* Having an especially high opinion of oneself; vain.

con·ceive /kən·sēv′/ *v.* **con·ceived, con·ceiv·ing** **1** To think of or develop, as an idea: A team of architects *conceived* the design for a new housing complex. **2** To imagine; to understand: I can't really *conceive* of taking a trip to Europe.

con·cen·trate /kon′sən·trāt/ *v.* **con·cen·trat·ed, con·cen·trat·ing,** *n.* **1** *v.* To fix one's full attention on something: It is hard to *concentrate* in a noisy room. **2** *v.* To gather or bring closely together: We *concentrated* our strength to move the car. **3** *v.* To make stronger or less diluted: We often buy orange juice that has been *concentrated* and frozen. **4** *n.* A concentrated solution: Frozen orange juice is a *concentrate*.

con·cert /kon′sûrt/ *n.* A musical performance or program.

con·crete /kon′krēt *or* kon·krēt′/ **1** *n.* A stonelike material made of cement, sand, gravel, and water. **2** *adj. use:* a *concrete* wall. **3** *adj.* Existing; real: A table is *concrete,* but an idea is not. **4** *adj.* Specific: Give *concrete* examples to support your argument.

con·fes·sion /kən·fesh′ən/ *n.* **1** The act of admitting something, especially faults or guilt. **2** That which is admitted or confessed.

con·fi·dence /kon′fə·dəns/ *n.* **1** Trust or faith. **2** Self-assurance; faith in oneself. **3** A secret.

con·science /kon′shəns/ *n.* The inner understanding that tells you when you are doing right or wrong.

con·scious /kon′shəs/ *adj.* **1** Awake; able to use your senses. **2** Aware of things.

con·se·quence /kon′sə·kwens/ *n.* Result or effect: the *consequences* of an action.

con·sid·er·a·ble /kən·sid′ər·ə·bəl/ *adj.* **1** To a large or great extent. **2** Worth recognizing or noticing.—**con·sid′er·a·bly** *adv.*

con·sid·er·a·tion /kən·sid′ə·rā′shən/ *n.* **1** The act of thinking something over carefully: After long *consideration,* he refused the job offer. **2** Thoughtful regard or concern for others: We appreciated your *consideration* for our feelings. **3** A reason: Your safety was my major *consideration.*

con·spic·u·ous /kən·spik′yōō·əs/ *adj.* Easily noticed; attracting attention.

con·spir·a·cy /kən·spir′ə·sē/ *n., pl.* **con·spir·a·cies** A secret plan made by two or more people to do something unlawful; a plot.

con·ta·gious /kən·tā′jəs/ *adj.* Easily spread from one person to another; catching; infectious.

con·tam·i·nate /kən·tam′ə·nāt/ *v.* **con·tam·i·nat·ed, con·tam·i·nat·ing** To make impure: Dumping waste *contaminated* the water.

con·tent·ment /kən·tent′mənt/ *n.* A state of being happy, satisfied, and content.

con·ven·tion /kən·ven′shən/ *n.* **1** A large meeting held for a specific purpose. **2** An accepted way of doing something; custom: Eating with a fork is a *convention.*

con·vert·i·ble /kən·vûr′tə·bəl/ **1** *adj.* Able to be changed: Coal is *convertible* into heat. **2** *n.* Something convertible, such as a car with a top that folds down or a sofa that can be opened into a bed.

con·vey /kən·vā′/ *v.* **1** To carry or move something from one place to another; to transport. **2** To communicate or make something known: She *conveyed* the message.

cor·dial /kôr′jəl/ *adj.* Friendly; warm; welcoming: We gave our friends a *cordial* greeting.—**cor′dial·ly** *adv.*

cor·du·roy /kôr′də·roi/ *n., pl.* **cor·du·roys**
1 A strong cloth with velvety stripes close together on one side. 2 (*pl.*) A pair of pants made of corduroy.

cor·po·ra·tion /kôr′pə·rā′shən/ *n.* A company that may be owned by many different people but functions legally as a single person.

cor·ral /kə·ral′/ *n., v.* **cor·ralled, cor·ral·ling**
1 *n.* A fenced-in space or pen for cattle, horses, etc. 2 *v.* To drive into a corral: to *corral* cattle. ▸ *Corral* is a Spanish word that comes from Latin *currere,* "to run."

cor·res·pond /kôr′ə·spond′/ *v.* 1 To be similar in function or nature: A bird's wing *corresponds* to a person's arm. 2 To exchange letters: He *corresponds* with his friend.

cor·ri·dor /kôr′ə·dər/ *n.* A long hallway with rooms opening onto it.

cos·me·tol·o·gist /koz′mə·tol′ə·jəst/ *n.* A person who is skilled in the use of cosmetics and beauty products; a beautician.

coun·cil /koun′səl/ *n.* 1 A meeting or assembly for discussion. 2 The legislative body of a city or town.

coun·sel /koun′səl/ *n., v.* **coun·seled, coun·sel·ing** 1 *n.* Advice: good *counsel.* 2 *n.* A lawyer or law firm handling a court case. 3 *v.* To give advice: to *counsel* a friend. *Alternate spellings:* **counselled, counselling.**

coy·o·te /kī·ō′tē/ *n., pl.* **coy·o·tes** A small wolf found on the western prairies of North America. *Alternate plural:* **coyote.** ▸ *Coyote* is a Mexican-Spanish word meaning "prairie wolf."

craft·y /kraf′tē/ *adj.* **craft·i·er, craft·i·est** Sly, clever: a *crafty* salesman. ● *Crafty* originally meant "skillful or good at a particular craft." A *crafty* weaver was a good weaver, not a sly one.

cram /kram/ *v.* **crammed, cram·ming** 1 To pack tightly into a small space; to stuff. 2 To study hard for a short period of time.

cred·it /kred′it/ 1 *n.* Admiration; honor: She deserves *credit* for her idea. 2 *v.* To give praise or recognition: He is *credited* with the discovery. 3 *n.* Financial reputation: Her *credit* is good. 4 *n.* Payment on a long-term basis: They bought the TV on *credit.*

crev·ice /krev′is/ *n.* A narrow opening caused by a crack or split.

crim·son /krim′zən/ *n., adj.* A deep red color.

crul·ler /krul′ər/ *n.* A doughnutlike Dutch cake made from a strip or twist of sweetened dough that is fried in deep fat and sprinkled with sugar.

crumb /krum/ *n.* 1 A small piece of bread or cake. 2 A bit or scrap.

cun·ning /kun′ing/ 1 *adj.* Clever or tricky: a *cunning* criminal. 2 *n.* Cleverness or slyness: He used *cunning* to defeat his enemy.—**cun′ning·ly** *adv.* ● *Cunning* comes from an Old English word for "know," and it did not always have the unpleasant associations it has now. Even now it can be used in such an expression as "What a cunning toy!"

cup·ful /kup′fool′/ *n., pl.* **cup·fuls** The amount that will fill a cup. A cup is usually equal to 8 ounces or 250 milliliters.

cur·tain /kûr′tən/ *n.* 1 Cloth hung at a window, door, or opening. 2 Cloth used to hide a stage from the audience.

cus·tom·er /kus′təm·ər/ *n.* A buyer of goods or services.

D

dai·ly /dā′lē/ *adj., adv., n., pl.* **dai·lies**
1 *adj.* Happening every day. 2 *adv.* Every day. 3 *n.* A newspaper that is published every day.

de·bris /də·brē′ or dā′brē/ *n.* The remains of something broken or destroyed; rubble: The entire town was littered with *debris* after the flood.

de·cade /dek′ād/ *n.* A period of ten years.

de·cay /di·kā′/ *v.* To rot; to fall apart or crumble.

de·ceive /di·sēv′/ *v.* **de·ceived, de·ceiv·ing** To trick into accepting something as true that is not true; to mislead or lie: An opossum *deceives* an enemy by pretending to be dead.

---

act, āte, câre, ärt;   egg, ēven;   if, īce;   on, ōver, ôr;   bŏŏk, fōōd;   up, tûrn;
ə=a in *ago,* e in *listen,* i in *giraffe,* o in *pilot,* u in *circus;*   yōō=u in *music;*   oil;   out;
chair;   si**ng**;   **sh**op;   **th**ank;   **th**at;   **zh** in *treasure.*

de·cent /dē'sənt/ *adj.* **1** Proper; acceptable: *decent* manners. **2** Good enough; adequate: a *decent* job. **3** Kind; good; charitable: *decent* people.

de·crease /*v.* di·krēs', *n.* dē'krēs *or* di·krēs'/ *v.* **de·creased, de·creas·ing,** *n.* **1** *v.* To make or become less. **2** *n.* A reduction: A serious *decrease* in rainfall causes drought.

de·feat /di·fēt'/ **1** *v.* To win or gain a victory. **2** *n.* A victory: the Panthers' *defeat* of the Bobcats. **3** *n.* A loss: the Bobcats' *defeat* by the Panthers. **4** *v.* To keep from succeeding: to *defeat* the purpose.

def·i·ni·tion /def'ə·nish'ən/ *n.* **1** The act of describing or explaining. **2** A statement that gives the meaning of a word.

de·lin·quent /di·ling'kwənt/ **1** *n.* A person who fails in a duty or breaks the law: a juvenile *delinquent.* **2** *adj.* Guilty of doing wrong or acting illegally: She works with *delinquent* children. **3** *adj.* Guilty of neglect or serious lateness: *delinquent* in paying a bill.

de·moc·ra·cy /di·mok'rə·sē/ *n., pl.* **de·moc·ra·cies** A system of government in which the people rule by voting directly or by electing representatives to hold government offices and make the laws. ▶ *Democracy* comes from two Greek words: *demos,* "the people," and *kratos,* "power."

dem·o·crat·ic /dem'ə·krat'ik/ *adj.* **1** Of or relating to a political system in which power is held by the people. **2** Treating all people as equals.

de·ni·al /di·nī'əl/ *n.* **1** A statement that something is not true: a *denial* of the accusation. **2** A refusal to grant or allow: *denial* of a license.

den·im /den'əm/ *n.* A strong cotton cloth used to make overalls, jeans, etc.

den·tist /den'tist/ *n.* A doctor whose job is to care for and keep teeth healthy.

de·part·ment /di·pärt'mənt/ *n.* A separate section of a larger whole, as of a corporation, government, hospital, etc.

de·pos·it /di·poz'it/ **1** *v.* To put or set down. **2** *n.* A store of minerals. **3** *v.* To put money into a bank. **4** *n.* Money put into a bank. **5** *n.* Money given as partial payment: Luis put a *deposit* on a new bicycle.

de·pot /dē'pō/ *n.* A railroad station.

de·scent /di·sent'/ *n.* **1** The process of coming down from a higher to a lower level; a decline: the *descent* of a kite. **2** Ancestry; family background: His parents are of Russian *descent.*

de·sir·a·ble /di·zīr'ə·bəl/ *adj.* Worth having or wanting.

de·sire /di·zīr'/ *v.* **de·sired, de·sir·ing,** *n.* **1** *v.* To wish or long for. **2** *n.* A wish or want. **3** *n.* Something wished for.

des·o·late /des'ə·lit/ *adj.* **1** Barren; lifeless: a *desolate* desert. **2** Having no people; deserted: a *desolate* ghost town. **3** Lonely; joyless: I spent a *desolate* weekend at home alone.—**des·o·late·ly** *adv.*

de·vice /di·vīs'/ *n.* **1** Something made to perform a specific task. **2** A scheme or plan: The offer of a free set of dishes is a *device* to bring people into the store.

de·vise /di·vīz'/ *v.* **de·vised, de·vis·ing** To figure out; to invent: to *devise* a scheme.

de·vote /di·vōt'/ *v.* **de·vot·ed, de·vot·ing** To give oneself or one's time to a person or an activity.

de·vot·ed /di·vō'tid/ *adj.* Feeling or expressing strong love or loyalty; dedicated.

dex·ter·i·ty /dek·ster'ə·tē/ *n.* **1** Skill and ease in using the hands. **2** Mental skill or quickness.

di·al /dī'(ə)l/ *n., v.* **di·aled, di·al·ing** **1** *n.* A flat surface with numbers or signs on it and a movable pointer that indicates time, temperature, etc. **2** *n.* A knob used to control a radio, television, etc. **3** *n.* The movable disc on some telephones. **4** *v.* To place a phone call by registering the numbers. *Alternate spellings:* **dialled, dialling.**

di·a·logue /dī'ə·lôg *or* dī'ə·log/ *n.* **1** Conversation involving two or more speakers. **2** Conversation in a play, novel, movie, etc.

dic·ta·tor·ship /dik·tā'tər·ship'/ *n.* A form of government in which a country is ruled by a dictator, who holds absolute power.

die /dī/ *v.* **died, dy·ing** **1** To stop living; to pass away. **2** To lose power or fade out or away: a *dying* fire. **3** To stop operating: Ben started the car, but the engine *died.* **4** To long for something: She is *dying* to take a vacation.

di·et /dī'ət/ **1** *n.* The foods a person or animal regularly eats. **2** *n.* A special selection of foods prescribed for health reasons, weight loss, etc. **3** *v.* To eat foods according to a special diet.

di·e·ti·tian /dī'ə·tish'ən/ *n.* A person trained in planning meals that provide proper nutrition. *Alternate spelling:* **dietician.**

dim /dim/ *adj.* **dim·mer, dim·mest,** *v.* **dimmed, dim·ming** **1** *adj.* Not bright: a *dim* light. **2** *adj.* Not clearly seen. **3** *v.* To make or grow dim.

direction   **efficient**

di·rec·tion /di·rek′shən *or* dī·rek′shən/ *n.*
1 Management; supervision.   2 Command;
order.   3 (*usually pl.*) Instructions for doing
something.   4 The line along which anything moves, faces, or lies.   5 A tendency:
the *direction* of the conversation.

dis- *prefix* Used with verbs, adjectives, and
nouns to give the opposite sense to or to
reverse the action or effect expressed in the
rest of the word; not: *disorder.*

dis·ad·van·tage /dis′əd·van′tij/ *n.*   1 A hindrance to success.   2 An unfavorable condition or position.

dis·a·gree /dis′ə·grē′/ *v.* **dis·a·greed, dis·
a·gree·ing**   1 To maintain a different opinion or belief.   2 To argue.   3 To be unsuit-
able or upsetting: The food *disagreed* with
her.

dis·arm·a·ment /dis·är′mə·mənt/ *n.* The act
or condition of removing or reducing a nation's fighting forces and weapons.   ► *Disarmament* comes from Latin *dis-*, "absence
of," and *arma,* "arms."

dis·con·nect /dis′kə·nekt′/ *v.* To break the
connection between; to separate.   ► *Disconnect* comes from Latin *dis-*, "apart," and *con-
nectere,* "to tie together."

dis·cour·age /dis·kûr′ij/ *v.* **dis·cour·aged,
dis·cour·ag·ing**   1 To cause to lose courage,
hope, or confidence.   2 To try to prevent by
showing disapproval.

dis·cus·sion /dis·kush′ən/ *n.* The act of discussing; consideration of a subject by exchange of ideas.

dis·hon·est /dis·on′ist/ *adj.*   1 Not honest, as
someone who lies or cheats: a *dishonest* person.   2 Showing a lack of honesty or truth:
a *dishonest* deed.—**dis·hon′est·ly** *adv.*

dis·in·fec·tant /dis′in·fek′tənt/ *n.* A chemical
substance used to destroy germs.

dis·may /dis·mā′/   1 *n.* A feeling of alarm or
disappointment.   2 *v.* To fill with alarm or
disappointment.

dis·miss·al /dis·mis′əl/ *n.*   1 The act of sending away: class *dismissal.*   2 The act of dis-
charging or firing someone from a job: Steal-
ing means immediate *dismissal.*   3 The act
of putting something aside or not considering it: the *dismissal* of an idea.

dis·po·si·tion /dis′pə·zish′ən/ *n.* The way an
individual or animal acts; nature; temperament: a friendly *disposition.*

dis·qual·i·fy /dis·kwol′ə·fī/ *v.* **dis·qual·i·fied,
dis·qual·i·fy·ing**   1 To make unfit or unqualified: His lack of education *disqualified*
him for the position.   2 To deny the right to
do something: The runner was *disqualified*
from the last race for breaking the rules.

dis·sim·i·lar /di·sim′ə·lər/ *adj.* Unlike; not
similar;   different.—**dis·sim·i·lar·ly**   *adv.*
► *Dissimilar* comes from Latin *dis-*, "not,"
and *similis,* "like."

dis·tract /dis·trakt′/ *v.* To draw attention
away: Do not *distract* your brother while he
is studying.   ► *Distract* comes from Latin
dis-, "apart," and *tractus,* "draw or pull."

dis·tri·bu·tion /dis′trə·byoo′shən/ *n.*   1 The
act of distributing or giving out.   2 The
manner in which something is distributed:
equal *distribution.*

do·nor /dō′nər/ *n.* A person who gives or do-
nates: a blood *donor.*

drive-in /drīv′in′/ *n.* Any business, such as a
bank, restaurant, or outdoor movie theater,
that can be used by customers while seated
in their cars.

drow·sy /drou′zē/ *adj.* **drow·si·er, drow·
si·est**   1 Sleepy.   2 Tending to cause sleepiness.

du·al /d(y)oo′əl/ *adj.* Of, having, or consisting
of two parts, sets, etc.; double.

dye /dī/ *v.* **dyed, dye·ing,** *n.*   1 *v.* To stain
something with a color by soaking it in a
liquid.   2 *n.* A coloring mixture dissolved in
liquid used for dyeing.

E

ea·sel /ē′zəl/ *n.* A three-legged frame, with a
narrow ledge, used to hold an artist's canvas
upright: Mary's latest painting was still on
the *easel.*

e·con·o·my /i·kon′ə·mē/ *n., pl.* **e·con·o·mies**
1 Use of money or other resources in a way
that avoids waste: We should exercise *economy* in our use of water.   2 The management of finances and resources: the national
economy.

ef·fect /i·fekt′/ *n.* A result; a change caused by
something else: One *effect* of the storm was
a loss of power.

ef·fi·cient /i·fish′ənt/ *adj.* Producing results
with little effort or waste; capable: an *efficient* worker.

---

act, āte, câre, ärt;   egg, ēven;   if, īce;   on, ōver, ôr;   boŏk, foōd;   up, tûrn;
ə=**a** in *ago,* **e** in *listen,* **i** in *giraffe,* **o** in *pilot,* **u** in *circus;*   yoō=**u** in *music;*   oil;   out;
chair; si**ng**; **sh**op; **th**ank; **th**at; **zh** in *treasure.*

eighteen

eight·een /ā'tēn'/ *n., adj.* A number equal to 10 + 8; seventeen plus one more; 18.

e·lect /i·lekt'/ **1** *v.* To select for an office by voting. **2** *adj.* Elected to an office but not yet sworn in: a mayor *elect*. **3** *v.* To decide: to *elect* not to go.

e·lec·tion /i·lek'shən/ *n.* **1** The selection of people for an office or an honor by voting. **2** A choice.

e·lec·tric /i·lek'trik/ *adj.* **1** Composed of or having to do with electricity. **2** Producing or transmitting electricity. **3** Operated by electricity. **4** Exciting; thrilling: an *electric* performance.

e·lec·tri·cian /i·lek'trish'ən/ *n.* A person who installs, maintains, operates, or repairs electrical equipment.

e·lim·i·nate /i·lim'ə·nāt/ *v.* **e·lim·i·nat·ed, e·lim·i·nat·ing** **1** To get rid of or remove. **2** To omit or exclude. **3** To remove from competition.

em·bar·rass /im·bar'əs/ *v.* To make self-conscious or uncomfortable.

em·blem /em'bləm/ *n.* **1** A symbol that stands for an idea, belief, nation, etc. **2** A badge or insignia.

em·i·grate /em'ə·grāt/ *v.* **em·i·grat·ed, em·i·grat·ing** To move out of a country or region in order to settle in another: My great-grandparents *emigrated* from the Netherlands.

em·pire /em'pīr'/ *n.* A group of countries or nations, often far away from each other, ruled by one person or government: the British Empire.

en·chi·la·da /en'chə·lä'də/ *n.* Cheese or ground meat flavored with chili peppers and rolled up in a tortilla, covered with seasoned tomato sauce. ► *Enchilada* is a Spanish word meaning "flavored with chili." The food itself is of Mexican origin.

exaggerate

en·cour·age·ment /in·kûr'ij·mənt/ *n.* Something that gives confidence; the act of giving confidence or assurance.

en·deav·or /in·dev'ər/ **1** *v.* To try hard; make an earnest attempt: to *endeavor* to win. **2** *n.* An earnest effort or project: We supported the *endeavor* to help the refugees.

en·er·gy /en'ər·jē/ *n., pl.* **en·er·gies** **1** Vigorous activity; power. **2** (*often pl.*) Power used in an effective way: We put all our *energies* into cleaning the garage. **3** The power to do work: electrical *energy*.

en·gi·neer /en'jə·nir'/ *n.* **1** A person who is trained in the planning, designing, and building of roads, bridges, etc. **2** A person who operates or drives a train.

en·joy·a·ble /in·joi'ə·bəl/ *adj.* Pleasant; satisfying.

en·large·ment /in·lärj'mənt/ *n.* **1** The act of increasing the size of something. **2** Something made bigger.

e·nor·mous /i·nôr'məs/ *adj.* Very large; huge; immense.

en·thu·si·as·tic /in·thoo'zē·as'tik/ *adj.* Full of enthusiasm; excited or interested.

en·ve·lope /en'və·lōp *or* än'və·lōp/ *n.* **1** A flat paper wrapper usually having a gummed flap. **2** Any outer covering.

-er *suffix* **1** A person or thing that does something: *swimmer*. **2** A person who lives in or comes from a certain place: *Southerner*. **3** A person practicing a trade or profession: *oceanographer*. This suffix is sometimes spelled *-ier* in words that come from French: *financier*.

e·rode /i·rōd'/ *v.* **e·rod·ed, e·rod·ing** To wear away, especially the earth by rain, ice, wind, etc.

es·sen·tial /ə·sen'shəl/ *adj.* **1** Basic; fundamental. **2** Absolutely necessary; vital. —**es·sen'tial·ly** *adv.*

e·val·u·ate /i·val'yoo·āt/ *v.* **e·val·u·at·ed, e·val·u·at·ing** To judge value or determine worth.

ev·i·dent /ev'ə·dənt/ *adj.* Easily seen or understood; apparent.

ex- *prefix* **1** Out: *exhale*. **2** Former (written with a hyphen): *ex-president*.

ex·ag·ger·ate /ig·zaj'ə·rāt/ *v.* **ex·ag·ger·at·ed, ex·ag·ger·at·ing** **1** To say that something is more than it is; to overstate: Parents often *exaggerate* when they talk about their children. **2** To make something appear larger than it really is: The trick mirror at the carnival *exaggerated* our heights.

examination   fiery

ex·am·i·na·tion /ig·zam′ə·nā′shən/ *n.* **1** Careful inspection. **2** A formal test.

ex·ceed /ik·sēd′/ *v.* **1** To be greater or better than what is anticipated or expected: Our success *exceeded* anything we had expected. **2** To go beyond what is allowed: The driver *exceeded* the speed limit.

ex·cept /ik·sept′/ *prep.* Leaving out; other than; but: Everyone is going *except* Larry.

ex·cess /*n.* ek·ses *or* ik·ses′, *adj.* ek′ses/ **1** *n.* An amount, degree, or supply of something beyond what is needed or proper: an *excess* of anger. **2** *adj.* Over what is usual, allowed, or needed: Don't carry *excess* weight while hiking.

ex·cur·sion /ik·skûr′zhən/ *n.* A short, pleasant trip; an outing.

ex·cus·a·ble /ik·skyoo′zə·bəl/ *adj.* Able to be forgiven; pardonable.

ex·hib·it /ig·zib′it/ **1** *v.* To display or put on public view. **2** *n.* A public display. **3** *n.* Something put on display. **4** *v.* To show signs of or demonstrate. **5** *n.* Something given as evidence in a court of law.

ex·hi·bi·tion /ek′sə·bish′ən/ *n.* **1** A public showing or display. **2** An open display or expression: an *exhibition* of poor manners.

ex·ile /eg′zīl *or* ek′sīl/ *v.* **ex·iled, ex·il·ing,** *n.* **1** *v.* To force someone to leave his or her native country. **2** *n.* A person who cannot return to his or her native country.

ex·it /eg′zit *or* ek′sit/ **1** *n.* A way out of an enclosed place, as a door. **2** *n.* A departure, especially of an actor from a stage. **3** *v.* To go out or leave. **4** *v.* To go offstage, used as a stage direction: *Exit* Peter Pan. ► *Exit* is a Latin word meaning "he or she leaves."

ex·pe·di·tion /ek′spə·dish′ən/ *n.* An organized journey made for a specific purpose: a military *expedition.*

ex·per·i·men·ta·tion /ik·sper′ə·men·tā′shən/ *n.* The act of experimenting or trying out.

ex·pla·na·tion /ek′splə·nā′shən/ *n.* **1** The act or process of explaining: She gave a clear *explanation* of the way a camera works. **2** A reason or cause.

ex·plor·er /ik·splôr′ər/ *n.* One who investigates in order to learn or discover.

ex·pres·sion /ik·spresh′ən/ *n.* **1** The act of putting into words. **2** A particular word or phrase. **3** A look on the face that shows what a person is feeling.

ex·ten·sion /ik·sten′shən/ *n.* **1** The act or condition of stretching or reaching out. **2** That which has been added to something; an addition.

ex·te·ri·or /ik·stir′ē·ər/ **1** *n.* The outside. **2** *adj.* On or for the outside. ► *Exterior* comes from the Latin word *exter,* "outward or being on the outside."

ex·tra /eks′trə/ **1** *adj.* Additional. **2** *n.* A person, thing, or charge in addition to what is needed or expected. **3** *adv.* Extremely: *extra* careful. **4** *n.* A special edition of a newspaper.

ex·trav·a·gant /ik·strav′ə·gənt/ *adj.* **1** Spending much more than necessary; wasteful. **2** Going beyond or exceeding the limits of reason or necessity: We greeted him with an *extravagant* display of enthusiasm.

eye /ī/ *n., v.* **eyed, eye·ing** **1** *n.* A part of the body by which humans and animals see. **2** *v.* To look at with interest; to watch carefully: The cat *eyed* the pigeons from the window. **3** *n.* Something like an eye; the center: the *eye* of a needle; the *eye* of the storm. *Alternate spelling:* **eying.**

F

fab·ric /fab′rik/ *n.* A material made of woven, knitted, or matted fibers.

fac·ul·ty /fak′əl·tē/ *n., pl.* **fac·ul·ties** **1** The people who teach in a school. **2** Ability or power of the body or mind: Reason is a human *faculty.*

fa·tigue /fə·tēg′/ *n., v.* **fa·tigued, fa·ti·guing** **1** *n.* Extreme tiredness or weariness. **2** *v.* To tire out.

fi·ber /fī′bər/ *n.* Threads or threadlike parts of cloth or of animal or plant tissue: cotton *fibers.*

field /fēld/ **1** *n.* A large area of open land. **2** *n.* A region of land that produces natural resources: an oil *field.* **3** *n.* An area of land used for sports events. **4** *v.* To catch and throw back a baseball. **5** *n.* An occupation or area of specialization: the *field* of teaching.

fierce /firs/ *adj.* **fierc·er, fierc·est** Cruel, violent, savage, or ferocious.

fier·y /fîr′ē *or* fī′ər·ē/ *adj.* **fier·i·er, fier·i·est** **1** Made up of or composed of fire. **2** Burning with fire or like fire; blazing: *fiery* sun. **3** Excitable; spirited: a *fiery* temper.

---

act, āte, câre, ärt;   egg, ēven;   if, īce;   on, ōver, ôr;   book, food;   up, tûrn;
ə=a in *ago,* e in *listen,* i in *giraffe,* o in *pilot,* u in *circus;*   yoo=u in *music;*   oil;   out;
chair;   **s**ing;   **sh**op;   **th**ank;   **th**at;   **zh** in *treasure.*

fiesta gazpacho

fi·es·ta /fē·es′tə/ *n.* A festival or celebration, especially a religious festival. ► *Fiesta* is a Spanish word meaning "feast."

fil·i·bus·ter /fil′ə·bus′tər/ **1** *n.* A means of blocking the passage of a bill in a legislature by long speeches or other delaying tactics. **2** *v.* To block the passage of a bill by this means. ► *Filibuster* comes from the Spanish word *filibustero*, "freebooter or pirate."

fin·an·cier /fin′ən·sir′/ *n.* A person who specializes in money management and investment, as a banker.

flex·i·ble /flek′sə·bəl/ *adj.* **1** Able to be bent or twisted easily. **2** Able to be changed; adaptable: a *flexible* schedule.

flim·sy /flim′zē/ *adj.* **flim·si·er, flim·si·est** Easily torn, broken, or damaged.

flock /flok/ **1** *n.* A large group of animals or birds. **2** *n.* A large crowd of people. **3** *v.* To move in a large group: People *flocked* to the beach.

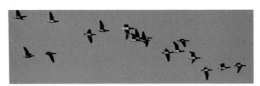

fo·cus /fō′kəs/ *n., pl.* **fo·cus·es,** *v.* **fo·cused, fo·cus·ing** **1** *n.* The point at which a lens brings light rays together to make a sharp image. **2** *v.* To adjust the focus to produce a clear image. **3** *n.* The main or central point of interest, attraction, or importance. **4** *v.* To concentrate one's energy, attention, etc. *Alternate plural:* **foci.** *Alternate spellings:* **focussed, focussing.**

fo·li·age /fō′lē·ij *or* fō′lij/ *n.* The leafy part of a tree or other plant; leaves.

for·bid /fər·bid′/ *v.* **for·bade, for·bid·den, for·bid·ding** Not to allow or permit.

for·bid·ding /fər·bid′ing/ *adj.* Unfriendly; threatening: a *forbidding* forest.

for·feit /fôr′fit/ **1** *v.* To lose or have to give up something as a penalty. **2** *n.* A penalty.

for·get /fər·get′/ *v.* **for·got, for·got·ten, for·get·ting** **1** To fail to remember or think of. **2** To leave behind.

for·mal·ly /fôr′mə·lē/ *adv.* In a formal or strict way; according to rule, ceremony, or custom: We have not been *formally* introduced.

for·mer·ly /fôr′mər·lē/ *adv.* In the past; once; previously: She was *formerly* mayor.

for·um /fôr′əm/ *n.* **1** The market or public place of an ancient Roman city where judicial and political business was conducted.

2 A court of law. **3** A meeting for the discussion of public affairs. ► *Forum* comes from the Latin word *foris,* "outside."

frag·ile /fraj′əl/ *adj.* Easily shattered or damaged; delicate: *fragile* china. ► *Fragile* comes from the Latin word *fragilis,* "easily broken."

fran·tic /fran′tik/ *adj.* Emotionally out of control; filled with fear and anxiety: I was *frantic* when I thought I had lost my wallet.

free·dom /frē′dəm/ *n.* **1** Liberty. **2** Ease: *freedom* of movement.

fre·quent /*adj.* frē′kwənt, *v.* fri·kwent′/ **1** *adj.* Often. **2** *v.* To go somewhere often.— **fre′quent·ly** *adv.*

friend·ly /frend′lē/ *adj.* **friend·li·er, friend·li·est** Like a friend; pleasant; helpful; neighborly.

friend·ship /frend′ship/ *n.* **1** The condition or fact of being friends. **2** Warm feelings.

fron·tier /frun·tir′/ *n.* **1** The border between two countries. **2** The part of a settled area that borders on an unsettled area. **3** Any unexplored area: the *frontiers* of medical research.

fu·el /fyoo′(ə)l/ *n., v.* **fu·eled, fu·el·ing** **1** *n.* A substance that is burned to produce energy in the form of heat. **2** *v.* To supply something with fuel: *fuel* a fire. *Alternate spellings:* **fuelled, fuelling.**

fun·da·men·tal /fun′də·men′təl/ **1** *adj.* Essential; basic; forming a foundation: Reading is a *fundamental* skill. **2** *n.* An essential part: The scouts learned the *fundamentals* of first aid.—**fun′da·men′tal·ly** *adv.*

fun·gus /fung′gəs/ *n., pl.* **fun·gi** /fun′jī/ A plant that has no chlorophyll, flowers, or leaves, such as mold, a mushroom, mildew, etc. *Alternate plural:* **funguses.** ► *Fungus* is a Latin word meaning "a spongy plant."

fur·lough /fûr′lō/ *n.* Permission to leave or take a brief vacation from official duty, granted to people in the armed forces.

G

gadg·et /gaj′it/ *n.* A small tool or mechanical device.

gai·e·ty /gā′ə·tē/ *n., pl.* **gai·e·ties** Cheerful liveliness or high spirits.

gar·bage /gär′bij/ *n.* Worthless material; trash.

gaz·pa·cho /gəz·päch′ō *or* gəs·päch′ō/ *n., pl.* **gaz·pa·chos** A cold vegetable soup of Spanish origin, made with tomatoes, cucumbers, garlic, onions, and spices.

gelatin   **gumbo**

gel·a·tin /jel′ə·tin/ *n.* A protein made by boiling the bones, skins, hoofs, etc., of animals. It forms a jelly when cooled and is used in foods, photographic films, etc. *Alternate spelling:* **gelatine.**

gen·er·a·tion /jen′ə·rā′shən/ *n.*   **1** People born during a given period of time: my grandfather's *generation.*   **2** A stage in the history of a family: Our family has been in this country for four *generations.*

gen·ius /jēn′yəs/ *n., pl.* **gen·ius·es**   **1** An extremely high degree of mental ability or creative talent.   **2** A person who possesses such ability or talent.   ► *Genius* is a Latin word meaning "the spirit of a person or place." This word is related to the English words *generation* and *generate.*

ger·mi·nate /jûr′mə·nāt/ *v.* **ger·mi·nat·ed, ger·mi·nat·ing**   **1** To grow or sprout or cause to grow or sprout.   **2** To develop or evolve, as an idea or thought.

ges·ture /jes′chər/ *n., v.* **ges·tured, ges·tur·ing**   **1** *n.* A motion made with some part of the body, usually the hands or arms, to express some feeling or idea.   **2** *v.* To make a gesture, especially to point: She *gestured* toward the broken plate on the floor.   **3** *n.* A deed that has a particular effect: a kind *gesture.*

glob·al /glō′bəl/ *adj.* Having to do with the whole world; worldwide: Clean air is a *global* concern.

go·ril·la /gə·ril′ə/ *n.* A large and powerful ape, found in Africa: The *gorilla* at the zoo likes to watch people.

gour·met /gŏor·mā′/ *n.* A person who appreciates and is knowledgeable about fine food.

gov·ern·ment /guv′ər(n)·mənt/ *n.*   **1** The administration of a country, state, city, etc.   **2** The system of this administration.   **3** The officials in this administration.

grad·u·al /graj′ōō·əl/ *adj.* Slowly; little by little: a *gradual* change. —**grad′u·al·ly** *adv.*

grad·u·ate /*v.* graj′ōō·āt, *n.* graj′ōō·it/ *v.* **grad·u·at·ed, grad·u·at·ing,** *n.*   **1** *v.* To complete school; to earn a diploma.   **2** *n.* A person who is graduating or has graduated.

graph·ics /graf′iks/ *n. pl.* (*used with singular verb*) The art of drawing, painting, and printmaking.

grav·el /grav′əl/ *n.* A mixture of small stones and pebbles.

grease /*n.* grēs, *v.* grēs *or* grēz/ *n., v.* **greased, greas·ing**   **1** *n.* Soft animal fat.   **2** *n.* Any thick, oily substance.   **3** *v.* To oil or lubricate; to apply grease.

greed·y /grē′dē/ *adj.* **greed·i·er, greed·i·est** Wanting much more than one needs.

growth /grōth/ *n.*   **1** The act or process of growing.   **2** The amount grown.   **3** Something that has grown or developed.

grudge /gruj/ *n.* A feeling of hatred or anger toward someone.

grue·some /grōō′səm/ *adj.* Horrible, especially in a disgusting way.

guar·an·tee /gar′ən·tē′/ *n., v.* **guar·an·teed, guar·an·tee·ing**   **1** *n.* A promise or pledge to replace or refund payment for a faulty item within a period of time.   **2** *v.* To give a guarantee.

guard·i·an /gär′dē·ən/ *n.*   **1** A person who watches over or protects.   **2** A person assigned by a court of law to care for someone else, especially a child.   **3** *adj. use: guardian* angel.

guer·ril·la /gə·ril′ə/ *n.*   **1** A member of a fighting group that uses surprise and sabotage as battle techniques.   **2** *adj. use: guerrilla* warfare. *Alternate spelling:* **guerilla.**   ► *Guerrilla* comes from the Spanish word *guerra,* "war."

gui·tar /gi·tär′/ *n.* A stringed instrument played by strumming or plucking the strings with fingers or a pick.   *Guitar* comes from the Greek word *kithara,* the name for an ancient stringed instrument.

gum·bo /gum′bō/ *n.*   **1** A stew often made with okra.   **2** Okra.   ► *Gumbo* comes from an African word in the Bantu language.

---

act, āte, câre, ärt;   egg, ēven;   if, īce;   on, ōver, ôr;   bŏok, fōōd;   up, tûrn;
ə=**a** in *ago,* **e** in *listen,* **i** in *giraffe,* **o** in *pilot,* **u** in *circus;*   y**ōō**=**u** in *music;*   **oi**l;   **out**;
chair; si**ng**; **sh**op; **th**ank; **th**at; **zh** in *treasure.*

H

hall·way /hôl′wā′/ *n.* A corridor or passage-way.

ham·bur·ger /ham′bûr′gər/ *n.* **1** Ground beef. **2** A cooked patty of ground beef, usually eaten as a sandwich on a bun. ► *Hamburger* once simply meant "of or coming from the city of Hamburg, Germany."

ham·mock /ham′ək/ *n.* A length of strong cloth or net hung between two trees, poles, etc., used for sitting or lying in. ► *Hammock* comes from the Spanish word *hamaca,* "a swinging, suspended bed."

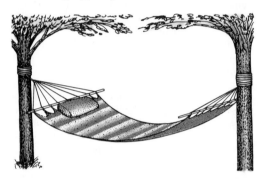

hand·ful /han(d)′fŏŏl/ *n., pl.* **hand·fuls** **1** The amount that can be held in the hand. **2** A relatively small number: Only a *handful* of people came to the meeting.

hand·ker·chief /hang′kər·chif/ *n.* A small piece of linen or other fabric used for personal or decorative purposes.

head·quar·ters /hed′kwôr′tərz/ *n. pl.* The place from which people direct an organization, such as a police force, military unit, election campaign, or large business.

hec·tic /hek′tik/ *adj.* Full of excitement; confused; rushed: a *hectic* day.

he·ro·ic /hi·rō′ik/ *adj.* Of or like a hero; brave, mighty, or courageous.

hes·i·tate /hez′ə·tāt/ *v.* **hes·i·tat·ed, hes·i·tat·ing** **1** To hold back; to pause before acting: The cat *hesitated* before leaping off the shelf. **2** To be unwilling, reluctant, or undecided: Do not *hesitate* to ask questions.

hin·der /hin′dər/ *v.* To interfere with; to block: The icy streets *hindered* our progress.

hin·drance /hin′drəns/ *n.* A person or thing that hinders or gets in the way; an obstacle: Bad weather is a *hindrance* to travelers.

his·to·ri·an /his·tôr′ē·ən/ *n.* A person who writes about historic events and is an authority on history: The *historian* is writing a book about the town during the Civil War.

his·tor·i·cal /his·tôr′ə·kəl/ *adj.* Of or having to do with the past; belonging to history: *historical* documents.

his·to·ry /his′tə·rē/ *n., pl.* **his·to·ries** Past events or the study or record of them, especially important events in the development of a nation, people, activity, etc.

hor·ri·fy /hôr′ə·fī/ *v.* **hor·ri·fied, hor·ri·fy·ing** To cause extreme fear or terror: The disaster *horrified* everyone.

hum /hum/ *v.* **hummed, hum·ming,** *n.* **1** *v.* To make a low, steady buzzing or whirring noise. **2** *n.* A buzzing or whirring noise. **3** *v.* To sing with the lips closed, using no words.

hun·ger /hung′gər/ **1** *n.* Weakness caused by lack of food. **2** *n.* A desire or need for food. **3** *n.* Any strong desire. **4** *v.* To have a strong desire.

hy·gi·en·ic /hī′j(ē·)en′ik/ *adj.* **1** Of or having to do with hygiene, the science of health. **2** Clean; sanitary.

I

-ian *suffix* A person who specializes in something: *veterinarian.*

-ible *suffix* Able to be: *corruptible.*

i·den·ti·fy /ī·den′tə·fī/ *v.* **i·den·ti·fied, i·den·ti·fy·ing** To recognize or show what something is or who someone is.

i·dle /īd′(ə)l/ *adj.* **i·dler, i·dlest,** *v.* **i·dled, i·dling** **1** *adj.* Not doing anything; not busy: *idle* hands. **2** *adj.* Not willing to work; lazy. **3** *v.* To waste time: to *idle* away an afternoon. **4** *v.* To run without transmitting power: The car *idled.*

i·dol /īd′(ə)l/ *n.* **1** An object that is worshiped, usually an image of a god. **2** A person who is very much admired and imitated: a movie *idol.*

-ier *suffix* See *-er.*

ig·ni·tion /ig·nish′ən/ *n.* **1** The act of catching fire. **2** The system that starts an engine by setting fire to the fuel.

il- *prefix* Form of *in-* (meaning "not") used before words beginning with *l: illegible.*

il·le·gal /i·lē′gəl/ *adj.* Not legal; unlawful. —**il·le′gal·ly** *adv.* ► *Illegal* comes from Latin *in-,* "not," and *legalis,* "legal."

il·lus·tra·tor /il′ə·strā′tər/ *n.* An artist who draws pictures or illustrations to explain or decorate a book, magazine, etc.

im-¹ *prefix* In, into, or on: *imprint.*

im-² *prefix* Form of *in-* (meaning "not") used before words beginning with *b, m,* and *p: improbable.*

imagination

indicator

im·ag·i·na·tion /i·maj′ə·nā′shən/ *n.* **1** The ability or power to picture absent things in the mind. **2** The ability to view things in new ways, develop new ideas, or create from thought.

im·ag·ine /i·maj′in/ *v.* **im·ag·ined, im·ag·in·ing** **1** To form a mental image or idea of. **2** To guess or suppose.

im·mense /i·mens′/ *adj.* Huge; vast; enormous: an *immense* amount.

im·mi·grate /im′ə·grāt/ *v.* **im·mi·grat·ed, im·mi·grat·ing** To come to a new country or region with the intention of living there permanently: My great-grandparents *immigrated* to this country.

im·mo·bile /i·mō′bəl/ *adj.* **1** Not able to be moved; fixed. **2** Not moving.

im·mor·tal /i·môr′təl/ *adj.* Living or remembered forever.

im·mun·i·ty /i·myōōn′ə·tē/ *n., pl.* **im·mun·i·ties** The state of being protected against or not affected by something, especially disease.

im·peach /im·pēch′/ *v.* **1** To challenge or bring doubt or suspicion upon. **2** To bring a legal charge against a public official for wrongdoing.

im·per·fect /im·pûr′fikt/ *adj.* Having faults; not perfect.—**im·per′fect·ly** *adv.* ▶ *Imperfect* comes from Latin *in-,* "not," and *perfectus,* "perfect."

im·po·lite /im′pə·līt′/ *adj.* Not polite; rude. —**im′po·lite′ly** *adv.*

im·pos·si·ble /im·pos′ə·bəl/ *adj.* **1** Not able to happen or be done. **2** Not to be tolerated or endured: It was *impossible* to listen to Jeff's constant complaining.

im·pres·sion /im·presh′ən/ *n.* **1** A strong effect on the mind, senses, or feelings: His honesty left a lasting *impression.* **2** A vague notion or idea: I had the *impression* that they were not going. **3** A mark left by pressure: The dentist made *impressions* of my teeth.

in-[1] *prefix* In, into, within, or on: *inborn.*

in-[2] *prefix* Not: *inadequate.*

in·a·bil·i·ty /in′ə·bil′ə·tē/ *n.* The act or condition of not being able to do something; lack of ability.

in·ac·cu·rate /in·ak′yər·it/ *adj.* Incorrect; not accurate; faulty: The suspect gave an *inaccurate* account of what happened.— **in·ac′cu·rate·ly** *adv.*

in·au·gu·ra·tion /in·ô′gyə·rā′shən/ *n.* A ceremony officially giving a person the powers and responsibilities of an office.

in·ca·pa·ble /in·kā′pə·bəl/ *adj.* Lacking the necessary ability or skill to do something: The injured horse was *incapable* of running.

in·come /in′kum/ *n.* Money received or earned through work or investments.

in·con·ven·ience /in′kən·vēn′yəns/ *n., v.* **in·con·ven·ienced, in·con·ven·ienc·ing** **1** *n.* Lack of convenience; trouble or bother. **2** *n.* Something that causes trouble or bother. **3** *v.* To trouble or bother: Don't let us *inconvenience* you.

in·cor·rect /in′kə·rekt′/ *adj.* Not right or correct; inappropriate.—**in′cor·rect′ly** *adv.*

in·crease /*v.* in·krēs′, *n.* in′krēs/ *v.* **in·creased, in·creas·ing,** *n.* **1** *v.* To make or become greater or larger. **2** *n.* A growing or becoming greater or larger in size, quantity, etc. **3** *n.* The amount added by an increase.

in·cred·i·ble /in·kred′ə·bəl/ *adj.* So strange or unusual as to be unbelievable; not to be believed or accepted as true.—**in·cred′i·bly** *adv.*

in·de·pen·dent /in′di·pen′dənt/ *adj.* **1** Not governed by another country: an *independent* nation. **2** Not influenced or swayed by others: He is an *independent* thinker. **3** Not dependent on anyone else for support or money: She has been financially *independent* since she graduated.—**in′de·pen′dent·ly** *adv.*

in·di·ca·tor /in′də·kā′tər/ *n.* Something that points out or indicates.

---

act, āte, câre, ärt; egg, ēven; if, īce; on, ōver, ôr; bŏŏk, fōōd; up, tûrn;
ə=a in *ago,* e in *listen,* i in *giraffe,* o in *pilot,* u in *circus;* yōō=u in *music;* oil; out;
chair; **s**ing; **sh**op; **th**ank; **th**at; **zh** in *treasure.*

in·dif·fer·ent /in·dif′rənt *or* in·dif′ər·ənt/ *adj.*
1 Not caring one way or another: an *indifferent* attitude. **2** Neither good nor bad: an *indifferent* artist.

in·dus·tri·al /in·dus′trē·əl/ *adj.* Having to do with industry or manufacturing.

in·dus·tri·al·i·za·tion /in·dus′trē·əl·i·zā′shən/ *n.* The act of making or becoming industrial.

in·dus·tri·ous /in·dus′trē·əs/ *adj.* Hardworking; working steadily.

in·ex·act /in′ig·zakt′/ *adj.* Not exact; not totally accurate or true.

in·fe·ri·or /in·fir′ē·ər/ **1** *adj.* Of little or less quality, worth, usefulness, etc. **2** *adj.* Lower in rank or position. **3** *n.* A person or thing that is less or not as good in some way. ▶ *Inferior* is a Latin word meaning "lower."

in·flate /in·flāt′/ *v.* **in·flat·ed, in·flat·ing**
1 To fill up with air or gas: *Inflate* the tires. **2** To puff up with importance or satisfaction: His good grades *inflated* his pride. **3** To increase or expand a great deal: Fuel prices were *inflated* by a shortage of oil.

in·fla·tion /in·flā′shən/ *n.* **1** The act or condition of being swelled or puffed out: Check the *inflation* of your tires. **2** A rise in price levels that comes from an increase in the amount of money available without a similar increase in the amount of goods: Prices are rising because of economic *inflation*. ▶ *Inflation* comes from Latin *in-*, "into," and *flare*, "to blow."

in·for·mal /in·fôr′məl/ *adj.* Not bound by strict forms or rules; relaxed: an *informal* meeting.—**in·for′mal·ly** *adv.*

in·her·i·tance /in·her′ə·təns/ *n.* **1** The act, fact, or right of inheriting or being left something upon the owner's death. **2** Something inherited.

in·jec·tion /in·jek′shən/ *n.* **1** The act of forcing fluid into the body with a hypodermic needle or syringe. **2** The fluid injected.

in·quire /in·kwīr′/ *v.* **in·quired, in·quir·ing**
1 To ask a question in order to obtain information. **2** To investigate or search: to *inquire* into the cause of the accident.

in·sig·ni·a /in·sig′nē·ə/ *n.*, *pl.* **in·sig·ni·a** A badge or emblem used to show membership, office, honor, or authority: military *insignia*. *Alternate plural:* **insignias.** ▶ *Insignia* comes from Latin *in-*, "upon," and *signum*, "a mark."

in·sig·nif·i·cant /in′sig·nif′ə·kənt/ *adj.* Unimportant; lacking meaning, size, or worth: an *insignificant* reason; an *insignificant* amount of rain.

in·som·ni·a /in·som′nē·ə/ *n.* The condition of being not able to sleep. ▶ *Insomnia* comes from Latin *in-*, "not," and *somnus*, "sleep."

in·stead /in·sted′/ *adv.* Rather than; in place of: Let's go on a camping trip *instead* of a ski trip.

in·sti·tu·tion /in′stə·t(y)oo′shən/ *n.* **1** An established organization with a specific purpose, as a school, bank, hospital, etc. **2** An accepted principle or rule.

in·struc·tion /in·struk′shən/ *n.* **1** The act of teaching. **2** Something that trains or teaches a lesson. **3** (*pl.*) Directions or orders.

in·stru·ment /in′strə·mənt/ *n.* **1** A mechanical device; tool. **2** A device for measuring, controlling, or recording, as one found in a plane. **3** *adj. use:* an *instrument* panel. **4** A device for producing musical sounds, as a piano or guitar: What kind of *instrument* do you play?

in·tel·li·gent /in·tel′ə·jənt/ *adj.* Able to learn; bright: His ideas show that he is an *intelligent* person.—**in·tel′li·gent·ly** *adv.*

inter- *prefix* Between: *intercede*.

in·ter·cept /in′tər·sept′/ *v.* To prevent from reaching a destination or point: Jack *intercepted* the ball and ran for a touchdown. I passed the popcorn to Ellen, but Mitch *intercepted* it. ▶ *Intercept* comes from Latin *inter-*, "between," and *capere*, "to take or seize."

in·ter·est /in′tər·ist *or* in′trist/ **1** *n.* A desire to learn or experience something. **2** *v.* To hold the attention. **3** *n.* Something that causes attention or curiosity. **4** *n.* Money paid for the use of money: Banks pay *interest* on savings accounts.

in·ter·fere /in′tər·fir′/ *v.* **in·ter·fered, in·ter·fer·ing** To meddle; to get in the way. ● It is possible to *interfere* for a good purpose: She *interfered* to break up the quarrel.

in·ter·fer·ence /in′tər·fir′əns/ *n.* **1** The act of getting in the way; interfering. **2** Something that gets in the way. **3** The act of hindering an opponent's play in sports. **4** A disturbance in radio and television reception.

in·te·ri·or /in·tir′ē·ər/ **1** *n.* The inside. **2** *adj.* Having to do with the inside; inner. ▶ *Interior* comes from the Latin word *interus*, "within, inward, or on the inside."

in·ter·me·di·ate /in′tər·mē′dē·it/ *adj.* In the middle of two things, levels, stages, or events. ▶ *Intermediate* comes from Latin *inter-*, "between," and *mediare*, "to mediate."

interpretation   juggle

in·ter·pre·ta·tion /in·tûr′prə·tā′shən/ *n.* The act, process, or result of interpreting, understanding, or explaining: I agree with Joe's *interpretation* of the poem.

in·ter·rup·tion /in′tə·rup′shən/ *n.* **1** The act of interrupting or breaking in. **2** Something that interrupts or breaks in: I hope we can see the show without *interruption.*

in·ter·state /in′tər·stāt/ *adj.* Happening or existing between or among two or more states: The *interstate* highway was closed for repairs.

in·ter·val /in′tər·vəl/ *n.* **1** A pause; the time between two events: There was a brief *interval* between the first and second acts of the play. **2** The distance between two objects or points: *intervals* of three feet. ► *Interval* comes from Latin *inter-*, "between," and *vallum*, "a defense structure; a rampart."

intra- *prefix* Within: *intravenous.*

in·tra·mu·ral /in′trə·myoo′rəl/ *adj.* Occurring between or among individuals of the same school, organization, etc.: an *intramural* basketball tournament.

in·tra·state /in′trə·stāt/ *adj.* Being or having to do with things within a single state: *intrastate* commerce.

in·trigue /*n.* in·trēg′ *or* in′trēg, *v.* in·trēg′/ *n., v.* **in·trigued, in·tri·guing 1** *n.* Scheming or plotting in secret: The king's court was full of *intrigue.* **2** *v.* To arouse interest or curiosity: The idea *intrigued* me. **3** *adj. use:* an *intriguing* idea.

in·trud·er /in·trood′ər/ *n.* A person who trespasses or enters without permission. ► *Intruder* comes from the Latin word *intrudere*, "to thrust in."

in·va·lid¹ /in′və·lid/ *n.* A person who is not well and cannot live a normal, active life.

in·va·lid² /in·val′id/ *adj.* Not true or sound; without force: an *invalid* decision. ► *Invalid* comes from Latin *in-*, "not," and *validus*, "strong."

in·ven·tor /in·ven′tər/ *n.* A person who thinks out or develops something for the first time: The *inventor* showed us how the machine worked.

-ion *suffix* **1** The act or process of: *rotation.* **2** The result of: *invention.* **3** The condition of being: *relation.*

ir- *prefix* Form of *in-* (meaning "not") used before words beginning with *r: irrelevant.*

ir·ra·tion·al /i·rash′ən·əl/ *adj.* Not reasonable or logical; senseless: George has an *irrational* fear of dogs.

ir·reg·u·lar /i·reg′yə·lər/ *adj.* **1** Not evenly shaped: an *irregular* pattern. **2** Not according to standard rules; unusual: an *irregular* procedure. **3** Lacking continuity; not following a regular pattern: *irregular* visits.— **ir·reg′u·lar·ly** *adv.* ► *Irregular* comes from Latin *in-*, "not," and *regularis*, "regular."

ir·re·sis·ti·ble /ir′i·zis′tə·bəl/ *adj.* Not able to be resisted or opposed: Those strawberries look *irresistible.*

ir·re·spon·si·ble /ir′i·spon′sə·bəl/ *adj.* Not responsible or reliable; not to be depended on: The *irresponsible* worker left before the job was done.

ir·ri·ga·tion /ir′ə·gā′shən/ *n.* A system for providing water through pipes, ditches, or canals. ► *Irrigation* comes from Latin *in-*, "to," and *rigare*, "to water."

-ist *suffix* A person who specializes in something: *sociologist.*

i·tem /ī′təm/ *n.* **1** One thing in a series. **2** A single thing. ► *Item* is a Latin word meaning "likewise or thus."

-ity *suffix* The condition or quality of being: *reality.*

J

jeal·ous /jel′əs/ *adj.* **1** Being afraid of losing someone's love to another person. **2** Feeling envy for what another person has.

jest /jest/ **1** *n.* A statement or action intended to provoke laughter; a joke. **2** *v.* To joke; to speak or act playfully: Don't be upset; I was just *jesting.*

jog·ger /jog′ər/ *n.* One who runs regularly for exercise.

jos·tle /jos′(ə)l/ *v.* **jos·tled, jos·tling,** *n.* **1** *v.* To push roughly or shove against. **2** *n.* A hard or rough push or shove.

ju·bi·lant /joo′bə·lənt/ *adj.* Overjoyed; extremely happy.

judg·ment /juj′mənt/ *n.* **1** A decision or serious opinion. **2** The ability to make a decision wisely; good sense. *Alternate spelling:* **judgement.**

jug·gle /jug′əl/ *v.* **jug·gled, jug·gling** To keep a number of objects in continuous motion in the air by tossing and catching.

---

act, āte, câre, ärt;   egg, ēven;   if, īce;   on, ōver, ôr;   book, food;   up, tûrn;
ə=a in *ago,* e in *listen,* i in *giraffe,* o in *pilot,* u in *circus;*   yoo=u in *music;*   oil;   out;
chair; sing; shop; thank; that; zh in *treasure.*

junior

leopard

jun·ior /jōōn′yər/ **1** *adj.* Younger or lower in rank. **2** *n.* The younger: usually abbreviated and used to show that a son is named after his father: Carl Bookstone, *Jr.* **3** *adj.* Pertaining to the next-to-last year of high school or college. **4** *n.* A student in this class or year.

jus·ti·fy /jus′tə·fī/ *v.* **jus·ti·fied, jus·ti·fy·ing** **1** To show something to be just, correct, or reasonable. **2** To give good reason for.

ju·ve·nile /jōō′və·nəl *or* jōō′və·nīl/ **1** *adj.* Young; childlike or immature. **2** *adj.* Something of, like, or for young people. **3** *n.* A young person.

K

ker·o·sene /ker′ə·sēn/ *n.* A colorless, thin oil produced from petroleum and used as fuel in lamps, stoves, etc.

kiln /kil(n)/ *n.* An oven or furnace used for drying and hardening pottery.

knowl·edge /nol′ij/ *n.* **1** The fact or condition of knowing or being aware. **2** The extent of a person's information or understanding. **3** All that is known by all people.

L

la·bor /lā′bər/ **1** *n.* Hard work. **2** *v.* To work hard. **3** *n.* Workers in general: That candidate has the support of *labor.*

land·scape /land′skāp/ *n., v.* **land·scaped, land·scap·ing** **1** *n.* A stretch of land viewed from a single point. **2** *n.* A picture of such scenery. **3** *v.* To beautify an area of land by reshaping its surface and planting trees and flowers.

la·sa·gna /lə·zän′yə/ *n.* **1** Wide, flat noodles. **2** An Italian dish made by baking layers of flat noodles, meat, cheese, and tomato sauce. ▸ *Lasagna* is an Italian word that means "flat noodle."

la·ser /lā′zər/ *n.* A machine that produces a light that can be used as a delicate tool to cut or burn holes.

las·so /las′ō/ *n., pl.* **las·sos,** *v.* **1** *n.* A long rope having a loop with a sliding knot at one end, used for catching horses and cattle. **2** *v.* To catch something with a lasso. *Alternate plural:* **lassoes** ▸ *Lasso* comes from the Spanish word *lazo,* "a snare."

lath·er /laᵗħ′ər/ **1** *n.* Suds made by soap mixed with water. **2** *v.* To cover with suds or foam.

law·yer /lô′yər/ *n.* A person licensed to advise clients about the law, act for them in court, draw up contracts, etc.

league[1] /lēg/ *n., v.* **leagued, lea·guing** **1** *n.* Persons, groups, countries, etc., joined together for a common purpose: the *League* of Nations. **2** *n.* A group of athletic teams that compete regularly with one another. **3** *v.* To form a league. ▸ *League* comes from the French word *liguer,* "to band together."

league[2] /lēg/ *n.* A measure of length equal to about three miles.

left·o·ver /left′ō′vər/ *n.* (*usually pl.*) An unused part, especially the food left after a meal.

le·gal·i·ty /li·gal′ə·tē/ *n.* The condition of being lawful or allowed by the law.

leg·end /lej′ənd/ *n.* **1** A story of strange or remarkable happenings that has come down from early times and may or may not have some basis in real incidents. **2** A key or guide accompanying a map, graph, etc.

leg·i·ble /lej′ə·bəl/ *adj.* Able to be read; clearly written: *legible* writing.—**leg′i·bly** *adv.*

leg·is·la·tion /lej′is·lā′shən/ *n.* **1** The act of making laws. **2** The laws made or enacted: Congress enacted *legislation* to clean up polluted rivers.

lei·sure /lē′zhər *or* lezh′ər/ **1** *n.* Free time; time away from work, study, or other duties. **2** *adj.* Free from work.

leop·ard /lep′ərd/ *n.* A large, fierce animal of the cat family, with a brownish-yellow coat and clustered black spots. It is found in Africa and Asia.

perceive   **plaid**

per·ceive /pər·sēv'/ *v.* **per·ceived, per·ceiv·ing** **1** To become aware of by means of the senses: I *perceived* a trace of perfume. **2** To come to understand or comprehend: to *perceive* the problem.

per·cus·sion /pər·kush'ən/ *n.* **1** The sharp striking of one thing against another. **2** Musical instruments played by striking.

per·form·ance /pər·fôr'məns/ *n.* **1** The act of performing or doing. **2** A play, concert, or other kind of entertainment. **3** A particular action or deed.

per·il /per'əl/ *n.* Danger; risk.

per·mis·si·ble /pər·mis'ə·bəl/ *adj.* Allowable; acceptable.

per·mis·sion /pər·mish'ən/ *n.* The act of allowing; approval to do something.

per·mit /*v.* pər·mit', *n.* pûr'mit/ *v.* **per·mit·ted, per·mit·ting,** *n.* **1** *v.* To allow; to give permission. **2** *n.* Written license to do something: a driving *permit*.

per·tain /pər·tān'/ *v.* **1** To refer or relate. **2** To belong or be associated with.

pet·al /pet'əl/ *n.* One of the leaflike segments of a flower.

pe·ti·tion /pə·tish'ən/ **1** *n.* A formal, written request made to a person or a group in authority. **2** *v.* To submit a petition.

phan·tom /fan'təm/ **1** *n.* A ghost or spirit; a shadowy vision. **2** *adj.* Having the qualities of a ghost or spirit; ghostlike.

phar·ma·cist /fär'mə·sist/ *n.* A person who is trained and licensed to prepare and sell drugs prescribed by doctors.

pho·tog·ra·pher /fə·tog'rə·fər/ *n.* A person who takes photographs, either as a hobby or as a business.

phy·si·cian /fi·zish'ən/ *n.* A medical doctor.

phys·i·cist /fiz'ə·sist/ *n.* A person who is an expert in the field of physics, a science dealing with matter, energy, and motion.

pic·co·lo /pik'ə·lō/ *n., pl.* **pic·co·los** A small flute with a high-pitched sound.

pick·le /pik'əl/ *n., v.* **pick·led, pick·ling** **1** *n.* A cucumber or other food soaked in salt water or vinegar. **2** *v.* To preserve or flavor by soaking in salt water or vinegar.

pic·tur·esque /pik'chə·resk'/ *adj.* Beautiful, unusual, or charming; resembling a picture: a *picturesque* village.

pier /pir/ *n.* **1** A structure extending out over water: The ship docked at the *pier*. **2** A massive structural support, as for the arch of a bridge.

pierce /pirs/ *v.* **pierced, pierc·ing** **1** To pass or go through or into, as by something sharp; to penetrate: We *pierced* the pie crust with a fork to let the steam out. **2** To poke through as something sharp; to affect sharply: The cold rain *pierced* our skin. **3** *adj. use:* a *piercing* wind; a *piercing* scream; *pierced* ears.

pi·geon /pij'ən/ *n.* A bird with a plump body, small head, and short legs.

pi·mien·to /pi·m(y)en'tō/ *n., pl.* **pi·mien·tos** A sweet mild-tasting red pepper, or the plant it grows on. *Alternate spelling:* **pimento.** ► *Pimiento* comes from the Spanish word *pimienta,* "pepper."

pit·y /pit'ē/ *n., pl.* **pit·ies,** *v.* **pit·ied, pit·y·ing** **1** *n.* A feeling of sorrow or compassion. **2** *v.* To feel sorry for; to have compassion or sympathy.

piz·za /pēt'sə/ *n.* An Italian dish made of a flat crust covered with cheese and tomato sauce and baked in a hot oven. ► *Pizza* in Italian is a word that is used for any open pie.

plaid /plad/ **1** *n.* A cloth woven with bands of various colors and widths crossing each other in patterns. **2** *adj.* Having a plaid pattern.

---

act, āte, câre, ärt;   egg, ēven;   if, īce;   on, ōver, ôr;   book, food;   up, tûrn;
ə=a in *ago,* e in *listen,* i in *giraffe,* o in *pilot,* u in *circus;*   yoo=u in *music;*   oil;   out;
chair;   sing;   shop;   thank;   that;   zh in *treasure.*

plan

plan /plan/ *n., v.* **planned, plan·ning** **1** *n.* A method for doing something. **2** *v.* To form a method for doing something. **3** *v.* To intend. **4** *n.* (*pl.*) Arrangements. **5** *v.* To make arrangements. **6** *n.* A drawing showing how the parts of something are arranged.

plan·e·tar·i·um /plan′ə·târ′ē·əm/ *n., pl.* **plan·e·tar·i·ums** A room or building with an apparatus that can project images of the stars and other celestial bodies onto a domed ceiling. *Alternate plural:* **planetaria.** ► *Planetarium* is made up of the base word *planet* and the Latin suffix *-arium,* "a place connected with." *Planet* comes from a Greek word that means "wanderer."

pla·za /plä′zə *or* plaz′ə/ *n.* An open square or shopping area in a city or town. ► *Plaza* is a Spanish word meaning "city square."

pli·ers /plī′ərz/ *n. pl.* A small pinching tool used for bending, cutting, or holding something.

plumb·er /plum′ər/ *n.* A person who installs and repairs pipes and fixtures connected with the water supply in a building.

plunge /plunj/ *v.* **plunged, plung·ing,** *n.* **1** *v.* To leap or fall suddenly or quickly. **2** *n.* A sudden or quick leap or fall, especially into water. **3** *v.* To rush or leap into something suddenly.

point /point/ *v.* **1** To show or indicate. **2** To aim or direct.

point·ed /poin′tid/ *adj.* **1** Possessing a sharp end or point. **2** Aimed at.

pol·i·ti·cian /pol′ə·tish′ən/ *n.* A person who works or is skillful in politics or the science of government.

pol·i·tics /pol′ə·tiks/ *n. pl.* The way government operates; the art or science of government.

pol·ka /pō(l)′kə/ *n.* **1** A lively dance. **2** A lively dance tune.

pon·der /pon′dər/ *v.* To think deeply about something.

pop·u·lar /pop′yə·lər/ *adj.* **1** Well liked by many people. **2** Representing the people: a *popular* government.

pop·u·lar·i·ty /pop′yə·lar′ə·tē/ *n.* The fact or condition of being well liked or popular.

pore /pôr/ *n.* A tiny natural opening in a leaf or in the skin.

por·trait /pôr′trit *or* pôr′trāt/ *n.* A painting or formal photograph of a person.

pos·ses·sion /pə·zesh′ən/ *n.* **1** The fact of owning or having something. **2** Something owned.

principal

post·age /pōs′tij/ *n.* A charge for sending mail.

po·ta·to /pə·tā′tō/ *n., pl.* **po·ta·toes** **1** The starchy stem or tuber of a cultivated plant, widely used as a vegetable. **2** The plant itself.

poul·try /pōl′trē/ *n.* Birds raised for meat or eggs, such as chickens, ducks, turkeys, etc.

pour /pôr/ *v.* **1** To cause liquid to flow. **2** To rain heavily; to drench. **3** To move in a constant stream.

pre- *prefix* Before in time or order: *predetermined.*

pre·cede /pri·sēd′/ *v.* **pre·ced·ed, pre·ced·ing** To be, go, or come before, especially in time or in arrangement: Soup *preceded* the main course.

pre·cip·i·ta·tion /pri·sip′ə·tā′shən/ *n.* **1** The falling of rain, snow, sleet, hail, etc., on the earth; also, the amount that falls. **2** The process of separating a solid substance from a solution.

pre·cise /pri·sīs′/ *adj.* **1** Exact; strictly accurate: the *precise* amount. **2** Very careful; strict about rules.

prej·u·dice /prej′oo·dis *or* prej′əd·əs/ *n.* An unfair opinion formed without examining facts or evidence.

pre·mi·um /prē′mē·əm/ *n.* **1** A prize, gift, or reward offered to persuade people to do or buy something. **2** An insurance payment. **3** A high value or regard; high quality: My teacher places a *premium* on neatness.

pres·sure /presh′ər/ *n., v.* **pres·sured, pres·sur·ing** **1** *n.* The force created by one thing pressing against another. **2** *n.* Strong effort to influence someone. **3** *v.* To influence as if by force. **4** *n.* Urgent demands: the *pressure* of everyday life.

pret·ty /prit′ē/ *adj.* **pret·ti·er, pret·ti·est,** *adv.* **1** *adj.* Attractive; pleasant. **2** *adv.* Somewhat: *pretty* certain.

pret·zel /pret′səl/ *n.* A crisp bread stick, usually in the shape of a loose knot, salted on the outside. ► *Pretzel* comes from the German word *brezel,* "having branches like arms."

priest /prēst/ *n.* **1** A person who has made a vow to serve God and is given authority by the Roman Catholic, Eastern Orthodox, or Anglican church to perform religious ceremonies and teach religious doctrine. **2** An individual who has the authority to practice sacred rites.

prin·ci·pal /prin′sə·pəl/ **1** *adj.* Most important: Their *principal* complaint was the lack of heat. **2** *n.* The head of a school.

principle   **quit**

prin·ci·ple /prin′sə·pəl/ *n.* **1** A basic rule or belief: the *principles* of English spelling. **2** A moral standard, such as fairness or honesty: a person of good *principles*.

prism /priz′əm/ *n.* **1** A transparent glass object that can split white light into rainbow colors. **2** A solid figure with ends that are identical polygons and sides that are parallelograms.

prob·a·bil·i·ty /prob′ə·bil′ə·tē/ *n., pl.* **prob·a·bil·i·ties** The likelihood that something will happen: What is the *probability* of rain today?

pro·ceed /prə·sēd′/ *v.* To go forward or go on, especially after a stop: We will *proceed* with the meeting after lunch.

pro·ceed·ing /prə·sē′ding/ *n.* (*often pl.*) **1** A series of actions: The *proceedings* of the meeting included electing a new board. **2** An action started in a court of law: legal *proceedings*.

pro·ce·dure /prə·sē′jər/ *n.* A way of proceeding; a method followed in doing something.

pro·duc·tion /prə·duk′shən/ *n.* **1** The act or process of making or producing something. **2** The amount of goods or services produced. **3** Something produced, as a theatrical entertainment.

pro·duc·tiv·i·ty /prō′dək·tiv′ə·tē *or* präd′ək·tiv′ə·tē/ *n.* The quality or state of producing; the amount or rate of production.

pro·fes·sion /prə·fesh′ən/ *n.* **1** An occupation requiring mental labor and a good educational background. **2** A group of people who work in such an occupation.

prom·ise /prom′is/ *n., v.* **prom·ised, prom·is·ing** **1** *n.* A statement that someone will or will not do something. **2** *v.* To give a promise.

prop·a·gan·da /prop′ə·gan′də/ *n.* **1** An attempt to persuade others to accept certain ideas, attitudes, or actions. **2** Anything used for this purpose. ► *Propaganda* comes from the Latin word *propagare,* "to spread, extend, or propagate."

prop·er·ty /prop′ər·tē/ *n., pl.* **prop·er·ties** **1** Anything that a person legally possesses. **2** A piece of land. **3** A particular characteristic: Hardness is a *property* of steel.

pro·po·sal /prə·pō′zəl/ *n.* **1** Something offered or suggested, as a plan: a budget *proposal*. **2** An offer of marriage.

pro·vi·sion /prə·vizh′ən/ *n.* **1** The act of supplying or preparing: We made *provision* for the winter. **2** (*pl.*) Food or a supply of food: We had *provisions* for a week. **3** A requirement or condition: a *provision* in a will.

pry[1] /prī/ *v.* **pried, pry·ing,** *n., pl.* **pries** **1** *v.* To force open with a wedge or lever. **2** *n.* A type of lever; crowbar.

pry[2] /prī/ *v.* **pried, pry·ing** To look too closely; to snoop.

psy·chol·o·gist /sī·kol′ə·jəst/ *n.* A person who studies the mind and human behavior.

pueb·lo /pweb′lō/ *n., pl.* **pueb·los** **1** An adobe or stone building or group of buildings built by Native American tribes living in the southwestern United States. **2** (*written* **Pueblo**) A member of one of the Native American tribes that live in such buildings. *Alternate plural:* **pueblo.** ► *Pueblo* is a Spanish word meaning "village."

pum·per·nick·el /pum′pər·nik′əl/ *n.* A coarse, dark German bread made with rye and whole wheat flours.

pu·pil[1] /pyoo′pəl/ *n.* The dark, central part of the eye, which admits light to the retina.

pu·pil[2] /pyoo′pəl/ *n.* One who is instructed by a teacher; a student.

pur·sue /pər·s(y)oo′/ *v.* **pur·sued, pur·su·ing** **1** To chase. **2** To follow; to proceed with: to *pursue* a career.

Q

quan·ti·ty /kwon′tə·tē/ *n., pl.* **quan·ti·ties** A large number, total, or sum of something.

quar·rel /kwôr′əl/ *n., v.* **quar·reled, quar·rel·ing** **1** *n.* An angry argument. **2** *n.* The reason or cause of such an argument. **3** *v.* To argue. *Alternate spellings:* **quarrelled, quarrelling.**

quar·ter /kwôr′tər/ **1** *n.* One-fourth of a whole. **2** *v.* To divide into four parts. **3** *adj.* Being one of four equal parts. **4** *n.* A coin worth 25 cents.

quench /kwench/ *v.* **1** To satisfy (a thirst) by drinking. **2** To extinguish a fire by throwing water on it.

ques·tion·naire /kwes′chən·âr′/ *n.* A printed list of questions used in gathering information.

quit /kwit/ *v.* **quit** *or* **quit·ted, quit·ting** **1** To stop. **2** To give up a job.

---

act, āte, câre, ärt;   egg, ēven;   if, īce;   on, ōver, ôr;   book, food;   up, tûrn;
ə=a in *ago,* e in *listen,* i in *giraffe,* o in *pilot,* u in *circus;*   yoo=u in *music;*   oil;   out;
chair;   sing;   shop;   thank;   that;   zh in *treasure.*

quiz /kwiz/ *n., pl.* **quiz·zes,** *v.* **quizzed, quiz·zing** **1** *n.* A short test. **2** *v.* To test by asking questions.

R

ranch /ranch/ **1** *n.* A large farm where cattle and horses are raised. **2** *v.* To run a ranch.

rare[1] /râr/ *adj.* **rar·er, rar·est** Not often seen or found; unusual.—**rare'ly** *adv.*

rare[2] /râr/ *adj.* **rar·er, rar·est** Not cooked thoroughly.

ras·cal /ras'kəl/ *n.* **1** An unprincipled or dishonest person; a scoundrel. **2** A mischievous child or animal.

rav·i·o·li /rav'ē·ō'lē *or* räv'ē·ō'lē/ *n.* An Italian dish made with small cases of pasta filled with meat or cheese and usually served with tomato sauce. ► *Ravioli* is an Italian word meaning "little turnips."

re- *prefix* **1** Again: *rewrite* **2** Back: *repay.*

re·al·is·tic /rē'əl·is'tik/ *adj.* **1** Having to do with the practical and real: Theo's ideas are not very *realistic.* **2** Showing things just as they are: a *realistic* picture.

rea·son·a·ble /rē'zən·ə·bəl/ *adj.* **1** Having, using, or exhibiting reason or fairness; sensible. **2** Moderate or fair in price: *reasonable* prices.

reb·el *n. or* **re·bel** *v.* /n. reb'əl, v. ri·bel'/ *n., v.* **re·belled, re·bel·ling** **1** *n.* A person who resists authority or fights against it. **2** *v.* To rise up against a governing power. **3** *v.* To resist or feel opposition toward.

re·build /rē·bild'/ *v.* **re·built, re·build·ing** **1** To make extensive repairs; to remodel. **2** To build again.

re·ceipt /ri·sēt'/ *n.* **1** A slip of paper that shows that something has been received or paid for. **2** The receiving of something.

re·ceive /ri·sēv'/ *v.* **re·ceived, re·ceiv·ing** **1** To get or accept something. **2** To experience: to *receive* attention. **3** To learn or gain information: to *receive* news. **4** To admit or welcome, especially guests or visitors.

re·cent /rē'sənt/ *adj.* Not long past; having happened only a little while ago.

re·cit·al /ri·sīt'(ə)l/ *n.* **1** The act of telling or explaining in great detail: We listened to a *recital* of all his problems. **2** A public performance of music or dance, usually by a single performer or by students.

reck·less /rek'lis/ *adj.* Careless.—**reck'less·ly** *adv.*

re·claim /ri·klām'/ *v.* To bring something useless to a usable condition: Irrigation has *reclaimed* much desert land for farming.

rec·om·mend /rek'ə·mend'/ *v.* **1** To praise or speak in favor of. **2** To advise or suggest.

re·fresh·ment /ri·fresh'mənt/ *n.* **1** The act of reviving or refreshing. **2** The condition or state of being revived or refreshed. **3** (*pl.*) Food and drink.

re·gion /rē'jən/ *n.* **1** A section of land, generally large: the northeast *region* of the country. **2** Any area: He sometimes felt pains in the *region* of his chest.

reg·is·ter /rej'is·tər/ **1** *n.* A list or book with official records entered in it. **2** *v.* To put something into a record. **3** *v.* To enroll or sign up. **4** *n.* A machine that prints out and adds up the prices of things purchased: The last *register* is for express only.

re·gret *v.* To be sorry or sad about something. **2** *n.* Sorrow or sadness.

reg·u·lar·i·ty /reg'yə·lar'ə·tē/ *n., pl.* **reg·u·lar·i·ties** The condition or quality of being regular, steady, or systematic.

re·hear·sal /ri·hûr'səl/ *n.* A practice session.

re·la·tion /ri·lā'shən/ *n.* **1** Kinship, or a person related by kinship, a relative. **2** A connection between two or more things, as in meaning or thought: This sentence has no *relation* to the paragraph. **3** (*pl.*) The connection between people or countries: international *relations.*

rel·a·tive /rel'ə·tiv/ **1** *n.* A member of one's family; connected by blood or marriage. **2** *adj.* Having to do with: books *relative* to the subject. **3** *adj.* Having meaning only in relation to something else and changing as that thing changes: The words *high* and *low* have *relative* meanings. **4** *adj.* By comparison; comparative: We discussed the *relative* merits of buying a new car or a used car.

re·li·a·ble /ri·lī'ə·bəl/ *adj.* Able to be trusted; dependable: a *reliable* friend.

re·li·gion /ri·lij'ən/ *n.* A belief in God or in gods.

re·pel /ri·pel'/ *v.* **re·pelled, re·pel·ling** **1** To force or drive back. **2** To cause someone to draw back in disgust.

re·pub·lic /ri·pub'lik/ *n.* A type of government in which power and authority are granted to officials elected by and representing the people.

re·sent /ri·zent'/ *v.* To feel angry, hurt, or displeased: I *resent* your remark.

re·spond /ri·spond'/ *v.* **1** To answer or reply. **2** To react in any way.

responsibility

sabotage

re·spon·si·bil·i·ty /ri·spon′sə·bil′ə·tē/ *n., pl.* **re·spon·si·bil·i·ties** **1** The condition of being accountable: It was your *responsibility* to make sure all the doors were locked. **2** A person or duty that one is supposed to take care of or be accountable for.

re·spon·si·ble /ri·spon′sə·bəl/ *adj.* **1** Obliged to take care of, as a duty, trust, etc: She is *responsible* for feeding the dog. **2** Deserving credit or blame; accountable: He is *responsible* for the accident. **3** Having to do with trust or importance: a *responsible* individual. **4** Reliable; trustworthy.

re·tire·ment /re·tīr′mənt/ *n.* The act of withdrawing from active involvement in a career.

re·trieve /ri·trēv′/ *v.* **re·trieved, re·triev·ing** **1** To get back. **2** To bring back: The dog *retrieved* the ball.

re·vers·i·ble /ri·vûr′sə·bəl/ *adj.* **1** Finished on both sides so that either side may be the outside. **2** Able to go either forward or backward: Is this chemical process *reversible*?

re·vi·val /ri·vī′vəl/ *n.* **1** A restoring or return to life or consciousness. **2** A renewal of interest in something neglected or forgotten. **3** A meeting for the purpose of stirring up religious faith.

rev·o·lu·tion /rev′ə·loo′shən/ *n.* **1** The overthrow of a government by the people. **2** Sudden change in condition, method, etc.: Computer technology has caused a *revolution* in society. **3** Circular movement around an axis or center: The scientists traced the path of the satellite's *revolution* around the earth. **4** One complete revolving movement.

re·wind /rē′wīnd′/ *v.* **re·wound** To wind again: Please *rewind* the string as you pull in the kite.

ri·dic·u·lous /ri·dik′yə·ləs/ *adj.* Silly; causing laughter; making no sense; foolish: He asked a *ridiculous* question.

ri·ot /rī′ət/ **1** *n.* A violent or wild disturbance involving a large group of people. **2** *v.* To take part in such a disturbance.

ri·val /rī′vəl/ *n., v.* **ri·valed, ri·val·ing** **1** *n.* A competitor. **2** *adj. use:* a *rival* chess player. **3** *v.* To try to excel or outdo: Ed *rivaled* Ann for first place. *Alternate spellings:* **rivalled, rivalling.**

ro·bot /rō′bot *or* rō′bət/ *n.* **1** A machine that resembles a human being, built to do work in place of human beings. **2** A person who acts and responds in a mechanical way.

ro·dent /rōd′(ə)nt/ *n.* Any member of a group of small mammals, including mice, rats, squirrels, and beavers, that have very sharp front teeth.

ro·de·o /rō′dē·ō *or* rō·dā′ō/ *n., pl.* **ro·de·os** **1** A public contest and entertainment in which people compete in bronco riding, calf roping, steer wrestling, etc. **2** Driving cattle together; a roundup. ► *Rodeo* is a Spanish word used in Mexico to mean "a roundup."

ro·tate /rō′tāt/ *v.* **ro·tat·ed, ro·tat·ing** **1** To turn or cause to turn on an axis. **2** To alternate: Farmers *rotate* crops.

rouge /roozh/ *n., v.* **rouged, roug·ing** **1** *n.* A cosmetic used to color the cheeks and lips. **2** *v.* To put rouge on. ► *Rouge* is a French word meaning "red."

run·ner-up /run′ər·up′/ *n., pl.* **run·ners-up** A person or team finishing second in a game or contest.

ru·ral /roor′əl/ *adj.* Having to do with the country rather than the city.

S

sab·o·tage /sab′ə·täzh/ *n., v.* **sab·o·taged, sab·o·tag·ing** **1** *n.* The act of damaging an enemy's machinery, factories, railroads, highways, etc., during a war: Blowing up the bridge was an act of *sabotage*. **2** *n.* Damage to work, tools, machinery, etc., as an attack against an employer by dissatisfied laborers. **3** *v.* To damage or destroy in this way: The dishonest racer *sabotaged* his opponent's car by putting sand in the gas tank.

---

act, āte, câre, ärt;   egg, ēven;   if, īce;   on, ōver, ôr;   boŏk, foŏd;   up, tûrn;
ə=a in *ago,* e in *listen,* i in *giraffe,* o in *pilot,* u in *circus;*   yoō=u in *music;*   oil;   out;
chair;   sing;   shop;   thank;   that;   zh in *treasure.*

sacrifice   **serial**

sac·ri·fice /sak′rə·fīs/ *n., v.* **sac·ri·ficed, sac·ri·fic·ing** **1** *n.* The act of offering something up to a god. **2** *v.* To give up something important for the sake of something one feels is more important: She *sacrificed* her life to save ours. **3** *n.* In baseball, a hit that puts the batter out but allows a runner to reach the next base.

sad·ness /sad′nis/ *n.* The condition of being sad.

sales·clerk /sālz′klûrk′/ *n.* A person hired to sell goods in a store.

sa·li·va /sə·lī′və/ *n.* Liquid produced by glands in the mouth. ▶ *Saliva* is a Latin word meaning "the fluid secreted in the mouth."

sal·vage /sal′vij/ *v.* **sal·vaged, sal·vag·ing** To save from destruction: We *salvaged* some old furniture that someone had thrown out.

sat·is·fac·tion /sat′is·fak′shən/ *n.* **1** The act of fulfilling or satisfying a need. **2** Contentment, pleasure.

sat·is·fy /sat′is·fī/ *v.* **sat·is·fied, sat·is·fy·ing** **1** To fill a need or desire completely. **2** To free from doubt; to convince.

sauer·kraut /sour′krout′/ *n.* A German dish made from shredded, pickled cabbage. ▶ *Sauerkraut* comes from two German words: *sauer,* "sour," and *kraut,* "cabbage."

sau·sage /sô′sij/ *n.* Highly seasoned minced or chopped meat, often packed into a thin tube or skin.

sax·o·phone /sak′sə·fōn/ *n.* A wind instrument with a single reed in the mouthpiece and a curved body.

sched·ule /skej′ōōl/ *n., v.* **sched·uled, sched·ul·ing** **1** *n.* A plan of the times when certain things are to be done or to take place. **2** *v.* To establish a time order; to set a time: We *scheduled* an appointment.

scheme /skēm/ *n., v.* **schemed, schem·ing** **1** *n.* A plan or plot, especially one that is underhanded. **2** *v.* To plan or plot, often in a sneaky way. **3** *n.* An arrangement of something based on a plan or design: the color *scheme* of a room.

sci·en·tist /sī′ən·tist/ *n.* A person who specializes in the study of science, especially one of the physical or natural sciences.

scis·sors /siz′ərz/ *n. pl.* A cutting tool with two sharp blades that are attached to resemble an X and close together to cut.

scrap¹ /skrap/ *n., v.* **scrapped, scrap·ping** **1** *n.* A small piece; fragment. **2** *v.* To throw out or abandon as useless.

scrap² /skrap/ *v.* **scrapped, scrap·ping,** *n.* **1** *v.* To fight or quarrel. **2** *n.* A quarrel.

sculp·tor /skulp′tər/ *n.* An artist who creates a sculpture from stone, clay, metal, or wood.

sculp·ture /skulp′chər/ *n., v.* **sculp·tured, sculp·tur·ing** **1** *n.* The art of carving or shaping stone, clay, metal, or wood. **2** *n.* A work of art formed in this way. **3** *v.* To form or create by carving or shaping.

sec·re·tar·y /sek′rə·ter′ē/ *n., pl.* **sec·re·tar·ies** A person whose duties involve writing or typing letters, keeping records, filing, etc., for a person, company, club, committee, etc.: My *secretary* will give you an appointment.

semi- *prefix* **1** Not fully; partly: *semitropical.* **2** Exactly half: *semicircular.* **3** Taking place twice within the given period of time: *semimonthly.*

sem·i·an·nu·al /sem′ē·an′yōō·əl/ *adj.* Issued or occurring two times a year.

sem·i·cir·cle /sem′ē·sûr′kəl/ *n.* A half circle.

sem·i·fi·nal·ist /sem′ē·fī′nəl·ist/ *n.* A person who participates in the next-to-last round or match in a contest or tournament.

sem·i·pre·cious /sem′ē·presh′əs/ *adj.* Indicating gems, such as jade, opal, etc., that are valuable but less rare than precious stones.

sem·i·sweet /sem′ē·swēt′/ *adj.* Somewhat or slightly sweetened: *semisweet* chocolate.

sen·ate /sen′it/ *n.* **1** A governing body, usually possessing law-making powers. **2** (*written* **Senate**) The upper house in the legislative branch of the U.S. government or of a state or other government. ▶ *Senate* comes from the Latin word *senatus,* "council of elders."

sen·a·tor /sen′ə·tər/ *n.* (*sometimes written* **Senator**) An elected member of a senate; a member of the upper house of the U.S. Congress.

sen·ior /sēn′yər/ **1** *adj.* Older, higher in standing, or longer in a position: a *senior* partner in the firm. **2** *n.* The father, especially when the son has the same first name; usually abbreviated: Juan Roys, *Sr.* **3** *adj.* Pertaining to the last year of high school or college. **4** *n.* A person in the last year of high school or college.

sen·si·ble /sen′sə·bəl/ *adj.* Having or showing good sense or good judgment.—**sen′si·bly** *adv.*

sen·ti·men·tal /sen′tə·men′təl/ *adj.* **1** Having, showing, or appealing to emotions. **2** Of or having to do with emotions rather than logic.

se·ri·al /sir′ē·əl/ **1** *n.* A story presented in parts: The third part of the *serial* will be in

series   **sleigh**

Tuesday's paper. **2** *adj.* In a series.

se·ries /sir′ēz/ *n., pl.* **se·ries** A number of things, one after another.

se·ri·ous /sir′ē·əs/ *adj.* **1** Solemn: a very *serious* expression. **2** Earnest; sincere: a *serious* interest. **3** Very important: a *serious* decision. **4** Giving cause for worry: a *serious* illness.

se·vere /si·vir′/ *adj.* **se·ver·er, se·ver·est** **1** Very harsh; strict. **2** Serious; major: a *severe* headache.

shears /shirz/ *n. pl.* A large cutting tool with two blades like scissors.

sher·bet /shûr′bit/ *n.* A frozen, usually fruit-flavored dessert, like ice cream but made with water and milk instead of cream. ► *Sherbet* comes from a Turkish word meaning "drink." In the Middle East sherbet is not completely frozen but is enjoyed as a sweet, chilled drink.

sher·iff /sher′if/ The chief law officer of a county.

shield /shēld/ **1** *n.* A large board or broad metal piece with a handle in back, once carried by warriors to protect themselves in battle. **2** *n.* Something that protects one from harm or injury. **3** *v.* To protect or guard from harm or injury.

shish ke·bab /shish′ kə·bäb′/ A Middle Eastern dish made of chunks of meat, tomatoes, and onions broiled or roasted on a stick or skewer.

shorts /shôrts/ *n. pl.* **1** Pants that end above the knees. **2** Underwear for men or boys.

shrimp /shrimp/ *n., sing. or pl.* Any of numerous types of small edible shellfish with thin shells and long tails. *Alternate plural:* **shrimps.**

siege /sēj/ *n.* An attempt to capture a fortified place by surrounding it; blockade: The castle was under *siege* by the enemy.

si·er·ra /sē·er′ə/ *n.* A range or chain of mountains, especially one with a series of jagged peaks. ► *Sierra* is a Spanish word meaning "saw" and suggests the "saw-toothed" appearance of these mountains.

si·es·ta /sē·es′tə/ *n.* An afternoon nap. ► *Siesta* is a Spanish word meaning "a nap taken during the hottest part of the day."

sign /sīn/ **1** *n.* A symbol, object, expression, or motion that has meaning or stands for something: The *sign* for subtraction is −. He nodded as a *sign* of approval. **2** *n.* A board or posted command with writing that gives information or a warning about something: a stop *sign* **3** *n.* A clue, symptom, or indication: A stuffy nose may be a *sign* of a cold. **4** *v.* To write one's name in one's own handwriting: *sign* your name.

sig·na·ture /sig′nə·chər/ *n.* **1** A person's name written by that person. **2** Symbols or signs in music that indicate key and time.

si·lent /sī′lənt/ *adj.* **1** Making no noise; soundless. **2** Remaining quiet; not speaking. **3** Not actively involved in something: a *silent* partner.

sin·cer·i·ty /sin·ser′ə·tē/ *n.* The quality or condition of being honest or genuine; meaning what one says.

sin·is·ter /sin′is·tər/ *adj.* **1** Threatening evil; ominous: a *sinister* look. **2** Wicked or evil: a *sinister* thought.

si·phon /sī′fən/ **1** *n.* A bent tube that is used to transfer liquid out of one container into another by means of air pressure and gravity. **2** *v.* To draw out using a siphon. ► *Siphon* comes from the Greek word *siphon,* "a small pipe or reed."

sis·ter-in-law /sis′tər·in-lô′/ *n., pl.* **sis·ters-in-law** **1** The sister of the person one is married to. **2** The wife of one's brother or of one's spouse's brother.

sketch /skech/ **1** *n.* A quick, rough, or unfinished drawing. **2** *v.* To make a rough drawing or outline.

slacks /slaks/ *n. pl.* Long pants or trousers worn by men and women.

sleigh /slā/ **1** *n.* A vehicle with runners for use on the snow or ice, usually drawn by a horse. **2** *v.* To ride or travel in a sleigh.

---

act, āte, câre, ärt;   egg, ēven;   if, īce;   on, ōver, ôr;   bŏŏk, fōōd;   up, tûrn;
ə=a in *ago,* e in *listen,* i in *giraffe,* o in *pilot,* u in *circus;*   yōō=u in *music;*   oil;   out;
ch in *chair;* sing; sh in *shop;* th in *thank;* th in *that;* zh in *treasure.*

slight   **squirrel**

slight /slīt/ **1** *adj.* Very little; minor or unimportant: Jessica had a *slight* temperature yesterday. **2** *adj.* Thin or weak: The child looked frail and *slight*. **3** *v.* To pay little attention to; to ignore: Bonnie *slights* her own achievements.

sliv·er /sliv′ər/ **1** *n.* A long slender piece cut or broken off something; splinter: a *sliver* of glass. **2** *v.* To cut, split, or break into slivers: to *sliver* almonds.

slo·gan /slō′gən/ *n.* An expression or motto used in advertising or campaigning: The campaign *slogan* was very catchy.

smor·gas·bord /smôr′gəs·bôrd′/ *n.* A Scandinavian meal with a large variety of salads, cheeses, meats, and smoked and pickled fish served as a buffet.

smudge /smuj/ *v.* **smudged, smudg·ing,** *n.* **1** *v.* To blur, smear, or soil: Be careful not to *smudge* the fresh paint. **2** *n.* A dirty mark or spot: The dog's paw print left a *smudge* on my pants.

so·ci·e·ty /sə·sī′ə·tē/ *n., pl.* **so·ci·e·ties 1** A group of people that depend on one another in various ways and have certain customs in common. **2** A group of people who join together for a common or specific purpose: The bird *society* will meet twice a month. **3** The fashionable or wealthy group in a particular place. **4** Companionship: The hermit avoided the *society* of other people.

sol·dier /sōl′jər/ *n.* A person who serves in an army, especially someone who is not an officer: After three years the *soldier* was returning home.

sor·row /sor′ō/ **1** *n.* Great sadness or grief. **2** *n.* The cause of great sadness or grief. **3** *v.* To feel or show sadness or grief.

south·ern /suth′ərn/ *adj.* Of, from, in, or toward the south: My apartment has a *southern* exposure.

sov·er·eign /sov′rən/ **1** *n.* A monarch or ruler. **2** *adj.* Possessing total or supreme power: a *sovereign* king. **3** *adj.* Best; greatest: the *sovereign* good of the nation. **4** *adj.* Free from being controlled by another; independent: The United States is a *sovereign* country.

spar·kle /spär′kəl/ *v.* **spar·kled, spar·kling,** *n.* **1** *v.* To shine or glitter as if giving off sparks of light. **2** *adj. use: sparkling* crystal. **3** *n.* A flash. **4** *v.* To be lively and bright.

spec·ta·tor /spek′tā·tər/ *n.* A person who watches an event but does not take part in it; observer.

spin·ach /spin′ich/ *n.* The large dark green leaves of a garden herb, used as a vegetable or salad green.

spi·ral /spī′rəl/ *n., adj., v.* **spi·raled, spi·ral·ing 1** *n.* A line on a flat plane that curls out from a central point, as the lines on a pinwheel or a jelly roll. **2** *n.* A curve or curl that winds around, as the thread of a screw. **3** *adj.* Winding: a *spiral* staircase. **4** *v.* To take or cause to take a winding path or form: The football *spiraled* high into the air. *Alternate spellings:* **spiralled, spiralling.**

sponge /spunj/ *n., v.* **sponged, spong·ing 1** *n.* A simple water animal whose dried skeleton is used for washing, cleaning, etc. **2** *n.* Any spongelike absorbent material. **3** *v.* To wipe or clean with a sponge.

spoon·ful /spoon′fool′/ *n., pl.* **spoon·fuls** The amount that fills a spoon.

sprawl /sprôl/ *v.* **1** To sit or lie with legs and arms spread out. **2** To spread out: The city *sprawls* over three counties.

squall /skwôl/ **1** *n.* A sudden, fierce wind, which often brings with it rain or snow. **2** *v.* To cry or scream loudly, as babies do.

squir·rel /skwûr′əl/ *n.* A small animal with sharp teeth and a long bushy tail.

stadium   **sukiyaki**

sta·di·um /stā′dē·əm/ *n., pl.* **sta·di·ums** A large structure with tiers of seats for spectators built around a playing field. *Alternate plural:* **stadia.**

stair /stâr/ *n.*   **1** One of a series of steps that go from one level to another.   **2** (*usually pl.*) A series of steps.

stam·i·na /stam′ə·nə/ *n.* Ability to endure; strength.   ► *Stamina* comes from the Latin word *stamen,* "the thread of life spun by the Fates."

stam·pede /stam·pēd′/ *n., v.* **stam·ped·ed, stam·ped·ing**   **1** *n.* A sudden rush or running of animals.   **2** *v.* To be a part of or to bring about a stampede.   ► *Stampede* comes from the American-Spanish word *estampida,* "stamping or trampling."

stand·by /stan(d)′bī′/ *n.*   **1** A person or thing ready to take another's place.   **2** Something you can always depend on.

stand·in /stand′in′/ *n.* A person who substitutes for another person in some way, especially a person who takes an actor's place.

stare /stâr/ *v.* **stared, star·ing,** *n.*   **1** *v.* To look hard at something, often without blinking.   **2** *n.* A steady, intense gaze.

sta·tion·ar·y /stā′shən·er′ē/ *adj.* Staying or keeping in one place; not moving or movable.

sta·tion·er·y /stā′shən·er′ē/ *n.* Materials used in writing, especially letter paper and envelopes.

stat·is·ti·cian /stat′is·tish′ən/ *n.* A person who is skilled in statistics, the science of collecting and analyzing numerical facts.

stat·ue /stach′o͞o/ *n.* A likeness of a person, animal, etc., that is carved, molded, or cast; figurine.

steal /stēl/ *v.* **stole, sto·len, steal·ing**   **1** To take another's property without permission; to rob.   **2** To win over or take by surprise or skill: The dog *stole* the show.   **3** To move or go secretly: to *steal* out of the room.   **4** In baseball, to reach a base without the help of a batted ball or an error.

stealth·y /stel′thē/ *adj.* **stealth·i·er, stealth·i·est** Acting in secret, or done in secret; sneaky.

steel /stēl/ *n.*   **1** A hard metal that contains iron, carbon, and sometimes other elements.   **2** *adj. use:* a *steel* wrench.   **3** A nature that is hard, cold, etc., like steel: nerves of *steel.*

stock·hold·er /stok′hōl′dər/ *n.* A person who owns shares in a corporation.

strug·gle /strug′əl/ *n., v.* **strug·gled, strug·gling**   **1** *n.* A strong effort.   **2** *v.* To strive or strain; to try hard, especially to overcome something or someone.   **3** *n.* A fight.

stun /stun/ *v.* **stunned, stun·ning**   **1** To knock unconscious; to make dizzy.   **2** To shock or astonish.

stur·dy /stûr′dē/ *adj.* **stur·di·er, stur·di·est** Strong; hardy; tough.

style /stīl/ *n., v.* **styled, styl·ing**   **1** *n.* The particular method in which something is done or created.   **2** *n.* A distinctive form of expression, as in writing, speaking, or painting.   **3** *n.* A currently accepted fashion.   **4** *v.* To design.   **5** *n.* A manner of living, especially one that is fashionable or elegant.

sub- *prefix* Under; beneath; below: *submarine.*

sub·mit /səb·mit′/ *v.* **sub·mit·ted, sub·mit·ting**   **1** To give up; to yield.   **2** To give in or present for approval.

sub·scrip·tion /səb·skrip′shən/ *n.* An agreement that a person will receive a certain number of issues of a publication, etc.: My *subscription* was renewed.

suc·ceed /sək·sēd′/ *v.*   **1** To accomplish what is planned or desired.   **2** To come after: She *succeeded* him as mayor.

suc·cess·ful /sək·ses′fəl/ *adj.* Achieving a favorable outcome or a desired goal.

sug·ges·tion /sə(g)·jes′chən/ *n.*   **1** The act of proposing or suggesting.   **2** Something that is proposed or suggested.   **3** A trace or hint.

su·ki·ya·ki /so͞o′kē·yä′kē/ *n.* A Japanese dish of lightly fried strips of meat and vegetables served with rice.

act, āte, câre, ärt;   egg, ēven;   if, īce;   on, ōver, ôr;   bo͝ok, fo͞od;   up, tûrn;
ə=a in *ago,* e in *listen,* i in *giraffe,* o in *pilot,* u in *circus;*   yo͞o=u in *music;*   oil;   out;
          chair; si**ng**; **sh**op; **th**ank; **th**at; **zh** in *treasure.*

sulky   tax

sulk·y /sul′kē/ *adj.* **sulk·i·er, sulk·i·est** Sullen; cranky; bad-tempered.

sum·mon /sum′ən/ *v.* **1** To send for; to command to come. **2** To stir into action; to arouse.

sun·glass·es /sun′glas′iz/ *n. pl.* Spectacles worn to protect the eyes from glare, usually made with colored glass or plastic: You should not wear *sunglasses* in the house.

super- *prefix* Over; above: *superhuman.*

su·per·fi·cial /soo′pər·fish′əl/ *adj.* **1** Of, on, or affecting only the surface: a *superficial* wound. **2** Not going past the surface or beyond the obvious; not deep or thorough; shallow or hasty: *superficial* understanding; a *superficial* search. **3** Not genuine: a *superficial* likeness.

su·per·flu·ous /soo·pûr′floo·əs/ *adj.* Extra and useless; unnecessary: *superfluous* words.

su·per·in·ten·dent /soo′pər·in·ten′dənt/ *n.* The person in charge of directing some work, organization, department, etc. ► *Superintendent* comes from Latin *super-,* "over or above," and *intendere,* "to attend or direct attention to."

su·pe·ri·or /sə·pir′ē·ər/ **1** *adj.* Much better than average; extremely good. **2** *adj.* Thinking oneself better than another; conceited. **3** *n.* A person with greater authority; boss: I have a meeting with my *superior* tomorrow. **4** *adj.* Higher in rank or authority. ► *Superior* is a Latin word meaning "higher or above."

su·per·la·tive /sə·pûr′lə·tiv *or* soo·pûr′lə·tiv/ **1** *adj.* Excellent to the highest degree; supreme: *superlative* work. **2** *n.* A grammatical term for the highest degree of comparison for an adjective or adverb: *Best, most,* and *greatest* are *superlatives.*

su·per·nat·u·ral /soo′pər·nach′ər·əl/ *adj.* Outside or having power over the known laws or forces of nature. ► *Supernatural* comes from Latin *super-,* "over or above," and *natura,* "nature."

su·per·sti·tion /soo′pər·stish′ən/ *n.* An unreasoning fear or belief that certain objects, places, or actions have power over the normal course of nature: Believing that horseshoes bring good luck is a *superstition.*

su·per·vi·sion /soo′pər·vizh′ən/ *n.* Direction; overseeing. ► *Supervision* comes from Latin *super-,* "over or above," and *videre,* "to see."

sup·ple·ment /*n.* sup′lə·mənt, *v.* sup′lə·ment/ **1** *n.* Something added, often to supply a lack: a vitamin *supplement.* **2** *v.* To provide or add what is missing: to *supplement* your diet. **3** *n.* An extra section of a newspaper, book, journal, etc., providing additional information: The newspaper had a *supplement* on the election.

sur·geon /sûr′jən/ *n.* A doctor whose practice is largely limited to the repair or removal of diseased or injured organs.

sur·plus /sûr′plus/ *n.* The amount remaining after a need has been met.

sur·round /sə·round′/ *v.* To enclose completely; to encircle.

sur·viv·al /sər·vī′vəl/ *n.* The act or condition of outliving, outlasting, or surviving.

sus·pi·cion /sə·spish′ən/ *n.* **1** An unproven idea, belief, or feeling that something is wrong or bad; the act of suspecting guilt. **2** The act of considering someone as a suspect.

sus·tain /sə·stān′/ *v.* **1** To maintain the strength or spirits of: Ellen's calm *sustained* us when we were afraid. **2** To supply with nourishment: Food and water are necessary to *sustain* life.

swap /swop/ *v.* **swapped, swap·ping,** *n.* **1** *v.* To give in exchange. **2** *n.* A trade.

sym·bol /sim′bəl/ *n.* **1** Something that stands for something else. **2** A mark or sign that has meaning, as a letter, number, dollar sign, etc.

sym·pa·thize /sim′pə·thīz/ *v.* **sym·pa·thized, sym·pa·thiz·ing** **1** To share someone else's feelings. **2** To have or express compassion or understanding.

sym·pho·ny /sim′fə·nē/ *n., pl.* **sym·pho·nies** A musical composition usually written in four parts or movements and played by an orchestra. ► *Symphony* comes from Greek *syn-,* "together," and *phone,* "voice, sound."

symp·tom /sim′təm/ *n.* Evidence of the existence of something; sign, indication.

T

ta·co /tä′kō/ *n., pl.* **ta·cos** A crisp tortilla folded over and filled with meat, cheese, chili peppers, etc. ► *Taco* is a Spanish word meaning "snack." The food itself is of Mexican origin.

tan·gi·ble /tan′jə·bəl/ *adj.* **1** Capable of being touched. **2** Real or concrete.

tan·trum /tan′trəm/ *n.* A fit of anger.

tar·iff /tar′if/ *n.* A tax or duty paid on imported or exported goods.

tax /taks/ **1** *n.* An amount of money paid by individuals, businesses, etc., and used for public purposes. **2** *v.* To put a tax on.

tech·ni·cian /tek·nish′ən/ *n.* A person skilled in the technical details of an art or science: a television *technician*.

tech·nique /tek·nēk′/ *n.* **1** Skill and control in doing something: The violinist worked hard to improve his *technique*. **2** A method of doing something: a new surgical *technique*.

tech·nol·o·gy /tek·nol′ə·jē/ *n., pl.* **tech·nol·o·gies** The use of technical methods to achieve practical purposes.

ten·sion /ten′shən/ *n.* **1** The act or condition of stretching tight or being stretched: Too much *tension* will cause a guitar string to snap. **2** Mental or emotional strain; anxiety.

ter·i·ya·ki /ter′ē·(y)äk′ē/ *n.* A Japanese dish of meat, chicken, or fish, soaked in a spicy sauce and broiled. ► *Teriyaki* comes from two Japanese words: *teri*, "sunshine," and *yaki*, "roast."

ter·mi·nal /tûr′mə·nəl/ **1** *adj.* At, forming, or having to do with a limit or end. **2** *n.* A boundary or end. **3** *n.* A railway or bus station: I'll meet you at the bus *terminal*. **4** *n.* The point at which electric current enters or leaves a device.

ter·ri·ble /ter′ə·bəl/ *adj.* **1** Distressing; severe: a *terrible* winter. **2** Extremely bad; awful: a *terrible* movie.

ter·ri·fy /ter′ə·fī/ *v.* **ter·ri·fied, ter·ri·fy·ing** To fill with terror or tremendous fear.

tex·tile /teks′til *or* teks′tīl/ **1** *n.* A woven or knitted cloth. **2** *adj.* Of or having to do with textiles.

ther·a·pist /ther′ə·pist/ *n.* A person whose work involves treating physical or psychological diseases, disabilities, etc.: My physical *therapist* said I am improving.

thief /thēf/ *n.* One who steals; robber.

threat /thret/ *n.* **1** A warning that one intends to hurt or punish another person or thing. **2** A sign that something bad or undesirable will happen: a *threat* of snow.

thun·der /thun′dər/ **1** *n.* The sound that follows a flash of lightning, caused by the expansion of air in the path of the electrical discharge. **2** *n.* A loud rumbling noise. **3** *v.* To speak with a thundering sound: to *thunder* orders.

tim·id /tim′id/ *adj.* Lacking self-confidence or courage; shy.

tis·sue /tish′oo/ *n.* **1** A group of cells in a plant or animal that are similar and have a specific function: lung *tissue*. **2** Light, absorbent paper used as a handkerchief. **3** Tissue paper: I wrapped his gift in brightly colored *tissue*.

to·ma·to /tə·mā′tō *or* tə·mä′tō/ *n., pl.* **to·ma·toes** A round, red, pulpy fruit, usually used as a vegetable: Please put *tomatoes* in my salad.

tongue /tung/ *n.* **1** A muscular organ attached at one end inside the mouth, used for eating, tasting, and speaking. **2** Power or manner of speech; way in which something is said: He has a sharp *tongue*. **3** A language: the French *tongue*. **4** The flap in a shoe that lies over the instep of the foot. ► *Tongue* comes from Middle English *tunge*, but its spelling was influenced by the French word for "tongue," *langue*.

tor·na·do /tôr′nā′dō/ *n., pl.* **tor·na·does** A violent, destructive whirling wind that forms a funnel-shaped cloud: The last *tornado* in Kansas was very destructive. *Alternate plural:* **tornados.**

tor·til·la /tôr·tē′yə/ *n.* A flat Mexican pancake made with coarse cornmeal: I had a *tortilla* for lunch. ► *Tortilla* is a Spanish word meaning "round loaf of bread." The food itself is of Mexican origin.

to·tal /tōt′(ə)l/ *n., adj., v.* **to·taled, to·tal·ing** **1** *n.* The whole amount: Find the *total* of the three numbers. **2** *adj. use:* the *total* amount. **3** *v.* To add up: We *totaled* our expenses for the week. **4** *v.* To amount to: Our expenses *totaled* $152.00. **5** *adj.* Complete in extent or degree: a *total* failure. *Alternate spellings:* **totalled, totalling.**

---

act, āte, câre, ärt;   egg, ēven;   if, īce;   on, ōver, ôr;   book, food;   up, tûrn;
ə=a in *ago*, e in *listen*, i in *giraffe*, o in *pilot*, u in *circus;*   yoo=u in *music;*   oil;   out;
chair; sing; shop; thank; that; zh in *treasure.*

tour·na·ment /tŏŏr′nə·mənt *or* tûr′nə·mənt/ *n.* **1** A medieval contest in which knights on horseback, armed with lances, attempted to knock their opponents off their horses. **2** A series of games or matches involving many players.

trace·a·ble /trā′sə·bəl/ *adj.* Able to be traced or followed: *traceable* evidence.

tra·di·tion·al /trə·dish′ən·əl/ *adj.* Following established social patterns or customs; customary: The dancers wore *traditional* costumes.—**tra·di′tion·al·ly** *adv.*

tram·ple /tram′pəl/ *v.* **tram·pled, tram·pling** To flatten by stepping on: The crowd *trampled* the flowers.

trans- *prefix* Across; through: *transatlantic.*

trans·ac·tion /trans·ak′shən *or* tranz·ak′shən/ *n.* The act of carrying out or doing, especially an exchange with other people: business *transactions.*

trans·fer /*v.* trans′fər *or* trans·fûr′, *n.* trans′fər/ *v.* **trans·ferred, trans·fer·ring,** *n.* **1** *v.* To move or send from one person or place to another: to *transfer* to another school. **2** *n.* The act of transferring.

trans·form /trans·fôrm′/ *v.* **1** To change significantly in appearance or condition: Heavy rains *transformed* the lawn into a giant mud puddle. **2** To change an electrical current; to convert electricity. ► *Transform* comes from Latin *trans-,* "across, through," and *formare,* "to form or shape."

trans·fu·sion /trans·fyŏŏ′zhən/ *n.* The process of transferring blood into a person or animal that has lost blood because of bleeding or illness. ► *Transfusion* comes from Latin *trans-,* "across, through," and *fundere,* "to pour."

tran·sis·tor /tran·zis′tər/ *n.* An electronic device that allows the current in one circuit to control the current in another, used in radios, television sets, computers, etc.

trans·late /trans·lāt′ *or* tranz′lāt/ *v.* **trans·lat·ed, trans·lat·ing** To change something written or spoken from one language into another: The book was *translated* from Italian into English. ► *Translate* comes from Latin *trans-,* "across, through," and *latus,* "carry."

trans·mis·sion /trans·mish′ən/ *n.* **1** The act of sending or passing something, as from one person to another. **2** A device that transfers power from the engine to the driving wheels in an automobile. ► *Transmission* comes from Latin *trans-,* "across, through" and *mittere,* "to send."

trans·par·ent /trans·pâr′ənt/ *adj.* **1** Able to be seen through: a *transparent* covering. **2** Easily seen through or detected: a *transparent* excuse. **3** Easily understood; obvious: The story's plot was too *transparent.* ► *Transparent* comes from Latin *trans-,* "across, through," and *parere,* "to show oneself."

trans·plant /trans·plant′/ *v.* **1** To remove a plant from the soil in which it is growing and plant it elsewhere. **2** To remove and reset an organ or tissue from one part of the body to another or from one person to another. ► *Transplant* comes from Latin *trans-,* "across, through," and *plantare,* "to plant."

trans·por·ta·tion /trans′pər·tā′shən/ *n.* **1** The act of transporting. **2** The state of being transported. **3** A means or system of transportation: public *transportation.*

trea·ty /trēt′ē/ *n., pl.* **trea·ties** A formal agreement between two or more countries regarding peace, trade, etc.

trek /trek/ *v.* **trekked, trek·king,** *n.* **1** *v.* To make a long, slow, hard journey: She *trekked* across the hot desert. **2** *n.* A long, hard journey or expedition. ● *Trek* is a word that is sometimes used humorously: I had to *trek* back home and get my baseball glove.

trem·ble /trem′bəl/ *v.* **trem·bled, trem·bling** To shake, as with fear, weakness, cold, etc.

tri- *prefix* Three: *tricycle.*

tri·an·gle /trī′ang′gəl/ *n.* **1** A plane figure that has three sides and three angles. **2** Something having this shape. **3** A metal musical instrument shaped like a triangle that produces a sound when struck with a metal rod.

tri·an·gu·lar /trī·ang′gyə·lər/ *adj.* Having the shape of a triangle; having three sides and three angles.

tri·um·phant /trī·um′fənt/ Proud or joyful over victory; successful: a *triumphant* smile.—**tri·um′phant·ly** *adv.*

trot /trot/ *n., v.* **trot·ted, trot·ting** **1** *n.* A moderately fast gait of a horse. **2** *v.* To move or cause to move in this gait. **3** *n.* A jogging gait of a human. **4** *v.* To move at this pace.

trout /trout/ *n., pl.* **trout** Any of several edible fishes found chiefly in fresh water.

tu·na /tŏŏ′nə/ *n., pl.* **tu·na** A large edible ocean fish. *Alternate plural:* **tunas.**

tune-up /t(y)ŏŏn′up′/ *n.* The adjustment of all the parts of a machine, especially an engine, so that it works smoothly.

tur·quoise /tûr′k(w)oiz/   **1** *n.* A sky-blue to greenish-blue mineral.   **2** *n., adj.* A greenish-blue color. *Alternate spelling:* **turquois.**

ty·rant /tī′rənt/ *n.*   **1** An all-powerful ruler.   **2** Someone who exercises power unfairly or cruelly.

U

ul·ti·ma·tum /ul′tə·mā′təm/ *n., pl.* **ul·ti·ma·tums** A final proposal, offer, or demand, with the likelihood that the consequences will be serious if refused: Joe gave me an *ultimatum. Alternate plural:* **ultimata.** ► *Ultimatum* comes from the Latin word *ultimatus,* "final."

um·pire /um′pīr/ *n., v.* **um·pired, um·pir·ing**   **1** *n.* A person who rules on plays in a sports contest, particularly baseball: The *umpire* said I was out at third base.   **2** *v.* To act as an umpire of a game.

un-[1] *prefix* Not; the opposite of: *unable.*

un-[2] *prefix* To do the opposite of: *untie.*

u·nan·i·mous /yōō·nan′ə·məs/ *adj.* In complete agreement; being of one mind: a *unanimous* decision. ► *Unanimous* comes from Latin *uni-,* "one," and *animus,* "mind."

un·cer·tain /un·sûr′tən/ *adj.*   **1** Not certain or sure; doubtful.   **2** Not capable of being predicted: The results are *uncertain.*   **3** Not to be depended on; apt to change suddenly: *uncertain* weather—**un·cer′tain·ly** *adv.*

un·cer·tain·ty /un·sûr′tən·tē/ *n., pl.* **un·cer·tain·ties** Lack of assurance; doubt.

un·con·sti·tu·tion·al /un′kon·sti·t(y)ōō′shən·əl/ *adj.* Violating the basic laws set out in the constitution of a country, organization, etc.

uni- *prefix* One: *unilateral.*

u·ni·corn /yōō′nə·kôrn/ *n.* A mythical animal that resembles a horse and has one long horn on its forehead: The circus claims to have a *unicorn.* ► *Unicorn* comes from Latin *uni-,* "one," and *corn(u),* "horn."

u·ni·cy·cle /yōō′nə·sī′kəl/ *n.* A pedaled vehicle similar to a bicycle but with only one wheel. ► *Unicycle* comes from Latin *uni-,* "one," and *cyclum,* "wheel."

u·ni·form /yōō′nə·fôrm/   **1** *adj.* Alike; not varying or changing.   **2** *n.* A specific outfit or dress worn by members of a group. ► *Uniform* comes from Latin *uni-,* "one," and *forma,* "shape."

u·ni·fy /yōō′nə·fī/ *v.* **u·ni·fied, u·ni·fy·ing** To bring together or form into one; to unite.

u·nique /yōō·nēk′/ *adj.*   **1** Unusual; rare: This is a *unique* gadget.   **2** Being one of a kind: This clock is *unique.*

u·ni·son /yōō′nə·sən/ *n.*   **1** Agreement in sound or motion: to sing in *unison.*   **2** Agreement: We were in *unison* about our decision. ► *Unison* comes from Latin *uni-,* "one," and *sonus,* "sound."

u·nit /yōō′nit/ *n.*   **1** A single person or thing, complete in itself but considered as part of a larger whole: The cell is the structural *unit* of animals and plants.   **2** A group of persons or things thought of as being complete in itself: a military *unit.*   **3** A part serving a special purpose: the cooling *unit* of a freezer.   **4** A standard quantity used as a measure: An hour is a *unit* of time.

u·ni·ver·sal /yōō′nə·vûr′səl/ *adj.* Common to all or occurring everywhere.

u·ni·verse /yōō′nə·vûrs/ *n.* Everything that exists, including the earth, sun, stars, planets, and outer space.

u·ni·ver·si·ty /yōō′nə·vûr′sə·tē/ *n., pl.* **u·ni·ver·si·ties** An institution of higher learning, usually including undergraduate colleges and schools for graduate and professional studies. ► *University* comes from the Latin word *universitas,* "whole."

un·nec·es·sar·y /un·nes′ə·ser′ē/ *adj.* Not needed or required; needless: It is *unnecessary* for you to drive me home.

un·pleas·ant /un·plez′ənt/ *adj.* Not pleasing; objectionable.

un·u·su·al /un·yōō′zhōō·əl/ *adj.* Uncommon; rare; not ordinary or usual.—**un·u′su·al·ly** *adv.*

un·wield·y /un·wēl′dē/ *adj.* Difficult or awkward to handle or manage.

---

act, āte, câre, ärt;   egg, ēven;   if, īce;   on, ōver, ôr;   bŏŏk, fōōd;   up, tûrn;
ə=a in *ago,* e in *listen,* i in *giraffe,* o in *pilot,* u in *circus;*   yōō=u in *music;*   oil;   out;
chair;   sing;   shop;   thank;   that;   zh in *treasure.*

upset
volcano

up·set /v., adj. up·set′, n., adj. up′set′/ v. **up·set, up·set·ting,** n., adj. **1** v. To overturn. **2** v. To disturb something arranged or ordered. **3.** v. To disturb or make uneasy. **4** adj. Disturbed or worried. **5** v. To defeat someone favored to win. **6** n. Such a defeat.

ur·ban /ûr′bən/ adj. Having to do with cities rather than the country.

V

vac·u·um /vak′yoo(·ə)m/ n. A space empty of all matter, even air.

vague /vāg/ adj. **va·guer, va·guest** **1** Blurry; not clear or definite: *vague* plans. **2** Not thinking or expressing oneself clearly: She was very *vague* about the details of the accident. ► *Vague* comes from the French word *vaguer,* "to roam or wander."

val·u·a·ble /val′y(oo·)ə·bəl/ **1** adj. Having worth, especially having a high value or price. **2** n. (usually pl.) Something worth a great deal, as jewelry, antiques, etc.: The *valuables* were kept in a safe.

va·nil·la /və·nil′ə/ n. A flavoring made from the seed pods of a tropical orchid. ► *Vanilla* comes from the Spanish word *vainilla,* "a little pod."

var·ied /vâr′ēd/ adj. **1** Changed or altered. **2** Made up of different parts.

var·y /vâr′ē/ v. **var·ied, var·y·ing** **1** To change or alter. **2** To be different in some way.

veg·e·tar·i·an /vej′ə·târ′ē·ən/ **1** n. A person who eats no meat. **2** adj. Made up of only fruits and vegetables.

ven·om /ven′əm/ n. **1** Poison, especially the kind produced by certain snakes, spiders, or other animals that bite or sting. **2** Hatred; bitterness.

ver·sus /vûr′səs/ prep. **1** Against: The basketball game featured the faculty *versus* the students. **2** In contrast to: fact *versus* opinion. *Abbreviation:* **vs.** ► *Versus* is a Latin word meaning "face to face, as with an opponent."

ves·sel /ves′(ə)l/ n. **1** A hollow container, as a bowl: He filled a *vessel* with water. **2** A boat that is larger than a rowboat. **3** A vein or artery for carrying blood through the body: a blood *vessel.*

vet·er·an /vet′ər·ən or vet′rən/ n. **1** A person who has served in the armed forces. **2** A person with long experience in something: *Veterans* of these cold winters know how to dress to keep warm. **3** adj. use: a *veteran* entertainer.

vet·er·i·nar·i·an /vet′ər·ə·nâr′ē·ən/ n. A doctor who treats animals: I have to take my dog to the *veterinarian* today.

ve·to /vē′tō/ n., pl. **ve·toes,** v. **ve·toed, ve·to·ing** **1** n. The right of a person in authority to reject a bill already passed by the legislature. **2** v. To reject a bill: The governor *vetoed* the bill. **3** v. To forbid, prohibit, or reject officially: The principal *vetoed* the party. ► *Veto* is a Latin word meaning "I forbid."

vic·to·ry /vik′tər·ē/ n., pl. **vic·to·ries** The defeat of an enemy or opponent; success: The *victory* was ours.

view /vyoo/ **1** v. To look at: They *viewed* the storm with alarm. **2** n. Area of vision: come into *view.* **3** n. What is looked at or seen: a beautiful *view.* **4** n. An opinion or belief: my *views* on the subject.

vig·il /vij′əl/ n. The act of keeping awake in order to watch, protect, or honor: The mourners kept a *vigil* all night long.

vig·i·lan·te /vig′ə·lan′tē/ n. A member of a citizens' group that, without authority, assumes the task of keeping order and punishing crimes.

vil·lain /vil′ən/ n. A wicked person; wrongdoer, especially an evil character in a play, novel, movie, etc.: Bruce will play the *villain* in the school play.

vi·rus /vī′rəs/ n. Any of a variety of tiny organisms that multiply in certain living cells, causing various diseases. ► *Virus* is a Latin word meaning "slimy liquid or poison."

vol·ca·no /vol·kā′nō/ n., pl. **vol·ca·noes** **1** An opening in the earth's surface through which lava, steam, ashes, etc., are released, forming a cone-shaped hill or mountain. **2** The hill or mountain itself. *Alternate plural:* **volcanos.**

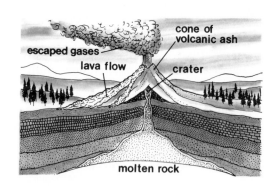

voyage   yogurt

voy·age /voi′ij/ *n.*, *v.* **voy·aged**, **voy·ag·ing**
1 *n.* A trip by water. **2** *n.* Any journey, as
one through air or space. **3** *v.* To travel on
a voyage.

W

waltz /wôlts/ **1** *n.* A graceful ballroom dance.
2 *v.* To dance a waltz. **3** *n.* Music for a
waltz.
watch·ful /woch′fəl/ *adj.* Watching carefully;
alert.
wedge /wej/ *n.*, *v.* **wedged**, **wedg·ing** **1** *n.*
Anything shaped like a triangle with two
equal sides: a *wedge* of cheese. **2** *v.* To
squeeze or pack into a small space.
weight /wāt/ *n.* **1** How heavy something is;
heaviness as measured in pounds, grams, or
other units. **2** A metal balance for a scale.
3 Having importance or significance: Her
decisions carry *weight*.
weird /wird/ *adj.* Strange or ghostly; eerie.
whim /(h)wim/ *n.* A sudden notion or desire
that has no important cause.
whis·tle /(h)wis′(ə)l/ *v.* **whis·tled**, **whis·
tling**, *n.* **1** *v.* To make a sound by blowing
air through the teeth or through puckered
lips. **2** *n.* The act of whistling. **3** *n.* A
small wind instrument that produces a
sound when air is blown through it.
wife /wīf/ *n.*, *pl.* **wives** A woman to whom a
man is married.
wit·ty /wit′ē/ *adj.* **wit·ti·er**, **wit·ti·est** Clever;
amusing; very funny.
won·ton /wän′tän′/ *n.* A flat, small Chinese
pie made from noodle dough filled with
meat and usually cooked in soup or fried.
► *Wonton* is a Chinese word meaning "pas-
try."
wood·cut /wŏŏd′kut′/ *n.* **1** A block of wood
on which a picture or design has been
carved. **2** A print made from a carved wood
block.

wrap /rap/ *v.* **wrapped** or **wrapt**, **wrap·ping**,
n. **1** *v.* To put a cover around something.
2 *v.* To wind around. **3** *n.* An outer garment.

X

xy·lo·phone /zī′lə·fōn/ *n.* A percussion instrument with bars of different lengths that produce musical sounds when struck by mal-
lets.

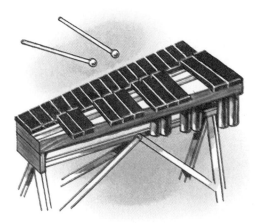

Y

yield /yēld/ **1** *v.* To give up or give way; to
surrender: He *yielded* to our coaxing and
came to the party. **2** *v.* To produce or give
in return for work or investment: The farm
yielded a good crop. **3** *n.* The amount
yielded or produced: The *yield* was one
hundred bushels per acre.
yo·gurt /yō′gŏŏrt/ *n.* A Middle Eastern food
made by adding special bacteria to milk.
Yogurt is thick like sour cream or custard.
Alternate spelling: **yoghurt.** ► *Yogurt* is a
Turkish word.

---

act, āte, câre, ärt;   egg, ēven;   if, īce;   on, ōver, ôr;   bŏŏk, fōōd;   up, tûrn;
ə=**a** in *ago*, **e** in *listen*, **i** in *giraffe*, **o** in *pilot*, **u** in *circus*;   yŏŏ=**u** in *music*;   oil;   out;
chair; si**ng**; **sh**op; **th**ank; **th**at; **zh** in *treasure*.

SPELLING THESAURUS

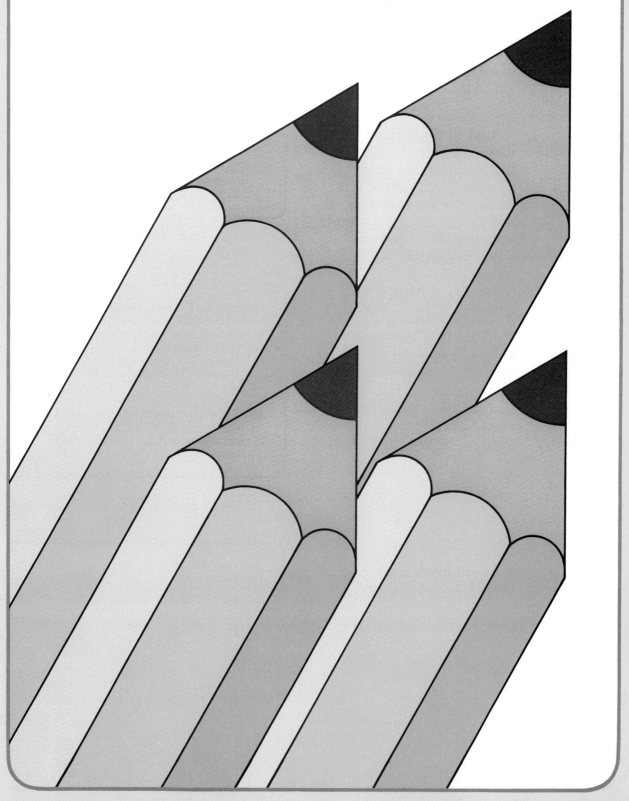

What Is a Thesaurus?

A **thesaurus** lists words and their synonyms. Like a dictionary, a thesaurus lists words in alphabetical order. Each of these words is called an **entry word.** A list of synonyms follows the entry words. Sometimes a thesaurus lists antonyms.

Look at the parts of this thesaurus entry for the adjective *generous*. The **entry word** is in red letters. It is followed by the part of speech and a definition. An **example sentence** shows how the word can be used.

> gradual *adj.* Slow; little by little. The scientist has measured the gradual progress of the glacier toward the town.

Synonyms for the entry word are in *italic* letters. Each synonym is followed by a definition and an example sentence.

> *consecutive* Following each other without a break. I prefer three *consecutive* weeks of vacation to three one-week vacations.
> *continuous* Going on without any interruption. The *continuous* flow of traffic made it impossible to cross the street.
> *steady* Moving and acting regularly and without sudden change. Charley has made slow but *steady* progress in math.

If an **antonym** is given, it is printed in dark letters.

> **ANTONYMS: abrupt, disconnected, sudden**

How to Use Your Spelling Thesaurus

Suppose you are writing a story about a person who is making steady progress in learning Spanish. You read over your work and see you have used the word *gradual* too many times. You decide to use the Spelling Thesaurus to find some synonyms. Here are the steps you should follow.

1. Look for the word in the Thesaurus Index. The Index lists every word in the Spelling Thesaurus.

2. Find the word in the Index. This is what you will find:

   gradual *adj.*

   The red print tells you that *gradual* is an entry word.

3. Turn to the correct page in the Spelling Thesaurus and read the entry carefully. Choose the synonym with the exact shade of meaning you want. Not every synonym will fit in the context of your story.

Remember: Each word has a slightly different meaning. Look at the sample entry for *gradual* on page 206. Which synonym for *gradual* makes most sense in a story about someone making progress without interruption?

- Sometimes a word is listed in the Index like this:

  continuous gradual *adj.*

  This means you will find the word *continuous* listed as a synonym under the entry word *gradual*. Since *continuous* is not printed in red, it is not an entry word. If you look for *continuous* in the Spelling Thesaurus as an entry word under the letter *C*, you will not find it!

- You will also see lines in the Index that look like this:

  abrupt gradual *adj.*

  This means that *abrupt* is listed as an antonym under the entry word *gradual*.

abandon

appeal

A

abandon *v.* To give up completely; to leave. We had to abandon our picnic plans when it started to rain.

desert To leave a person, place, or thing, especially if one has a duty to stay. Jules *deserted* the car in the intersection, obstructing traffic for blocks.

evacuate To move out of; vacate. The firefighters *evacuated* the employees from the burning building.

quit To cease from; stop. The bell was the signal to *quit* work and go home.

renounce To give up, especially by formal statement. He *renounced* the throne so that his son could be king.

ANTONYMS: cherish, support

achievement *n.* Something achieved or accomplished. In 1921 Einstein received the Nobel Prize for outstanding achievement in physics.

accomplishment A skill or ability, especially a social grace. They honored Willie Mays's *accomplishments* by electing him into the Baseball Hall of Fame.

deed Anything done; an act. Alice won the mayor's medal for her brave *deeds* at the scene of the fire.

feat A remarkable act or deed, as one showing great skill, endurance, or daring. Bonzo the Bold performed his greatest *feat*—juggling blindfolded—at the end of the show.

ANTONYMS: defeat, failure

advisable *adj.* Fit to be done, sensible, wise. It's advisable to read any paper before you sign it.

desirable Worth having because good, helpful, or very pleasing. The most *desirable* part of the job was the high pay.

recommended Advantageous or beneficial; praised as good. I don't find "Joe's Place" on the list of *recommended* restaurants.

suitable Proper for the purpose or occasion; fitting. The most *suitable* route is the most direct one.

ANTONYMS: reckless, unwise

aggressive *adj.* Quick to fight or attack. Most snakes are not aggressive and will strike only when threatened.

assured Confident. Mario's handshake was firm, brisk, and *assured*.

forceful Full of or done with force; vigorous; strong. Her *forceful* personality makes her a natural leader.

hostile Showing dislike; unfriendly. In a *hostile* mood, he refused to share the information with anyone.

insistent Demanding or holding the attention; demanding with determination. He wore down the secretary with his *insistent* demands to see her boss.

ANTONYMS: agreeable, friendly, harmonious

apparent *adj.* Obvious, able to be seen by anyone. Her dislike of turnips was apparent from the way she looked at her plate.

clear Plain and understandable. The tea dumped in the harbor was a *clear* message of defiance to the king.

evident Easily seen or understood. They whistled, cheered, and clapped in *evident* delight.

obvious Easily perceived; clear; visible. The deer left an *obvious* trail of footprints in the snow.

plain Easy to understand; clear; obvious. To get your message across, use simple sentences and *plain* words.

transparent Easily understood; obvious. His motive was *transparent;* he wanted the fortune for himself.

ANTONYMS: indefinite, obscure, unclear, vague

appeal *v.* To be attractive or pleasing. The freer, looser fashions appealed to the women of the 1920's.

attract To draw or invite. Red flowers, especially, *attract* hummingbirds.

charm To delight or fascinate. The friendliness of the villagers *charmed* the travelers.

engage To attract; gain. He *engaged* the attention of the other diners by tapping his glass with a spoon.

entice To attract or lure by offering or tempting with something attractive or desirable. The smell of baking bread *enticed* her to enter the shop.

tempt To attract or invite. The promise of a promotion *tempted* me to take the job.

ANTONYMS: disgust, repel, revolt

argument *n.* An angry discussion; a quarrel. To avoid an argument, I didn't contradict her.

debate A discussion for or against a cause, especially in a formal way, by persons taking opposite sides of a question. The class held an animated *debate* on whether all students should be required to take computer courses.

disagreement A difference in views; failure to agree. Amy and the cashier had a *disagreement* about the correct price of canned tomatoes.

discord Lack of harmony; angry or quarrelsome disagreement. The source of *discord* between the two countries was the exact location of the boundary between them.

discussion Argument or consideration of a subject. The previously calm *discussion* grew heated when the mayor proposed a tax increase.

ANTONYMS: agreement, harmony, understanding

B

baffle *v.* To confuse completely; bewilder. The writing of the ancient Egyptians baffled everyone until the discovery of the Rosetta Stone.

bewilder To puzzle or confuse. Joanne's strange symptoms *bewildered* the doctor.

confuse To perplex; mix up. The speaker's rambling lecture *confused* the audience.

mystify To puzzle; bewilder. The crafty general *mystified* the enemy by pretending to retreat.

perplex To cause to hesitate; confuse; bewilder; puzzle. Oedipus solved the riddle of the Sphinx, which had *perplexed* the people of Thebes for years.

ANTONYMS: clarify, enlighten, explain, simplify

basis *n.* The foundation or essential part of something. The basis for Halley's prediction was the orbit he calculated for the comet.

foundation An underlying basis, as for a belief. Your theory has no *foundation* in fact.

groundwork A foundation. President Truman laid the *groundwork* for his victory by visiting small towns across America.

support A person or thing that supports. The loser underestimated his rival's *support* among the voters of the Ninth District.

benefit *v.* To be helpful or profitable. The scholarship fund benefits poor but deserving students.

advance To help onward; further; promote. The unions *advanced* the interests of the workers.

avail To be of use; help or profit. Bowie's best efforts did not *avail* him in defending the Alamo.

gain To profit or advance. In chess you *gain* nothing by taking the bishop if you lose your queen in return.

serve To promote the interest of; work for; aid; help. The antipollution laws *serve* the cause of preserving wildlife.

ANTONYMS: hinder, obstruct, retard

C

commerce *n.* The exchange or buying and selling of goods, especially on a large scale, as between nations. Bands of robbers interrupted commerce between Persia and the Byzantine empire.

business The buying, selling, and other details of trade or industry. The store opened for *business* at nine o'clock.

enterprise A systematic, purposeful activity. Selling raffle tickets was a time-consuming but profitable *enterprise*.

trade The buying and selling of goods. Caravans from India stopped at Mecca, making that city an important center of *trade*.

transaction Something carried out, as a business deal. They ended the *transaction* by signing a contract.

compel *v.* To force; to demand. The defeat of the Armada compelled the Spanish to give up their plan of seizing the English throne.

drive To force into some act or condition. The dripping faucet began to *drive* him crazy.

enforce To require to be obeyed. After adopting the rule, they found that they couldn't *enforce* it.

oblige To bind or force. Unable to climb out of the canyon, they were *obliged* to wait for the helicopter to rescue them.

pressure To urge or influence as if by force. We hoped the petition would *pressure* the city council into action.

compete *v.* To strive to do better than another; to take part in a contest. Three nations competed for the rich fishing grounds off Nova Scotia.

combat To fight or struggle. The two groups *combated* for control of the legislature.

contest To fight for or challenge. The colonists *contested* the right of the king to tax them.

oppose To act or be against; resist; fight. Many people *oppose* air and water pollution.

ANTONYMS: assist, boost, support

compose *v.* To create or write. Though German, Handel composed many operas in English.

conceive To think of or develop, as an idea. The Pied Piper *conceived* a plan to help the town.

construct To make by putting parts together; build. They *constructed* the walls out of wattle, a combination of sticks, twigs, and mud.

fashion To make, shape, or form. The potters *fashion* small animal-shaped bowls out of the local clay.

forge To produce or form; shape. The question was how best to *forge* one nation from thirteen colonies.

produce To bring into being, often by mental effort. Belgian mills *produce* high-quality linen.

ANTONYMS: demolish, destroy, wreck

conceive *v.* To imagine; to understand. Isaac Newton conceived parts of his theory of gravity before he saw an apple fall from a tree.

comprehend To understand; grasp. No human being can fully *comprehend* the size of the universe.

consider To take into account; make allowance for. Nowadays most people would not *consider* living without a refrigerator.

speculate To think seriously or wonderingly; form theories; conjecture. Mark *speculated* about the meaning of the mysterious message he found in a bottle.

See also **compose.**

concrete *adj.* Existing; real. It's hard to imagine a concrete object being made up of millions of whirling atoms.

material Of or having to do with physical or worldly things rather than ideas or things of the spirit. Though the *material* reward for his work was money, John received greater satisfaction from the people's gratitude.

substantial Of or having substance; actual; real. Many people ridiculed Winston Churchill for believing Germany posed a *substantial* danger to Great Britain.

tangible Capable of being felt by the sense of touch; real; definite. There is no *tangible* proof that the Loch Ness monster exists.

ANTONYMS: abstract, ideal, imaginary

conscious *adj.* Aware of things. Marco Polo was conscious of the riches that lay in the East, and so he set off to find a land route.

acquainted Familiar with. Before you judge him, take time to become *acquainted* with the facts.

aware Realizing or knowing fully. In the dark, I wasn't *aware* of the deep puddles.

knowledgeable Having considerable knowledge or information. Some Americans are quite *knowledgeable* about Chinese literature.

ANTONYMS: ignorant, unaware, unconscious

conspicuous *adj.* Easily noticed; attracting attention. Life jackets are usually yellow, orange, or a color that will be conspicuous in the water.

crafty

desolate

notable Worthy of note; remarkable; famous. Lewis Carroll, the author of *Alice in Wonderland,* was a *notable* mathematician of his day.

noticeable Attracting one's attention; easily seen. The soldiers showed a *noticeable* lack of enthusiasm for the dull assignment.

outstanding More excellent or important than others of its kind. The first prize went to Mrs. Simon's *outstanding* roses.

prominent Easily seen. Abraham Lincoln had a *prominent* nose.

striking Appealing strongly to the eye or the imagination; impressive. The red flower against her black hair made a *striking* contrast.

ANTONYMS: **common, humble, modest, ordinary**

crafty *adj.* Sly; clever. In one of Aesop's fables, a crafty fox outwits a raven.

clever Exhibiting skill, wit, or sharp thinking. Always extremely *clever* with words, Alice made up a funny rhyme on the spot.

cunning Clever or tricky. Raised in the forest, the boy grew as *cunning* in the ways of nature as the wild animals.

sly Clever in a secret, stealthy, or sneaky way; artful in deceiving. The *sly* raccoon snatched the bait but avoided being caught.

ANTONYMS: **aboveboard, genuine, sincere**

D

deceive *v.* To cause to take as true something that is not true; fool or mislead, as by lying. We hoped to deceive the dog by hiding the pill in a meatball.

mislead To lead into an error or wrong judgment. The weather report *misled* many people into leaving their raincoats at home.

swindle To cheat of money or property. In the play, the professor tries to *swindle* the townspeople out of their tax money.

decrease *v.* To make or become less. The Panama Canal greatly decreased the distances ships had to travel.

diminish To make smaller or less; to grow smaller or weaken. All hurricanes *diminish* in force as soon as they pass over land.

dwindle To grow steadily smaller or less; shrink; diminish. The stream *dwindled* to a trickle during the dry summer.

lessen To make or become less. Her dislike of the new coach *lessened* as she grew to know him.

reduce To make less in size or amount. The government hoped to *reduce* the national debt by taxing imports.

ANTONYMS: **enlarge, expand, increase, magnify**

defeat *v.* To win or gain a victory. After the Greeks defeated the Persians at Marathon, a runner set off to bring the news to Athens.

conquer To win control of. After hearing tales of a golden city, Spanish adventurers set off to *conquer* the New World.

overcome To get the better of; triumph over. Roald Amundsen and four men had to *overcome* bitter cold and hunger in their march to the South Pole.

overthrow To bring down or remove from power by force. They planned to *overthrow* the emperor by accusing him in front of the Senate.

triumph To be successful; win a victory. At the end of the story, good *triumph*s over evil.

vanquish To overcome. The Sioux *vanquished* Custer and his men near a river called Little Big Horn.

ANTONYMS: **fail, lose, yield**

desolate *adj.* Barren, lifeless. The first pictures of Mars showed a desolate landscape.

barren Not yielding fruit or crops. Irrigation brought the once *barren* fields to life.

bleak Exposed to wind and weather; bare. The lighthouse keeper didn't seem to mind living alone on the *bleak* cliff.

lifeless Lacking vitality; dull; dead. The party was *lifeless* until the band arrived.

uninhabited Having no living beings.

The *uninhabited* town had been abandoned soon after the Gold Rush was over.

ANTONYMS: fertile, fruitful, lush, teeming

dim *adj*. Not clearly seen. Only one candle lit the dim hallway.

blurred Indistinct in form or outline. Through the frosted glass, I saw the *blurred* figure of a deer.

faint Weak or slight. I could barely see my own hand in the *faint* light.

fuzzy Blurry; not clear. The poor organization of the report was a sign of *fuzzy* thinking.

ANTONYMS: distinct, recognizable, straightforward

direction *n*. The line along which anything moves, faces, or lies. How does a weathervane show the direction of the wind?

course Line of motion; something, as a path, passed over. They headed on a new *course* downstream toward the rapids.

path A track or course along which a thing moves. Appearing on that television show was her first step on the *path* to fame.

tendency A leaning or inclination toward some condition or action. Most plants have a natural *tendency* to grow toward light.

turn A change of position; the point along which that change occurs. Signing up with the Giants marked a *turn* in his career.

disagree *v*. To argue. The archbishop disagreed with King Henry, who wanted to be head of the English church.

clash To be in opposition; conflict. I think your orange skirt *clashes* with your pink blouse.

contradict To deny; state the opposite of. Dr. Chang *contradicted* the reporter's story and threatened to sue the newspaper.

dispute To argue or challenge in debate. Citing evidence of their slow disappearance, the scientist *disputed* the theory that dinosaurs died off suddenly.

quarrel To take part in an angry or violent dispute. The two politicians had *quarreled* bitterly twenty years ago and hadn't spoken to each other since.

ANTONYMS: agree, concur, cooperate

discussion *n*. The act of discussing; consideration of a subject by exchange of ideas. The ancient Greeks believed in testing their ideas through open discussion

conference A meeting for the purpose of consulting on a particular subject. The generals were invited to a *conference* to discuss the final terms of peace.

conversation An exchange of ideas by informal talk. She enjoyed the *conversation* so much that she returned to the park every day.

meeting A gathering of persons, as for religious worship or some other common purpose. We held a *meeting* to decide how to raise money for the dance.

E

effect *n*. A result; a change caused by something else. One effect of World War II was a very strong postwar economy.

consequence Result. An important *consequence* of the Lewis and Clark expedition was that thousands of adventurous Americans moved west.

outcome A result or conclusion. The *outcome* of the game is hard to predict because the teams are so evenly matched.

product A result. Edgar Allan Poe's poems were the *product* of inspiration and hard work.

result An outcome; consequence. The price of lettuce has gone up as a *result* of the dry weather.

ANTONYMS: cause, reason, source

eliminate *v*. To get rid of or remove. Sue used steel wool to eliminate the rust.

discard To throw away or get rid of as useless or not wanted. Elena decided to *discard* all the clothes that no longer fit her.

disqualify To declare not qualified. The judges *disqualified* all paintings that weren't original.

exterminate To destroy (living things) entirely; kill. Scientists know of nothing that will *exterminate* the destructive gypsy moth.

extinguish To wipe out; destroy. Lack of books didn't *extinguish* his desire to learn.

ANTONYMS: encourage, foster

enjoyable *adj.* Pleasant; satisfying. Janet felt better after playing an enjoyable game of tennis.

agreeable Giving pleasure; pleasing. An *agreeable* companion helps make a trip pleasant.

comforting Giving ease or freedom from pain or worry. Far from home, David found Uncle Malcolm's letters *comforting*.

gratifying Giving pleasure or satisfaction. It's *gratifying* to see that my work has paid off.

pleasurable Pleasant. Some people find roller coasters *pleasurable,* but they make me dizzy.

ANTONYMS: annoying, disagreeable, unpleasant

enormous *adj.* Very large; huge; immense. Four enormous faces are carved on Mount Rushmore.

colossal Of immense size; huge. A *colossal* two-story gate guarded the entrance to the city.

gigantic Like a giant; huge; mighty. Ultrasaurus, the most *gigantic* of dinosaurs, had ribs that were almost as long as a car.

immense Huge, vast. An *immense* country, the Soviet Union has eleven time zones compared to four in the United States.

mammoth Huge; colossal. Imagine the *mammoth* effort that went into building the pyramids.

tremendous Overwhelming. The sinking of the *Titanic* was a *tremendous* disaster.

ANTONYMS: minute, tiny

examination *n.* Careful inspection. After a close examination of the painting, Professor Smith declared it to be genuine.

analysis The separation or breaking up of something into its smaller parts or elements so as to be able to study or describe the thing more closely. Our *analysis* shows that the drinking water is pure.

inspection Careful or critical study of something. The fuzzy black dots proved, on closer *inspection,* to be a mirage.

investigation A thorough search or inquiry to find out facts or details. The fire department is conducting an *investigation* to determine the cause of the fire.

observation The act of observing scientifically and making notes on what is observed. After careful *observation* of the heavens, they built Stonehenge, a colossal rock calendar.

survey A brief but thorough study. The home buyer took a *survey* of the house and grounds.

excursion *n.* A short, pleasant trip; an outing. We took a four-hour excursion on a Mississippi River steamboat.

expedition An organized journey made for a specific purpose. During the 1871 *expedition,* Henry M. Stanley searched Africa to find the missing explorer, Dr. David Livingston.

jaunt A short journey for pleasure. Our morning *jaunt* through the woods ended at the inn.

outing A short pleasure trip. We'll vote on whether to go to the wildlife preserve or the planetarium on our class *outing*.

trek A long, hard journey or expedition. We reached the top of the hill after a tiring *trek*.

explanation *n.* The act or process of explaining. I didn't understand the explanation of how an automobile engine works.

clarification The act or process of making clear or understandable. These jumbled instructions need *clarification*.

demonstration An example as proof. Horace Wells planned a *demonstration* of the pain-killing effects of the gas.

fatigue

illustration An example or comparison used to explain. Your last report card is a good *illustration* of what you can do when you study.

justification The act of showing to be just, right, or reasonable. The chairman asked for a *justification* of why so much money was budgeted for entertainment.

F

fatigue *n.* Extreme tiredness or weariness. After two hours of running, I had to fight off fatigue if I was going to win the race.

boredom The condition of being made weary by something dull or tiresome. Cervantes overcame the *boredom* of prison life by writing parts of *Don Quixote.*

drowsiness Sleepiness. Doctors have proved that warm milk does cause *drowsiness.*

exhaustion Extreme weariness. Long-distance swimmers must pace themselves to avoid *exhaustion.*

sluggishness Lack of activity or energy. The boy blamed his *sluggishness* on lack of sleep.

weariness Tiredness; discontentment or boredom. She looked with *weariness* at all the work still left to do.

ANTONYMS: energy, stamina, vigor

fierce *adj.* Cruel, violent, savage, or ferocious. The fierce arctic wind slowed their progress toward the North Pole.

barbaric Uncivilized; cruel. The Romans greatly feared Attila the Hun because of the *barbaric* acts he was said to commit.

ferocious Extremely savage. The small but *ferocious* wolverine can fend off a bear or wolf.

savage Ferocious or untamed; wild; cruel. The *savage* expression on the mask frightened the children.

untamed Not tamed; wild. Alaska has more *untamed* country than any other state.

ANTONYMS: friendly, tame

flexible *adj.* Able to be bent or twisted easily. The next step is to connect the hollow glass rods with this flexible rubber tubing.

friendly

elastic Able to return to a former size or shape. First reported by the Spanish in Central America in the 1500's, rubber was prized for its *elastic* qualities.

limber Pliant; agile or supple. Stretching will make you *limber,* and you'll be less likely to injure yourself when exercising.

springy Able to snap back; elastic. He walked with a *springy* stride and breathed in the cold, clear air.

ANTONYMS: inflexible, rigid

fragile *adj.* Easily shattered or damaged; delicate. Although the shell is fragile, the shape of the egg makes it strong.

brittle Likely to break or snap. As people grow older, their bones become *brittle* and more likely to break than before.

dainty Delicately pretty or graceful. Don't put this *dainty* lace handkerchief in the washing machine.

delicate Fine, as in structure, design, or shape; easily injured. The rain washed away the *delicate* spider web.

flimsy Ready to fall apart or tear; easily damaged or broken. The *flimsy* hut leaned and seemed about to fall over.

frail Easily damaged in body or structure; weak. She lived to be ninety even though her health had always been *frail.*

ANTONYMS: strong, sturdy

friendly *adj.* Like a friend; pleasant; helpful; neighborly. Amy relaxed in the friendly atmosphere of the room.

cordial Warm and hearty; sincere. He gave the visitors a warm smile and a *cordial* welcome.

courteous Polite and considerate. It is *courteous* to take off your shoes before entering a Japanese home.

kindhearted Kind and sympathetic. The *kindhearted* grocer always fed the stray dog.

neighborly Being like a good or pleasant neighbor; considerate. Bringing soup to the sick man was a *neighborly* gesture.

ANTONYMS: aggressive, hostile, unfriendly, warlike

G

gesture *n.* A motion made with some part of the body, usually the hands or arms. The police officer's gesture told me to stop.

nudge A gentle push or poke. The dog had a habit of giving your hand a *nudge* when it wanted to be petted.

pantomime Expression without speech. By turning his empty pocket inside out, he used *pantomime* to tell me he had no money.

shrug The act of drawing up the shoulders to show doubt, dislike, or indifference. "Go ahead," he said with a *shrug,* "there's nothing I can do to stop you anyway."

signal A sign agreed on as a way of sending a message. The secret *signal* was two short whistles.

government *n.* The system of administering a country, state, city. A problem for the future may be attracting qualified people to the field of government.

democracy A form of government in which the people rule, either by voting directly or by electing representatives to manage the country and make the laws. The club was run like a *democracy,* with each member having one vote.

dictatorship A form of government in which a country is ruled by a dictator, who holds absolute power. With the support of the army, he unseated the elected president and set up a *dictatorship* with himself as head.

empire A group of countries or nations, often far away from each other, ruled by one person or government. Julius Caesar added England to the *empire* of lands ruled by Rome.

reign The period during which a king or queen rules. England became a superpower during the eventful *reign* of Elizabeth I.

republic A government in which the power is given to officials elected by and representing the people. The government of the United States is a democratic *republic*.

gradual *adj.* Slow; little by little. The scientist has measured the gradual progress of the glacier toward the town.

consecutive Following each other without a break. I prefer three *consecutive* weeks of vacation to three one-week vacations.

continuous Going on without any pause or interruption. The *continuous* flow of traffic made it impossible to cross the street.

steady Moving and acting regularly and without sudden changes. Charley has made slow but *steady* progress in math.

ANTONYMS: abrupt, disconnected, sudden

gruesome *adj.* Horrible, especially in a disgusting way. Two cars were involved in the gruesome collision.

ghastly Horrible or terrifying. Ellen woke up screaming from her *ghastly* nightmare.

grim Stern or forbidding; ghastly or repulsive. The nation was shocked by the *grim* photographs of the famine.

horrible Causing horror; frightful. After hearing the *horrible* horror story, the children were afraid to go to sleep.

monstrous Horrible, atrocious. The criminal was punished for his *monstrous* acts.

ANTONYMS: attractive, delightful

H

hesitate *v.* To hold back; to pause before acting. Never hesitate to say that you don't understand.

balk To stop and refuse to move or act. Rags *balked* at the door of the vet's office, and we had to carry him in.

dilly-dally To take one's time; dawdle; loiter. Don't *dilly-dally* over breakfast or you'll be late.

falter To be uncertain or give way. His balance *faltered,* and he slipped on the last step.

waver To be uncertain or undecided. Alan *wavered* for five days before finally deciding to accept the invitation.

ANTONYMS: act, decide

hinder *v.* To interfere with; to block. To *hinder* the growth of algae, keep your aquarium out of direct sunlight.

check To hold back; curb. The city sprayed the trees to *check* the spread of the beetle.

hamper To interfere with the movements of; obstruct. The slippery ice *hampered* the flow of traffic.

obstruct To block; cut off; be in the way of. An enormous building *obstructed* our view of the beach.

restrain To hold back; repress. I had to *restrain* myself from talking about the party.

ANTONYMS: **encourage, stimulate, support**

horrify *v.* To cause extreme fear or terror. Photographs of the bombed city *horrified* the people.

dismay To fill with uneasiness and alarm. The high cost of our hotel room *dismayed* us.

shock To disturb the feelings or mind of suddenly and violently; disgust. News of the accident *shocked* the world.

startle To frighten, surprise, or excite suddenly. A loud pop *startled* the cat.

terrify To fill with extreme fear; frighten greatly. The thought of spending a night alone in that large house *terrifies* me.

ANTONYMS: **delight, enchant, fascinate**

I

identify *v.* To recognize or show what something is or who someone is. Dr. Watson correctly *identified* the mysterious powder as chalk dust.

distinguish To recognize or point out a difference. How do you *distinguish* the harmless scarlet king snake from the deadly coral snake?

perceive To come to understand or comprehend. She *perceived* me as honest, and we became good friends.

recognize To know, as if from previous acquaintance. After all those years, I hardly *recognized* my own sister at the airport.

reveal To make known, disclose, or make visible. Leon drew back the curtain to *reveal* his new creation.

ANTONYMS: **mistake, misunderstand**

idle *adj.* Not doing anything; not busy. After being *idle* all morning, Paul wanted to get out and do something.

inactive Not active or in use; inert. The volcano had been *inactive* for centuries before coming back to life.

slack Lacking activity; not busy. Sales have been *slack* since the new store opened for business.

sluggish Not active or energetic; lazy or dull. *sluggish* after his long day at work, he wanted only to eat dinner and go to sleep.

ANTONYMS: **active, busy, energetic**

illegal *adj.* Not legal; unlawful. It was *illegal* to park on the street after dark.

criminal Consisting of or guilty of crime. *Criminal* activity lessened when they put in the street lights.

lawless Refusing to obey or pay attention to the law. The new sheriff promised to rid the town of the *lawless* band of robbers.

outlawed Made unlawful; prohibited; banned. The sheriff collected the *outlawed* weapons from the cowhands.

prohibited Forbidden, especially by authority or law. *Prohibited* behaviors include playing radios and talking to the bus driver.

ANTONYMS: **lawful, legal**

impossible *adj.* Not able to happen or be done. Traveling to the moon, they thought, was an *impossible* dream.

absurd Unreasonable; ridiculous. Although it seems *absurd* to us, many people believed lead could be turned into gold.

ridiculous Making no sense; foolish. It's *ridiculous* to believe that you'll lose thirty pounds in just six days.

ANTONYMS: **believable, likely, possible, reasonable**

increase *v.* To make or become greater or larger. Researchers found that loud noise *increases* people's blood pressure.

enhance To add to; heighten. Washing the old car *enhanced* its appearance.

incredible

enlarge To make or become larger; expand. During World War II the United States *enlarged* its armed forces by drafting young men.

exaggerate To make something appear larger than it really is. The cat's fur stood on end, which *exaggerated* its actual size.

inflate To raise (prices or the like) a great deal. The freeze in Florida *inflated* the price of oranges.

magnify To cause to seem greater or more important; exaggerate. Eager to impress the strangers, he *magnified* the importance of his job.

ANTONYMS: decrease, diminish, lessen, reduce

incredible *adj.* So strange or unusual as to be unbelievable; not to be believed or accepted as true. The movie is funny if you can accept the incredible plot.

bizarre Very different from the usual; fantastic. The engine started making *bizarre* grinding noises as we climbed the hill.

fantastic Odd, original, weird, or unreal. The artist's *fantastic* style gives her paintings a dreamlike quality.

miraculous Amazing or wondrous. Houdini's escape from the locked trunk seemed *miraculous*.

odd Strange or unusual; peculiar; queer. The *odd* appearance of the rhinoceros startled the first Europeans to see one.

outrageous Fantastic or unbelievable. No one could believe such an *outrageous* story.

questionable Likely to be questioned or debated. The findings are *questionable* because the researchers did not conduct the study properly.

unbelievable Not to be believed. Because germs can't be seen, many people found the theory that germs cause disease *unbelievable*.

ANTONYMS: believable, credible, normal, ordinary, usual

inquire *v.* To investigate or search. In this book, the author inquires into the causes of the Great Depression.

interruption

interrogate To question, usually in a formal examination. The police *interrogated* a man who was seen running from the scene of the crime.

pry To look too closely; to snoop. I locked my desk drawer so that others wouldn't *pry* into my private papers.

question To have doubt about or an objection to. She *questioned* my ability to drive after only three lessons.

quiz To examine by asking questions. The reporters *quizzed* the couple who jogged across the country for peace.

institution *n.* An established organization with a specific purpose, as a school, bank, or hospital. Sixty-five institutions of higher learning received grants of money.

association An organization of persons with a common purpose. An *association* of nurses defines the standards that nurses must live up to.

league A number of persons, groups, or countries united for some common purpose. Six nations formed a *league* to encourage trade among themselves.

organization A number of people systematically united for some work or purpose. The purpose of the *organization* is to preserve historic buildings in the city.

society A group of people who join together for a common purpose. The *society* of stamp collectors meets every Tuesday night.

union An association, as of persons, nations, or states. The waiters had to decide whether to join a *union* of restaurant workers.

interruption *n.* Something that interrupts or breaks in. Mrs. Green does not stand for interruptions during her lectures.

interval A pause; the time between two events. There will be a short *interval* between the two acts of the play.

intrusion The act of coming in without being invited or wanted. The reporter's visit was an unwelcome *intrusion* on Shirley's free time.

lull A time of quiet or calm during a period of noise or activity. Linda waited for a *lull* in the conversation to announce that she was leaving.

pause A brief stop or short rest. After a *pause* to sip some water, the speaker continued.

recess A short period of time during which work is stopped. We'll begin the meeting again after a fifteen-minute *recess*.

ANTONYMS: continuation, continuity, link

J

jest *n.* A statement or action intended to provoke laughter; a joke. Don't be angry; Vicky was speaking in jest.

farce A comedy using exaggeration and ridiculous situations to be funny. Everyone enjoyed the *farce* the seventh-grade class performed.

lark A carefree adventure; a good time. Never thinking he would win, Sean entered the contest just for a *lark*.

merriment Laughter; fun. They added to the merriment by making up a new dance.

prank A mischievous, playful act or trick. They played a *prank* on the babysitter by hiding her car keys.

ridicule Words or actions intended to make another thing or person seem foolish. He refused to wear the loud shirt because he feared the *ridicule* of his classmates.

jubilant *adj.* Overjoyed; extremely happy. The jubilant crowd celebrated the team's victory.

ecstatic Full of great happiness or delight. *Ecstatic* people danced in the streets to celebrate the birth of the prince.

elated Filled with joy or pride. *Elated* by the success of his new product, Carl decided to start his own business.

gleeful Full of glee; mirthful; joyous. The children were *gleeful* at the first snowfall of the year.

overjoyed Greatly pleased or delighted. The new father was *overjoyed* with his first daughter.

ANTONYMS: dejected, depressed, unhappy

judgment *n.* The ability to make a decision wisely; good sense. His decision not to delay showed good judgment.

decision A conclusion. When did America make the *decision* to enter World War I?

insight The ability to see into the heart or inner nature of something or someone. Your wise remark shows that you have real *insight* into the problem.

verdict Any conclusion or decision; the decision of a jury after a trial. The jury was evenly divided and so could not reach a *verdict*.

See also **opinion.**

K

knowledge *n.* All that is known by all people. All the knowledge of the ancient world was collected in the library at Alexandria.

education Instruction or training. Making certain all children are given a quality *education* is a priority.

information Facts about a subject or subjects. I need more *information* to make that decision.

learning Information gotten by study or instruction. The monasteries became centers of *learning* during the Dark Ages.

lore Facts or stories about a subject. Barbara collected their sayings and traditions into a book of Indian *lore*.

L

labor *n.* Hard work. Mining the coal was a dangerous and uncomfortable labor.

drudgery Dull, hard, unpleasant work. Cleaning the oven is my idea of *drudgery*.

effort The use of physical or mental energy or power to get something done. Digging up the ruins of ancient Troy took great *effort*.

exertion Great effort. Even with the greatest *exertion*, they weren't able to budge the stone.

toil Hard, tiring work. Imagine the *toil* it must have taken to dig the tunnel using only shovels.

ANTONYMS: ease, leisure, relaxation

legend *n.* A story of strange or remarkable happenings that has come down from early times and may or may not have some basis in real incidents. Most people now believe that dragons exist only in legends.

narrative An account, story, or tale. The stranger continued his *narrative* of how he had lost his way and stumbled across our campground.

saga An ancient Scandinavian story of heroes and their deeds. The movie is based on a Norse *saga* of a hero who sailed to the Western Isles.

tale A story; narrative or account of real or imaginary events. In one of the *tales,* Paul Bunyan had a giant blue ox named Babe.

tradition The passing down of customs, beliefs, and tales from one generation to the next. According to Irish *tradition,* kissing the Blarney Stone gives one the gift of easy speech.

limit *v.* To restrict. Please limit your calls to five minutes.

bound To form the boundary of; enclose. Lark Avenue *bounds* the park on the north.

confine To shut in or keep shut in. The doctor *confined* Sue to bed until her fever passed.

enclose To close in on all sides; surround. A tall fence *enclosed* their yard.

restrict To hold or keep within the boundary of; confine. The board voted to *restrict* trucks to nonresidential streets.

ANTONYMS: liberate, release

M

manager *n.* An individual who oversees or manages something, as a business or institution. The manager handed out the work assignments for the day.

chief A person highest in command or authority. Henry was made *chief* of fifteen salespeople.

commander A person who is in command, as of a ship or military force.

George Washington was an able *commander* of troops.

director A person who directs, as one in charge of the production of a movie or play. The *director* of the project was in charge of three departments.

governor A person who governs, rules, guides, or manages. Four candidates are running for the position of *governor* of this state.

marvelous *adj.* Causing wonder; amazing. At first, the people didn't believe the stories of the marvelous carriage that could move without being pulled by horses.

amazing Astonishing; wonderful. "I've had an *amazing* stroke of good luck," she said.

astonishing Amazing. Her ability to memorize long passages quickly is *astonishing*.

enchanting Charming; delightful. The audience sat motionless during the *enchanting* violin solo.

exceptional Not ordinary; unusual. The *exceptional* tomato crop broke last year's harvest record.

See also **unusual.**

ANTONYMS: horrible, humdrum, terrible

minute *adj.* Very tiny. Many species of whales feed on minute animals called krill.

compact Closely and firmly put together. The computer is *compact* enough to fit under an airplane seat.

microscopic Very small; tiny. When you consider the size of the galaxy, the Earth is like a *microscopic* grain of sand on a vast beach.

miniature Very small; tiny. Dorothy bought *miniature* furniture for her doll house.

trifling Lacking size, quantity, or value; trivial. The young Franklin worked for *trifling* wages: less than ten cents a day.

ANTONYMS: colossal, enormous, gigantic, huge

monotonous *adj.* Repetitious; boring because there is no change. The monotonous tone of his voice put the audience to sleep.

repetitious Full of repetition, especially in a useless or tiresome way. Too many chase scenes made the movie *repetitious* and boring.

routine Habitual; customary. It started as a *routine* day, and we had no idea that it would change our lives.

uniform Always the same; not varying or changing. A square has four sides of *uniform* length.

ANTONYMS: exciting, fascinating, lively, stimulating, vivacious

mysterious *adj.* Filled with or suggesting something not known or strange; unexplained. People still wonder about Amelia Earhart's mysterious disappearance.

baffling Confusing completely; bewildering. The last three math problems were *baffling* to Tomás.

obscure Not clear to the mind; hard to understand. No one had a clue about the meaning of the *obscure* message.

perplexing Confusing; bewildering; puzzling. It's easy to get lost in that *perplexing* tangle of winding streets.

puzzling Confusing; perplexing; mystifying. I'd find the assignment *puzzling*, too, if I hadn't read the directions.

ANTONYMS: clear, straightforward, understandable

N

necessary *adj.* Needed; essential. Revising is a necessary part of writing.

compulsory Required; enforced. These English and math courses are *compulsory* for graduation.

essential Absolutely required; vital. Making an outline is an *essential* step in writing any paper.

indispensable Absolutely required; essential. Cereal, fruit, and vegetables are *indispensable* to a healthy diet.

pressing Needing immediate attention. With only one hospital, the county has a *pressing* need for more.

required Needed; insisted upon. This guidebook should be *required* reading for anyone planning a trip to France.

ANTONYMS: dispensable, needless, nonessential

nervous *adj.* Showing anxiety or tension; uneasy. Some people say horses become nervous just before an earthquake.

anxious Worried; uneasy; filled with anxiety. The miners were *anxious* that the ceiling of the mine might collapse.

fearful Full of fear; frightened. *Fearful* of the threat from the North, the Chinese built a great wall.

fidgety Restless; impatient; nervously active. Ten minutes into the story, the children started to get *fidgety*.

jittery Anxious; fearful. After the wild ride, we were all too *jittery* to get on the roller coaster again.

restless Unable to rest or be still; anxious; uneasy. We finally began to grow *restless* five days after we were snowed in.

ANTONYMS: calm, composed, cool, relaxed, unruffled

nonessential *adj.* Not necessary or essential. When you carry a backpack, you soon learn to leave nonessential items behind.

insignificant Unimportant; lacking meaning, size, or worth. "For the *insignificant* amount of twelve cents a day," the ad read, "you can buy the great music of the Western world."

needless Not needed or necessary; useless. Buying the second television set was a *needless* extravagance.

unimportant Not important or significant. Missing the baseball game was *unimportant* to Harry.

ANTONYMS: essential, necessary, needed

nonsense *n.* Words or action that make no sense. *Alice in Wonderland* is full of delightful nonsense

folly Lack of sense; foolishness. Robert Fulton's steamboat was called "Fulton's *Folly*" because few people thought it would work.

foolishness Silly behavior. The teacher said, "I won't stand for any *foolishness* in this class."

gibberish Rapid or senseless talk or chatter. Wally listened patiently to the excited child's *gibberish*.

stamp To affect in some way by or as if by stamping; crush. The forest ranger *stamped* out the campfire and then threw water on the ashes.

tread To step or walk on, over, or along. Imagine how it would feel to *tread* the boards of this stage.

transparent *adj.* Able to be seen through. The transparent outer layer of the eye is the cornea.

cloudless Free of clouds. The beaches shimmered under the *cloudless* sky.

crystal Resembling crystal; very clear. The advertisement promised scuba diving in *crystal* waters.

glassy Like glass; clear, shiny, and brittle. The sun reflected off the *glassy* frozen pond.

sheer Very thin and fine. We could see the sky through the *sheer* fabric of the curtains.

See also **apparent.**

ANTONYMS: **cloudy, murky**

tremble *v.* To shake, as with fear, weakness, cold. The dog trembled with anticipation as I filled its bowl with the table scraps.

quake To shake, often with great force. Sensing the bear, the campers *quaked* with fear.

shiver To shake, as with cold or fear; quiver. I *shivered* so violently that my teeth chattered.

shudder To shake, as from fear or cold; shiver. The lawnmower engine *shuddered* and then died.

vibrate To move back and forth rapidly; quiver. The whole house *vibrated* as heavy trucks passed outside.

U

uncertain *adj.* Not certain or sure; doubtful. If you're uncertain of the spelling of a word, look it up in a dictionary.

doubtful Unsure; undecided. The outcome is *doubtful,* but everyone is hoping that we'll win.

hesitant Doubtful; undecided. The child was *hesitant* to walk past the dog even though it was on a leash.

indecisive Not able to decide; hesitant or wavering. My father was *indecisive* about whether to bring an umbrella to work.

undecided Not having the mind made up; not yet decided or settled. Most of the public is *undecided* about whom they will vote for, and either candidate could win.

wavering Lacking certainty; undecided. Many colonists held *wavering* opinions about whether or not to break with England.

ANTONYMS: **certain, decisive, definite, doubtless, unwavering**

unusual *adj.* Uncommon, rare; not ordinary or usual. The car was painted an unusual color he called "pencil yellow."

extraordinary Remarkable; surprising. Mozart's *extraordinary* gift for music was evident by the time he was six years old.

rare Not often seen or found; uncommon. Gold is valuable in part because it is *rare.*

remarkable Worthy of notice; extraordinary. Joan has a *remarkable* memory for numbers.

singular Extraordinary; uncommon. Sarah Bernhardt's *singular* ability to move her audience made her the greatest actress of her time.

unique Being one of a kind. Its duck bill makes the platypus *unique* among mammals.

See also **marvelous.**

ANTONYMS: **common, ordinary, unremarkable, usual**

V

vague *adj.* Blurry; not clear or definite. I couldn't place him, but I had a vague memory of having met him before.

indefinite Not definite or precise. Because we don't know when our passports will arrive, our departure date is *indefinite.*

indistinct Not clear or distinct; dim or faint. Through the haze, we could make out the *indistinct* outline of the hills.

shadowy Like a shadow in being unclear or dim. We saw the *shadowy* figure of the driver as the car raced by.

uncertain Not certain or sure; doubtful. The origin of the word is *uncertain,* but it is probably related to an old Indian word for *grain.*

ANTONYMS: clear, distinct, exact, precise

valuable *adj.* Having worth, especially having a high value or price. Rubies are the most valuable gems.

advantageous Giving an advantage; favorable; profitable. From her *advantageous* position, Frances could see what everyone else was doing.

beneficial Tending to help or benefit; useful or helpful. The doctor pointed out the *beneficial* effects of exercise.

profitable Bringing advantage or gain. The business was so *profitable* that the partners were forced to expand.

useful Having a use; giving service; helpful; beneficial. A flashlight is a *useful* tool to have if your car breaks down at night.

ANTONYMS: useless, worthless

varied *adj.* Made up of different parts. Bears eat a varied diet of plants, nuts, insects, fruit, meat, and fish.

assorted Of various sorts; of different kinds and varieties. The shirt is available in *assorted* colors and sizes.

irregular Not evenly shaped. From the bridge, we could see the *irregular* pattern of the skyline.

miscellaneous Composed of many different things or elements. The record store featured a *miscellaneous* selection of music from classical to popular.

various Different from one another; of different kinds. Eating *various* foods from all of the basic food groups will help you maintain a balanced diet.

ANTONYMS: identical, uniform, unvaried

W

watchful *adj.* Watching carefully; alert. The watchful sentry sounded the alarm.

alert Very aware and ready. The zebra pack is always *alert* to danger.

cautious Very careful or alert. *Cautious* with money, Lucille spent very little on her trip.

wary Cautious and suspicious; very careful. The *wary* dog sniffed the food and turned away.

ANTONYMS: careless, heedless, inattentive

Y

yield *v.* To give up or give way; to surrender. Motorboats must always yield the right of way to sailboats.

bend To give in. The committee had no choice except to *bend* to the demands of the parents.

concede To grant; give in. Before the debate, the candidate for governor *conceded* that his rival was more experienced.

submit To give up; surrender. After a long struggle, the dog *submitted* to the bath.

surrender To abandon or give up possession of. Father wouldn't *surrender* the keys to the car until Pete promised to have it back by ten o'clock.

ANTONYMS: mutiny, rebel, revolt

WRITER'S GUIDE

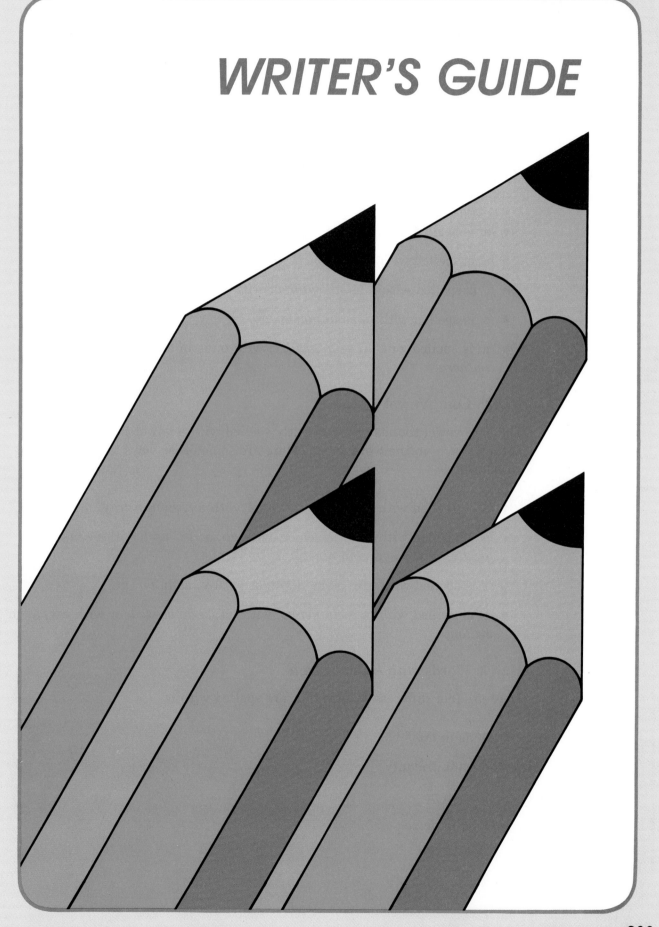

SPELLING RULES

Unit 1: **Short Vowel Sounds**

The short vowel sounds are usually spelled with one vowel letter each. However, two letters are sometimes combined to spell a short vowel sound. Here are some ways to spell the short vowel sounds.

- /a/ is spelled with **a,** as in *lather,* or with **ai,** as in *plaid.*
- /e/ is spelled with **e,** as in *method,* or with **ea,** as in *instead.*
- /i/ is spelled with **i,** as in *whim,* or with **y,** as in *symbol.*
- /o/ is spelled with **o,** as in *notch.*
- /u/ is spelled with **u,** as in *grudge,* with **o,** as in *tongue,* or with **ou,** as in *southern.*

Unit 2: **Long Vowel Sounds**

The long vowel sounds are frequently spelled with a vowel-consonant-*e* pattern, as /ā/ in the word *inflate.* Here are some other ways to spell the long vowel sounds.

- /ā/ is spelled with **ai,** as in *sustain,* or with **ay,** as in *betray.*
- /ē/ is spelled with **e,** as in *senior,* with **ea,** as in *easel,* with **ee,** as in *greedy,* or with **y,** as in *ninety.*
- /ī/ is spelled with **igh,** as in *slight,* or with **y,** as in *tyrant.*
- /ō/ is spelled with **o,** as in *heroic,* with **oa,** as in *coaxed,* or with **ow,** as in *mellow.*

Unit 3: **Words with *ie, ei,* or *eigh***

Here are four different sounds that are spelled with *ie.*

- /ē/ as in *thief*
- /e/ as in *friendly*
- /ī/ as in *fiery*
- /i/ as in *fierce*

Unit 4: **The Sound /j/**

Here are six ways to spell /j/.

- with **j,** as in *jubilant*
- with **g,** as in *gesture*
- with **ge,** as in *salvage*
- with **d** before **u,** as in *graduate*
- with **di,** as in *cordial*
- with **dge,** as in *smudge*

Unit 5: **The Sounds /k/ and /kw/**

Here are five ways to spell /k/.

- with **k,** as in *king*
- with **c,** as in *corduroy*
- with **cc,** as in *occupy*
- with **ch,** as in *monarch*
- with **ck,** as in *clock*

Here are two ways to spell /kw/.

- with **qu,** as in *quantity*
- with **cho,** as in *choir*

Unit 7: **Words with Shifting Accents**

- Many English words are spelled with "silent" letters, or letters that are not pronounced. To remember "silent" letters, think of a related word in which the letter is pronounced.

    sign—signature   muscle—muscular

- Schwa /ə/ is a weak vowel sound. The schwa can be written with any vowel letter. To spell a word with a schwa, think of another word with the same root.

    competition—compete   major—majority

Unit 8: **Foods from Many Nations**

- In Spanish, the sound /y/ as in *yet* is spelled with *ll*.

  tortilla   /tôr·tē′yə/

- In Italian, the letters *gn* before a vowel are pronounced /ny/ as in *onion*. The letter *z* is sometimes pronounced /ts/ as in *cats*.

  lasagna   /lə·zän′yə/   pizza   /pēt′sə/

Unit 9: **Plurals**

- Some words have only a plural form.

  scissors   politics

- To form the plural of a compound word written as one word, add *s* or *es*.

  hourglass—hourglasses   cupful—cupfuls

- To form the plural of a hyphenated compound word, add *s* to the end of the word.

  tune-up—tune-ups   drive-in—drive-ins

- If the first word in a hyphenated compound word is a noun, form the plural by adding *s* to the first word.

  runner-up—runners-up

Unit 10: **Homophones**

- **Homophones** are words that sound alike but are spelled differently and have different meanings.

  stationary   stationery

  To decide on the correct spelling of a homophone, think about the context in which the word is used.

Unit 11: **Easily Confused Words**

- Words that sound similar and have similar spellings can be easily confused. To decide on the correct spelling of certain words, listen to the word and think about the context in which the word is used.

Unit 13: **The Sounds /ən/ and /əm/**

Here are three ways to spell /ən/.

- with **an,** as in *slogan*
- with **on,** as in *abandon*
- with **ain,** as in *bargain*

Here are four ways to spell /əm/.

- with **um,** as in *pendulum*
- with **em,** as in *emblem*
- with **om,** as in *venom*
- with **im,** as in *denim*

Unit 14: **The Sounds /ər/ and /əl/**

Here are three ways to spell /ər/.

- with **er,** as in *commuter*
- with **ar,** as in *caterpillar*
- with **or,** as in *narrator*

Here are four ways to spell /əl/.

- with **el,** as in *panel*
- with **le,** as in *muffle*
- with **al,** as in *classical*
- with **il,** as in *peril*

Unit 15: **Words from Spanish**

- In Spanish the sound /k/ is spelled with *c* or *qu.*

    mosquito   bronco   corral

▶ WRITER'S GUIDE

Unit 16: **Inflectional Endings**

The inflectional endings *er, est, s, ed,* and *ing* can be added to the end of a base word to change or add to its meaning.

- If a base word ends in *e,* drop the final *e* if the inflectional ending begins with a vowel.

     devote   devoted   devoting

- ☐ The words *eyeing* and *dyeing* are exceptions to this rule.

     eye   eyed   eyeing

- If a base word ends in a consonant and *y,* change the *y* to *i,* unless the inflectional ending begins with *i.*

     pity   pitied   pitying

- If a word ends in a vowel and *y,* just add the inflectional ending.

     dismay   dismayed   dismaying

Unit 17: **Music and Art Words**

- Many words used in music and art come from Greek words. The word *guitar* comes from the Greek word *kithara,* which means "lyre, lute."

Unit 19: **More Inflectional Endings**

If a word ends with one vowel followed by one consonant, double the final consonant before adding *ed* or *ing* if:

- it is a one-syllable word.

     stun   stunned   stunning

- it is a compound word and the second word has one syllable.

     outfit   outfitted   outfitting

- it is a two-syllable word and the accent is on the final syllable.

     permit   permitted   permitting

Do not double the final consonant of a word that ends in one vowel followed by one consonant if the final syllable is not accented.

     benefit   benefited   benefiting

Do not double the final consonant when a word ends with a consonant cluster or digraph or with *two* vowel letters and one consonant.

succeed   succeeded   succeeding

Unit 20: Synonyms and Antonyms

- A **synonym** is a word that has the same or almost the same meaning as another word.

    corridor   hallway

- An **antonym** has the opposite meaning of another word.

    rarely   frequently

Unit 21: Double-Letter Spellings

- Double consonant letters often follow a short vowel sound.

    intelligent   immense

- Double consonant letters also occur when a prefix that ends with a consonant is added to a base word that begins with the same consonant letter.

    un + necessary = unnecessary

Unit 22: Prefixes

- A **prefix** is a word part added to the beginning of a word to make a new word. A prefix comes *before* the base word. Here is a chart of some prefixes and their meanings.

Prefix	Meaning	Example
in-	"not"	*incapable*
non-	"not"	*nonessential*
dis-	"not"	*discouraged*

- When the prefix *in-* is added to base words that begin with *m, b,* or *p,* the *n* is changed to *m.*

    perfect—imperfect

- When *in-* is added to words beginning with *l,* the *n* is changed to *l.*

    legal—illegal

- When *in-* is added to words beginning with *r,* the *n* is changed to *r.*

    regular—irregular

Unit 23: More Prefixes

Here is a chart of some prefixes and their meanings.

Prefix	Meaning	Example
uni-	"one"	*uniform*
mono-	"one"	*monotonous*
para-	"alongside of"	*parallel*
bi-	"two"	*bisect*
semi-	"half"	*semiannual*

Unit 25: Latin Prefixes

Some prefixes come from Latin. Here is a chart of some prefixes and their meanings.

Prefix	Meaning	Example
circum-	"around"	*circumference*
inter-	"between"	*interstate*
intra-	"within"	*intrastate*
super-	"over, above"	*supervision*
trans-	"across, through"	*transparent*

Unit 26: Social Studies Words

- Many of the words used in social studies come from Greek or Latin. The words *social* and *society* come from the Latin word *socius,* which means "companion."

Unit 27: Words from French

French words in English usually keep their French spellings. Here is a chart that shows French spellings.

Spelling	Sound	Example
et	/ā/	*ballet*
gue	/g/	*league*
que	/k/	*boutique*
ch	/sh/	*chandelier*
ge	/zh/	*beige*

- In many French words, the final consonant is not pronounced.

  depot   /dē′pō/

Unit 28: **Adjective Suffixes**

The suffixes *-ible, -able,* and *-ous* are adjective-forming suffixes.

- If a word ends with *e,* drop the final *e* before adding a suffix that begins with a vowel letter. However, if a word ends with *ce* or *ge,* keep the final *e.*

    believe—believable   notice—noticeable

- If a word ends with a consonant and *y,* change the *y* to *i* before adding a suffix that begins with a vowel.

    mystery—mysterious   industry—industrious

- ☐ The words *anxious* and *numerous* do not fit these rules. *Anxious* is related to the noun *anxiety.* The *b* in *number* is dropped when *-ous* is added to form *numerous.*

Unit 29: **Noun Suffixes**

Nouns are often formed by adding suffixes to another part of speech.

- Sometimes the final *e* is dropped before the suffix *-ment* is added to a verb.

    argue—argument   judge—judgment

- If the suffix *-ity* is added to a word that ends in *ble,* insert an *i* between *b* and *l.*

    probable—probability

- The suffix *-an* or *-ian* is added to a word that is already a noun. It adds the meaning "a specialist."

    library—librarian   history—historian

- ☐ The word *vegetarian* is formed from the noun *vegetable* and the suffix *-arian,* which means "a believer."

Unit 31: **More Noun Suffixes**

- The suffixes *-al* and *-ion* may be added to verbs to form nouns.

    arrive—arrival   confess—confession

- To make the noun form of *admit,* change the final *t* to *s* and add *-sion.* To make the noun form of *examine,* drop the *e* before adding *-ation.*

    admit—admission   examine—examination

Unit 32: **Syllable Patterns**

- When a word has two consonant letters between vowel letters, divide between the consonants except in the case of a consonant digraph.

    lug·gage   fab·ric

- When a word has two vowel sounds between consonant sounds, divide between the vowel letters. The words *dial* and *fuel* are often pronounced as one-syllable words, but they still follow the same pattern as *liar*.

    li·ar   di·al   fu·el

- When a word has one consonant letter between two vowel letters, divide *before* the consonant if the first vowel sound is long.

    fi·ber   mo·lar

- When a word has one consonant letter between two vowel letters, divide *after* the consonant if the first vowel sound is short and the first syllable is accented.

    log·ic   grav·el

Unit 33: **Words from Latin**

- Some words that were borrowed from Latin entered English through French, Spanish, or Italian. *Virus* is a word that was borrowed from Latin.

Unit 34: **Multisyllabic Words**

- Multisyllabic words have many syllables. To remember the spelling and meaning of multisyllabic words, divide them into word parts. Think of the meanings, pronunciations, and spellings of the smaller parts.

Unit 35: **Career Words**

- The noun-forming suffixes *-er, -or, -ian,* and *-ist* mean "one who does" or "one who specializes in."

    illustrate—illustrator   photograph—photographer

TROUBLESOME WORDS TO SPELL

already	have	quite	today
am	haven't	receive	together
and	hello	remember	tomorrow
are	her	right	tonight
awhile	here	school	too
because	I'll	some	two
before	I'm	sometimes	until
can't	isn't	stationery	very
close	it's	suppose	want
couldn't	know	teacher	we
cousin	letter	Thanksgiving	went
didn't	maybe	that's	we're
don't	Mr.	their	won't
down	Mrs.	there	would
everybody	name	there's	write
football	now	they're	writing
for	off	think	you
friend	our	thought	your
from	outside	time	you're
Halloween	pretty	to	yours

LANGUAGE: A Glossary of Terms and Examples

Grammar

Sentences

- A **sentence** is a group of words that expresses a complete thought. It always begins with a capital letter. It always ends with a punctuation mark.

- A **declarative sentence** makes a statement. It ends with a period (.).

    The seventh-grade class planned a picnic.

- An **interrogative sentence** asks a question. It ends with a question mark (**?**).

    Where will it be held?

    An **exclamatory sentence** shows strong feeling or surprise. It ends with an exclamation point (!).

    What a wonderful idea!

- An **imperative sentence** gives a command or makes a request. It ends with a period (.).

    Bring the baseball equipment with you.

- The **subject** of a sentence is the part about which something is being said. All the words that make up the subject are called the **complete subject.**

    <u>Inez and Ricardo</u> discussed their plans for the picnic.

- The **predicate** of the sentence is the part that says something about the subject. All the words that make up the predicate are called the **complete predicate.**

    Each person <u>would bring a different kind of food.</u>

Nouns

- A **noun** is a word that names a person, place, thing, or idea.
- A **common noun** names any person, place, thing, or idea. It is a general word that begins with a lowercase letter.

> nurse   corridor   chandelier   friendship

- A **proper noun** names a particular person, place, thing, or idea. It begins with a capital letter.

> Kitty O'Neil   Chicago   Arbor Day

- A **singular noun** names one person, place, thing, or idea.
- A **plural noun** names more than one person, place, thing, or idea.
- To form the plurals of most nouns, add *s*.

> statue—statues   guitar—guitars

- To form the plurals of nouns ending in *s, z, x, ss, sh,* or *ch,* add *es*.

> chorus—choruses   wish—wishes

- To form the plurals of nouns ending in *y* preceded by a consonant, change the *y* to *i* and add *es*.

> activity—activities   monopoly—monopolies

- To form the plurals of most nouns ending in *o* preceded by a consonant, add *es*.

> tomato—tomatoes   mosquito—mosquitoes

- To form the plurals of some nouns ending in *f* or *fe,* change the *f* to *v* and add *es*.

> knife—knives   half—halves

- For some nouns the plurals are formed by changing a vowel sound or by adding a syllable.

> mouse—mice   child—children

- Some nouns are the same in the singular as they are in the plural.

> sunglasses   headquarters

- To form the plural of a hyphenated compound noun, make only the most important noun plural.

> sister-in-law—sisters-in-law   runner-up—runners-up

Possessive Nouns

- A **possessive noun** shows ownership. To form the possessive of a singular noun, add an apostrophe and *s*.

  secretary's desk   Les's book

- To form the possessive of a plural noun ending with *s*, add only an apostrophe.

  the lawyers' debate   the dentists' instruments

Verbs

- A **verb** is a word that expresses an action or a state of being.

  juggle   wrapped   raced   became

- An **action verb** is a verb that expresses a physical or mental action.

  tremble   thinks   whistle   resent

- A **linking verb** does not show action, but it connects the subject to the other words in the predicate.

  am   are   is   were   appears   sounds

- A **verb phrase** is a verb that consists of more than one word.

  was trotting   has benefited   is struggling

- The **main verb** is the verb that expresses the action or state of being.

  was <u>trotting</u>   has <u>benefited</u>   is <u>struggling</u>

- The **helping verb** is the verb that helps the main verb make its statement.

  <u>was</u> trotting   <u>has</u> benefited   <u>is</u> struggling

Verb Tenses

- **Tense** is the time expressed by a verb.

- The **present tense** expresses action that is taking place *now*.

    The football game <u>proceeds</u>. Everyone <u>stares</u> at the quarterback.

- The **past tense** expresses action that took place at some *definite time in the past*.

    Someone <u>inflated</u> the football incorrectly.

- A verb with an *ing* ending tells what *is* or *was* happening. The following forms of *be* are often used with *ing* verbs.

    am   is   are   was   were

    The quarterback <u>was passing</u> the ball.

Regular and Irregular Verbs

- The three basic forms of a verb are the **present,** the **past,** and the **past participle.** The past and past participle of **regular verbs** are formed by adding *d* or *ed* to the present form.

Present	Past	Past Participle
pass(es)	passed	(have, has, had) passed
accept(s)	accepted	(have, has, had) accepted
inquire(s)	inquired	(have, has, had) inquired

- The past and past participle forms of **irregular verbs** are not formed by adding *d* or *ed* to their present forms. Their past and past participles are formed in a variety of ways, as shown on this chart.

Present	Past	Past Participle
catch(es)	caught	(have, has, had) caught
forget(s)	forgot	(have, has, had) forgotten
lose(s)	lost	(have, has, had) lost
lie(s)	lay	(have, has, had) lain
lay(s)	laid	(have, has, had) laid

WRITER'S GUIDE

Adjectives

- An **adjective** is a word that modifies a noun or pronoun.

  That is a <u>colossal</u> mountain. It is <u>enormous</u>.

- The **positive degree** of an adjective is used when only *one* thing is being described.

  Look at that <u>muddy</u> lagoon. Its water is certainly <u>dirty</u>.

- The **comparative degree** of an adjective is used when *two* things or ideas are being compared. To compare two things, add *er*.

  This fish is <u>swifter</u> than that one.

- Some adjectives of two syllables and most adjectives of three or more syllables use the word *more* to form their comparative forms.

  This park is <u>more popular</u> than the other one.

- The **superlative degree** of an adjective is used when *three or more* things are being compared. Add *est* to form the superlative.

  Grant Park has the <u>loveliest</u> scenery of all.

- Some adjectives of two syllables and most adjectives of three or more syllables use the word *most* to form their superlative forms.

  It is also the <u>most popular</u> park in our area.

- A **participle** is a word that looks like a verb form but is used as an adjective.

  The <u>devoted</u> servant prepared a <u>satisfying</u> meal for all the campers.

Adverbs

- An **adverb** is used to modify a verb, an adjective, or another adverb. Adverbs answer the questions *where, when, how, how often,* and *to what extent.*

  She wrote <u>frequently</u>. (modifies the verb *wrote*)
  He was <u>very</u> annoyed. (modifies the adjective *annoyed*)
  She answered <u>too</u> quickly. (modifies the adverb *quickly*)

- Some adverbs can be formed by adding *ly* to the end of an adjective. When you add *ly* to most words, do not change the spelling of the base word.

  rare—rarely   frequent—frequently

  However, when a word ends with *le,* drop the *le* before adding *ly.*

  legible—legibly

- The **positive degree** of an adverb is used when *one* action is being described.

  Ellen can swim quite <u>far</u>.

- The **comparative degree** of an adverb is used when *two* actions are being compared.

  Ellen can swim <u>farther</u> than Sam.

- The **superlative degree** of an adverb is used when *three or more* actions are being compared.

  In the last contest Ellen swam <u>farthest</u> of all.

Pronouns

- A **pronoun** is a word used in place of one or more nouns.

  Ted is going to Topeka on Saturday. <u>He</u> is looking forward to the trip.

- A **possessive pronoun** takes the place of a possessive noun or possessive noun phrase. The words *my, your, his, her, our, their, its, mine, hers, yours, ours,* and *theirs* are possessive pronouns.

  <u>My</u> ticket is in <u>her</u> desk. Where is <u>yours</u>?

Agreement

- A verb must agree with its subject in number. If the subject of a sentence is singular, it takes a singular verb. If the subject is plural, it takes a plural verb.

    The <u>scientist</u> <u>is</u> in the laboratory.
    The <u>scientists</u> <u>are</u> in the laboratory.

- Some nouns may be singular in meaning although plural in form. These words take a singular or plural verb depending on their meaning in the sentence.

    The <u>headquarters</u> for his campaign <u>is</u> in that building.
    The <u>headquarters</u> for every candidate <u>were bustling</u>.

- Other nouns always take a plural verb no matter what their meaning is in context.

    Her <u>sunglasses</u> <u>were</u> red.
    The <u>sunglasses</u> displayed in the window <u>were</u> dazzling.

- The word *clothes,* which has only a plural meaning, always takes a plural verb.

    Her <u>clothes</u> <u>are</u> always neat and clean.

Vocabulary

Compound Words

- A **compound word** consists of two or more words used as a single word.

    carloads   sunglasses

- A **hyphenated compound** is a compound word connected by hyphens.

    runners-up   so-called

Antonyms

- **Antonyms** are words with opposite meanings.

    interior—exterior   confidence—uncertainty

Synonyms

- **Synonyms** are words with similar, but not identical, meanings.

    meddle—interfere   trek—expedition

Prefixes

- A **prefix** is a syllable or syllables added to the beginning of a word to change its meaning.

  <u>semi</u>circle   <u>dis</u>please
  <u>post</u>date   <u>il</u>legal

Suffixes

- A **suffix** is a syllable or syllables added to the end of a base word. Suffixes change the way words are used as parts of speech.

  attach<u>ment</u>   success<u>ful</u>   depend<u>able</u>

Word Families

- When you add a prefix or a suffix to a base word, you create a new word. The basic meaning of the base word remains the same in each word, but the meanings of the new words are different. These words belong to a **word family.**

  state   statement   understatement

Homographs

- **Homographs** are words that are spelled alike but have different meanings and sometimes different pronunciations.

  We could hardly see the <u>minute</u> snowflakes.
  Dad said he'd be ready in a <u>minute</u>.

Homophones

- **Homophones** are words that sound alike but have different meanings and spellings.

  principle—principal   pore—pour

Analogies

- An **analogy** shows a similarity between two sets of ideas.

  <u>Friendly</u> is to <u>hostile</u> as <u>cautious</u> is to <u>reckless</u>.

  Friendly and *hostile* are antonyms. They have the same relationship to each other as *cautious* and *reckless* do.

Rhyme Stymes

- A riddle that has two rhyming words for the answer is called a **rhyme styme.** Here is an example of a rhyme styme.

    What do you call oil that is used to heat a junior high?
    Answer: *school fuel*

Malapropisms

- A **malapropism** is a mix-up in the use of words that is often quite funny. A word that has a similar sound is used instead of the correct word.

    I love to eat <u>synonym</u> toast for breakfast. (cinnamon)

DICTIONARY: A Glossary of Terms and Examples

Alphabetical Order

- The order of letters from A to Z is called **alphabetical order.** Words in a dictionary are listed in alphabetical order. These words are in alphabetical order.

  anyway   chandelier   juvenile   kayak   narration   unwieldy

Guide Words

- There are two **guide words** at the top of each dictionary page. The word on the left is the first word on the page. The word on the right is the last word. All the other words on the page are in alphabetical order between those words.

---

burro   **chemistry**

bur·ro /bûr′ō/ *n., pl.* **bur·ros** A small donkey, usually used to carry packs.   *Burro* comes from the Spanish word for a small horse or donkey, *borrico.*

cau·tious /kô′shəs/ *adj.* Very careful or watchful.

Entry Word

- On a dictionary page, an **entry word** is a word in dark print that is followed by its meaning. Entry words appear in alphabetical order.

  caf·e·te·ri·a /kaf′ə·tir′ē·ə/ *n.* A restaurant in which customers pick up their own food and carry it to the tables.

  cal·en·dar /kal′ən·dər/ *n.* **1** A chart showing dates, days of the week, months of the year, etc., in order. **2** An orderly list; a schedule of things. ▶ *Calendar* comes from the Latin word *calendae,* "the first day of the Roman month."

  cam·ou·flage /kam′ə·fläzh/ *n., v.* **cam·ou·flaged, cam·ou·flag·ing** **1** *n.* A coloring or covering that conceals or protects. **2** *v.* To change the appearance of, in order to conceal.

Pronunciation

- A **pronunciation** follows each entry word. Special spellings and symbols called **diacritical marks** show how to pronounce the word.

  cer·tain /sûr′tən/ *adj.* **1** Entirely sure. **2** Known, but not named or stated: A *certain* person called today. **3** Some: *certain* things to do.

Part of Speech

- A **part of speech** tells whether the word is a noun, a verb, or some other part of speech. The names are abbreviated.

Definition

- A **definition** tells what a word means. Many words have more than one definition. Sometimes an example sentence follows the definition.

Example

- An **example** shows you how to use the word.

Pronunciation Key

- A **pronunciation key** explaining the diacritical marks appears at the beginning of a dictionary. A brief key is often found at the bottom of a dictionary page as well.

act, āte, cȃre, ärt;   egg, ēven;   if, īce;   on, ōver, ôr;   bo͞ok, fo͞od;   up, tûrn;
ə=a in *ago,* e in *listen,* i in *giraffe,* o in *pilot,* u in *circus;*   yo͞o=u in *music;* oil;   out;
chair; sing; shop; thank; that; zh in *treasure.*

Syllables

- A word is made up of several parts called **syllables.** Each syllable has a vowel sound.
- In a word with two or more syllables, the **accent mark** (′) in the pronunciation shows which syllable is said with the most force.
- The syllable with the accent mark is called the **accented syllable.**
- A **secondary accent** shows a syllable said with less force.

Etymology

- An **etymology** is a word history. It explains how a word came into our language. It also tells how the meaning of a word has changed and developed. Some dictionaries provide etymologies. They often use a special symbol such as an arrow to show where the etymology begins.

> **chan·de·lier** /shan′də·lir′/ *n.* A decorative lighting fixture that hangs from the ceiling.
> ► *Chandelier* is the French word for "candlestick."

Composing

Use this checklist as you write.

- Read over your plan.
- Think about your purpose and audience.
- Use your plan to put your ideas on paper quickly.
- Do not worry about spelling, punctuation, or grammar at this time.
- Remember that you may get more ideas as you write.
- Add new ideas as you think of them.

Revising

Use this checklist when you edit and proofread your work.

Editing

- Read over your work.
- Be sure your audience has enough information.
- Be sure the order of your sentences makes sense.
- Check that each sentence is a complete thought.
- Be sure each paragraph has a clear topic sentence.
- Check that all the detail sentences support the main idea.
- Be sure the words are lively and interesting.

Proofreading

- Be sure you used capital letters correctly.
- Be sure you used punctuation marks correctly.
- Check the spelling of each word.
- Be sure you used each word correctly.
- Be sure the grammar is correct.
- Be sure the first line of each paragraph is indented.
- Be sure your handwriting is neat and readable.

WRITER'S GUIDE

Editing and Proofreading Marks

- Use **Editing and Proofreading Marks** when you revise your writing. These marks help you see the changes you want to make.

- Remember that you can go back and change words or sentences as many times as you want or need to.

Editing and Proofreading Marks

☰	capitalize
⊙	make a period
∧	add something
⋏	add a comma
⌄⌄	add quotation marks
ഉ	take something away
◯	spell correctly
⊓	indent the paragraph
/	make a lowercase letter
∼ tr	transpose

The school fair will be held next tuesday afternoon. All students are going to attend. There will be a contest and a crafts show. Science projects will also be displayed. Teachers families. and friends will be invited. The school band will play The Star-Spangled Banner. Then the principal and the coach will give a speech. Prizes will be given for the best compositions and drawings. The fair has always been a highlight of the school year. Plans are already being made for the fair next year. It will place take in April instead of in May.

A Glossary of Terms and Examples

Kinds of Sentences

- A **sentence** is a group of words expressing a complete thought. Each sentence begins with a capital letter and ends with a punctuation mark.

- A **declarative sentence** makes a statement. It ends with a period (.).

    The comedian is very funny.

- An **interrogative sentence** asks a question. It ends with a question mark (**?**).

    Is it permissible to swim in the lake?

- An **imperative sentence** gives a command or makes a request. It ends with a period (.).

    Please return the novel you borrowed.

- An **exclamatory sentence** shows strong feeling or surprise. It ends with an exclamation point (!).

    How delighted I am!

Paragraph

- A **paragraph** is a group of sentences that develops a single topic or **main idea.** Paragraphs can describe, explain, narrate, and persuade.

- The **topic sentence** expresses the main idea of the paragraph.

- The other sentences in a paragraph, called **detail sentences,** help develop the main idea.

- The first line of every paragraph is indented.

Descriptive Paragraph

- A descriptive paragraph describes a person, place, or thing.

- The **topic sentence** often gives a general impression of the subject.

- **Detail sentences** must support the topic sentence. They should be arranged in some kind of logical order.

- Using vivid descriptive words helps set the **tone** for this type of paragraph. The tone is the mood of the paragraph.

- Where appropriate, words that help the reader *see, hear, smell, touch,* and *feel* are used in a description.

- Using personality traits as well as physical characteristics when describing people and animals adds to a description.

- Comparisons can make descriptions more vivid.

Here is an example of a descriptive paragraph.

> It was so hot outside that by noon, none of us had the energy to go anywhere. The window shades had been pulled all the way down and were glowing yellow. Through a tear in one, the sky could be seen like a piece of blazing tin. The drawn shades made the rooms dim but did not cool them. The air seemed heavy and thick with old smells brought up by the heat: melted crayons, cooked tomatoes, and dusty wool. My skin felt slick and sticky, and when I moved, I felt as if I were swimming through a tank of warm, murky water.

Narrative Paragraph

- A **narrative paragraph** often relates an anecdote. An **anecdote** is a brief and sometimes amusing story from the life of a person. It presents an account of an interesting incident or event.

- In a narrative paragraph, a **topic sentence** tells what the story will be about, introduces the main characters, and describes the setting.

- **Detail sentences** briefly tell the story and support the main idea.

- Adding dialogue can make a story more interesting.

- The **concluding sentence** is often amusing or surprising.

Here is an example of a narrative paragraph.

Pioneers on the central plains sometimes found it difficult to scratch a living out of the land. However, their wit often turned their hardships into humor. One favorite tale was about the poor farmer who one day went into the town hardware store and bought three hammer handles for a dollar apiece. The next week he bought ten, and a few weeks later he came back for twenty. The store owner had to ask the farmer what he was doing with so many handles.

"I'm selling them to my neighbors for fifty cents," replied the farmer.

Shocked, the store owner exclaimed, "But you're losing fifty cents apiece that way!"

The farmer shrugged and said, "That's a whole lot better than I was doing when I was dirt-farming."

How-to Paragraph

- **How-to paragraphs,** or directions, explain to a reader how to do something.

- The **topic sentence** tells which process will be explained.

- Necessary materials for the process are included in the topic sentence or the first detail sentence.

- **Detail sentences** that explain the steps of the process are given in the correct order. Unfamiliar or hard-to-understand words are defined.

- **Transitional expressions** such as *first, next, then,* and *finally* help simplify the steps to be followed.

Here is an example of a how-to paragraph.

To learn how to do word processing, you will need a computer, a keyboard, a monitor, and perhaps a printer. The easiest way to learn is to memorize only a few keyboard commands at a time. To begin with, learn the simple set of commands that tells the computer to get ready to let you write. Then look up the commands that tell how to move the cursor, or place marker, on the screen. Type two or three sentences, and practice moving the cursor up and down and left and right. Next, learn and practice the command that lets you erase letters. End your first lesson by memorizing the command that tells the computer to make a record of the work you want to save.

Comparison Paragraph/Contrast Paragraph

- A **comparison paragraph** shows the ways in which two things are alike.

- A **contrast paragraph** points out the ways in which two things are different.

- The **topic sentence** expresses the main idea and states whether the paragraph will compare or contrast. The qualities to be discussed are named in this sentence.

- **Detail sentences** explain the qualities mentioned in the topic sentence in the order in which they are named in the topic sentence.

Here is an example of a comparison paragraph.

> A native of the west coast of the United States would find the same climate, natural vegetation, and crops on the central coast of Chile. For a start, both coastal regions are located about the same distance from the equator. Thus, each has a warm, humid climate with dry summers and winter rainfall. In addition, both are covered with the same kinds of natural vegetation, which range from Mediterranean woodland and scrub to mixed forests of evergreens and deciduous trees. In their rich, well-watered farmlands, many of the same crops thrive.

Here is an example of a contrast paragraph.

> My uncle Ram and his brother Dev differ both in physical characteristics and in the sounds of their voices. My Uncle Ram is a short, compact man full of enthusiasm, like a bulldog pup, while Uncle Dev is more like a lean, sleepy cat. Not only do they look quite different, they sound quite different. Uncle Ram talks in an excited voice— "faster than he can think," according to my mother. On the other hand, each sentence that comes out of Uncle Dev seems as if it were slowly drawn up out of a deep well.

Persuasive Paragraph

- The purpose of a **persuasive paragraph** is to convince the audience that the writer's opinion and reasons are correct and should be acted upon.

- The **topic sentence** states the issue and offers an opinion on it.

- The **detail sentences** present the reasons for the opinion.

- The strongest reason is usually saved for last because the audience is most likely to remember the final reason.

- The **conclusion** of the paragraph includes a restatement of the writer's reasons. It calls upon the audience to take action on the issue.

Here is an example of a persuasive paragraph.

> If Montoya High School is going to prepare students for today's job market, it must modernize its foreign language program. Of its offerings—Latin, French, Spanish, and German—only Spanish is clearly useful in the Western Hemisphere. The curriculum should be expanded to include languages like Japanese and Chinese, which are far more necessary to trade and communication than German or French. Trade figures show that the United States does three times as much business with Japan as with Germany or France. Moreover, statistics show that there are 900 Chinese speakers for every 75 French speakers and every 100 German speakers in the world. You can help Montoya High's students prepare for today's job market by signing our petition for modernization of the foreign language program.

Friendly Letter

- **Friendly letters** and **social notes,** such as **invitations** and **thank you notes,** have five parts.

- The **heading** is in the upper right-hand corner. It contains the letter writer's address and the date. A comma is used between the city and the state and between the day and the year.

- The **salutation** is next to the left margin. It begins with a capital letter and is followed by a comma.

- The **body** is organized in paragraphs. Each paragraph is indented.

- The **closing** is in line with the heading. The first word of the closing is capitalized. A comma follows the closing.

- The **signature** is in line with the closing.

Here is an example of a friendly letter.

1500 Garden St. Kansas City, Missouri 64118 August 14, 19--	**Heading**
Dear Joann,	**Salutation**
It sounds as though you are having a good time at camp. I sure miss you. I can't wait for you to come home. School will start before we know it. I met two new girls who will be in our class. You will like them, too. See you soon.	**Body**
Love, Chris	**Closing** **Signature**

Business Letter

- A **business letter** is formal and brief. It can be a letter of request or it can call attention to a problem or an error. A business letter has six parts.

- Except for the salutation, the punctuation in a business letter is the same as that in a friendly letter.

- The **heading,** which includes the writer's address and the date, is in the upper right-hand corner.

- The **inside address** starts at the left margin. It tells who is receiving the letter.

- The **salutation** begins at the left margin. It begins with a capital letter and is followed by a colon.

- The **body** tells why the letter is being written. It should briefly and clearly give all the facts that the business needs to answer the letter or fill an order.

- The **closing** is in line with the heading.

- The **signature** of the writer is in line with the closing.

Here is an example of a business letter.

15 Granite Street Indianapolis, Indiana 46220 March 15, 19——	**Heading**
Ms. Sharon Westfall Patterns Plus 3300 19th Street Milwaukee, Wisconsin 53222	**Inside Address**
Dear Ms. Westfall:	**Salutation**
I am very interested in receiving your catalog of quilt patterns. Please send me the catalog and an order form at your earliest convenience.	**Body**

Sincerely yours,
          Barbara Edwards
          Barbara Edwards
	Closing
	Signature

Journal

- A **journal** contains daily writing about personal activities.

- A journal is a good place to write personal thoughts and feelings.

- Each journal entry starts with a day and date.

Here is an example of a journal entry.

> *Tuesday, January 6, 19--*
> *I tried out for the school play today. I was really scared. I actually think I'll be chosen for a small part, at least! Boy, were my knees shaking!*

Story

- A story has a beginning, a middle, and an ending.

- The **beginning** presents the setting and characters and introduces the plot.

- The **middle** shows how the plot unfolds, presenting a conflict, or problem.

- The **ending** tells how the problem is solved and ends the story.

- A story has a **title.** The first word and each important word in the title begin with a capital letter.

Here is an example of the beginning paragraph for a story.

<u>The Contraption</u>

On Monday after dinner, Kristin carried all the materials for her science research project into the living room. She'd spent every spare minute of the last four weeks studying and planning for it. She had researched library materials, interviewed teachers and university professors, and scoured the town for some very scarce and unusual-looking supplies. When her family asked what she was building, all that Kristin said was, "a contraption."

Book Report

- One way of sharing information about a book is to write a **book report.** A book report gives enough information about a specific book to enable a person to decide whether he or she would enjoy reading that book.

- A book report includes the **title, author,** and **setting** of the book, and the **main character** and minor characters.

- The report includes a **summary** of the plot of a fiction book or the contents of a nonfiction book. It does not give away too much.

- The reader's **opinion** of whether the book is good or not is part of the report.

- The opinion is supported with **reasons** and examples from the book.

Here is an example of a book report.

Hidden Treasure

The novel <u>Hidden Treasure</u> was written by Lou Guthrie. It tells how Danielle and Bree Russo, along with their friends Kristy Fraser and Chad Burnett, search for treasure in Key West, Florida. Bree and Danielle are sisters who are spending the summer with relatives in Florida. While playing on the beach, the girls stumble on a box half-buried in the sand. Inside is an old map to a treasure hidden on the island years ago by pirates. The sisters enlist the help of their new friends, Kristy and Chad, and set out on an adventure to find the hidden treasure.

I loved the book. It is suspenseful and full of action. It keeps the reader guessing until the very end about what and where the treasure is. The friends even find an old pirate ship and a haunted house!

Conversation

- A **conversation** is a written dialogue between two or more persons.

- A new paragraph begins each time the speaker changes.

- The speaker's exact words are set off by **quotation marks.** If the quotation is divided into two parts by other words, place quotation marks only around the quoted words.

- If the speaker's words consist of several sentences, without any interrupting words, do not close the quotation until the speaker is finished.

- Always place commas and periods inside the closing quotation marks. Place question marks and exclamation points inside the closing quotation marks if the quotation itself is a question or an exclamation.

Here is an example of written conversation, or dialogue.

"What did you do today?" Debbie asked.

"I went to the zoo with my class," Sharon answered.

"That's great!" Debbie exclaimed. "What animals did you see?"

"We spent a lot of time looking at the big cats," Sharon responded. "There were lions, tigers, leopards, pumas, and cheetahs. We even saw a lioness playing with her two cubs. Then we went to the pool and watched the keepers feed the seals."

"That sounds really exciting," Debbie remarked. "I hope our class can go on a trip like that soon."

Interview

- A conversation to learn specific information is called an **interview.** It is often recorded.

- The first step in setting up an interview is to make an appointment with the person to be interviewed.

- The questions for the interview should be prepared in advance.

- Interviews are often used to obtain direct quotations for news stories or biographies.

News Story

- The most important information in a **news story** is presented first, in the **lead,** or opening section of the story.

- The answers to the questions *who, what, when, where, how,* and *why* are included in the lead sentence or paragraph.

- Some news stories include **quotations** and **details** that give the article a firsthand flavor.

- Every news story has a headline. The **headline** sums up the contents of a news story.

Here is an example of a lead for a news story.

Independence High Honors Luis Valdez

Last Friday, playwright and director Luis Valdez was the guest of honor at a special performance staged by the students of Independence High School in San José. Valdez was obviously moved as he expressed his appreciation, addressing his audience from the stage of the new theater building named for him. The Luis Valdez Center for the Performing Arts had been dedicated as a tribute to the man who founded and fought for the survival of El Teatro Campesino, which was the first and is today the foremost successful Hispanic theater company in the United States.

"I am truly honored," Mr. Valdez commented, "that young people know my work and think enough of it to name their theater after me."

Biography

- A **biography** is the story of a person's life written by someone else.

- A biography is written from the **third-person point of view.**

- A biography often starts with a person's birth and continues to his or her death.

- **Anecdotes** are short, entertaining accounts often included in biographies.

Here is an example of an introductory paragraph for a biography.

> The August sun glinted on the waters of Boston Harbor as an expectant crowd gathered on the deck of the <u>Constitution</u>. Among the faces in the crowd, some were smiling and some were solemn. Today the Navy's oldest active officer was retiring. Heads turned as a double row of young sailors snapped to attention and raised their hats in salute. Gravely, 79-year-old Rear Admiral Grace Hopper returned their salute and came forward. Beyond the sailors' young faces she could see older, familiar faces. There were the officials whose rules she had challenged again and again in her forty-three years of service. And there were some of her old teammates with whom she had created a new mathematical language and helped bring about the computer revolution. Grace Hopper drew herself even more erect. It would be a difficult leave-taking.

Research Report

- A **research report** is a presentation of facts about a certain topic.

- An **outline** of the research notes helps organize the material before the report is written.

- Each outline heading serves as an idea for the topic sentence of a paragraph.

- The subheadings and other facts from the notes help form the detail sentences supporting the main idea.

- A rough draft is usually written based on the outline.

- Transitional expressions or sentences are added where necessary.

An example of the beginning of a research report is on the next page.

How American English Has Changed

Three hundred years ago someone could sail from London to Boston and hear nearly the same language being spoken in both cities. Now, as everyone knows, British and American English sound very different. However, the difference is more than a matter of accent. Our vocabularies are sometimes different, too. For centuries, the American language has been growing and changing on its own. Native Americans and settlers from all over the world contributed words like caribou, tote, kosher, and mesa. When words for certain concepts or experiences did not exist, Americans invented words like boost, ballpark figure, gang, and nitty-gritty.

Poetry/Rhymes

- In many poems, the words at the ends of some lines sound alike. This is called **rhyme.**
- A **rhyme scheme** in a poem is the pattern of the rhymes.
- Most poems have **rhythm,** or a regular beat.
- The pattern of beats in a poem is its **meter.**
- **Alliteration** is the repetition of beginning consonant sounds in words. Alliteration is often used in poetry.

Susie sympathized with her sulky sister.

Here is an example of part of a poem.

A sudden storm raged through town.
Wild winds whipped tall trees down.

Its angry roar and jagged light
Sent people scurrying home in
fright.

MECHANICS: A Glossary of Rules

Capitalization

Names and Titles of People and Places

- Capitalize names of people, including initials, titles, and abbreviations of titles.

    Mr. Harold C. Barrett   Dr. Ruth Lorenson

- Capitalize names of nationalities and languages.

    Some Peruvians and Bolivians speak Quechua.

- Always capitalize the pronoun *I*.

    After I wrote the letter, I signed my name.

- Capitalize geographical names.

    Fifth Avenue   Lookout Mountain   Reno, Nevada

- Capitalize abbreviations of parts of addresses.

    St. (Street)   Ave. (Avenue)   Dr. (Drive)

Names of Days, Months, and Holidays

- Capitalize days of the week and months of the year and their abbreviations.

    Monday   Tues.   September   Nov.

- Capitalize the names of historical events.

    War of 1812   Age of Reason

- Capitalize each important word in the name of a holiday.

    Fourth of July   Columbus Day

The Beginning of Sentences and Titles of Written Work

- Capitalize the first word of every sentence.

- Capitalize the first word, the last word, and all other important words in the title of a written work.

    Popular Science (magazine)
    The Game of Baseball (book)
    "Yesterday" (song)
    "Spring" (short poem)

Punctuation

Period

- Place a period at the end of a declarative or an imperative sentence.

    The activity is difficult. Please concentrate on it.

- Place a period after an abbreviation.

    Pres.   P.M.   Hon.   Sun.

- Place a period after an initial.

    Franklin D. Roosevelt   R. M. Keller

- Place a period after each number or letter in an outline.

    I. Purebred cats
       A. Oriental cats
          1. Siamese
          2. Burmese

Question Mark, Exclamation Point, Underlining

- Place a question mark at the end of an interrogative sentence.

    Do you paint with acrylics or oils?

- Place an exclamation point at the end of an exclamatory sentence.

    The expedition is finally over!

- Place an exclamation point after a strong interjection.

    <u>Aha</u>! I found your hiding place.

- Underline titles of books, plays, newspapers, magazines, movies, records, works of art, musical compositions, TV shows, and long poems.

    <u>Finian's Rainbow</u> (play, movie, record)
    <u>Orlando Sentinel</u> (newspaper)
    Ravel's <u>Mother Goose Suite</u> (musical composition)

Comma

- Place a comma between the day and year in a date. If the year is followed by more words in the sentence, place a comma after the year.

    The politician won the election on June 4, 1985.
    On August 24, 1985, he signed his first bill.

- Place a comma between the city and the state within an address.

    Kansas City, Missouri   Hartford, Connecticut

- If the address or place name is in a sentence, place a comma after the street address, a comma between the city and state, and a comma after the state.

    We stayed at the Southern Hotel, International Drive, Orlando, Florida, for a week.

- Place a comma after the salutation of a friendly letter and after the closing of any letter.

    Dear Angela,   Sincerely yours,   Yours truly,

- Use commas to separate three or more items in a list or series in a sentence.

  Ron, Angela, Linda, and Ed are invited to Bob's party.
  Go out the gate, through the gardens, over the bridge, and past the iron fence.

- Place a comma before the conjunctions *or, and,* and *but* in a compound sentence.

  First we'll vacuum the rug, and then we'll wash the floor.

- Place a comma between the closing marks of a direct quotation and the rest of the sentence unless a question mark or exclamation point is needed.

  "I am anxious about the test," she told me.

- Use commas to set off most appositives.

  Ms. Dobbs, our senator, is visiting our city.

Apostrophe

- Use an apostrophe for possessive nouns but not for possessive pronouns.

  | Dominic's | government's | the Millers' |
  | his | its | theirs |

- Use an apostrophe and an *s* after the last word of a singular hyphenated compound to form the possessive.

  sister-in-law's hat   commander-in-chief's office

- Use an apostrophe to form contractions of pronouns and verbs and of verbs with the adverb *not.*

  they're   he's   can't   shouldn't

Semicolon and Colon

- Use a semicolon to connect independent clauses in a compound sentence.

    I plan to take a siesta this afternoon; however, I may have to work.

- Place a colon after the salutation of a business letter.

    Dear Ms. Whitney: Gentlemen:

- Place a colon between the hour and the minute in the time of day.

    8:15 A.M.   4:23 P.M.   5:30 P.M.

- Place a colon before a list of items, especially when the list follows expressions such as *the following* or *as follows*.

    My favorite snacks are as follows: grapes, cheese, and apples.

Hyphen

- Use a hyphen to divide a word between syllables at the end of a line.

    phar-ma-cist   char-ac-ter   to-bog-gan

Quotation Marks

- Place quotation marks around the titles of songs, articles, short stories, chapters in books, and short poems.

    "Who Wants to Be a Millionaire?" (song)
    "Big Red" (short story)
    "How to Make Raisin Bread" (article)

- Place quotation marks directly before and after each direct quotation in a conversation or dialogue. If the quotation is divided into two parts by other words, place quotation marks only around the quoted words.

    He said, "I'm going to order a salad."
    "I'll have a salad, too," she said, "and a bowl of soup."

- If a direct quotation consists of several sentences, do not close the quotation until the speaker is finished.

    Pierre said, "I'm getting tired. Why don't we stop hiking now and eat our lunch?"

- Always place commas and periods inside the closing quotation marks. Place question marks and exclamation points inside the closing quotation marks if the quotation itself is a question or an exclamation.

> The cashier said, "It is five dollars."
> "Wow, what a great opportunity!" she exclaimed.
> "Do you want to go to the symphony?" he asked.
> Did Laura say, "I'll be there at five"?

HANDWRITING: Letter Forms

Uppercase and Lowercase Manuscript Letters

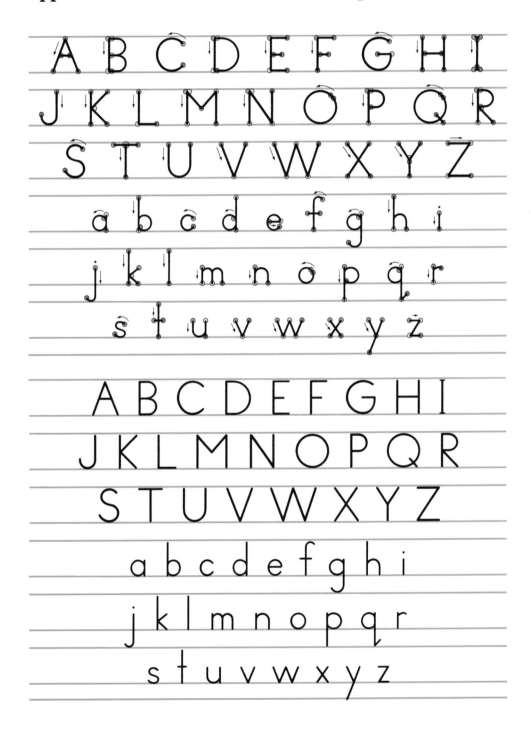

Uppercase and Lowercase Cursive Letters

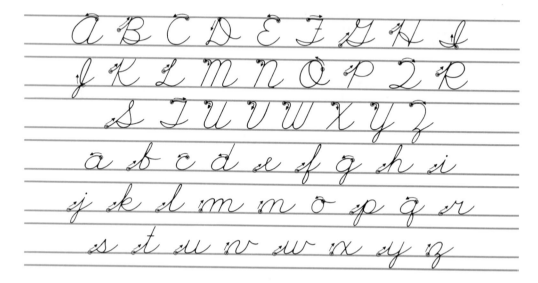